Matthew C. Moen is Assistant Professor of Political Science at the University of Maine and author of *The Christian Right and Congress*. *Lowell S. Gustafson* is Assistant Professor of Political Science at Villanova University and author of *The Sovereignty Dispute Over the Falkland/Malvinas Islands*.

The
Religious Challenge
to the State

THE RELIGIOUS CHALLENGE TO THE STATE

Edited by

Matthew C. Moen and Lowell S. Gustafson

Temple University Press

PHILADELPHIA

Temple University Press, Philadelphia 19122
Copyright © 1992 by Temple University. All rights reserved
Published 1992
Printed in the United States of America

The paper used in this publication meets the minimum requirements of American
National Standard for Information Sciences—Permanence of Paper for Printed Library
Materials, ANSI Z39.48-1984

Library of Congress Cataloging-in-Publication Data
The Religious challenge to the state / edited by Matthew C. Moen and Lowell S.
   Gustafson.
      p.   cm.
   Includes bibliographical references.
   ISBN 0-87722-856-6 (alk. paper)
   1. Religion and state. 2. Religion and politics. I. Moen, Matthew C.,
   1958–   . II. Gustafson, Lowell C.
   BL65.S8R45   1992
   291.1′77—dc20   90-29160

With gratitude and love,
to my wife, Donna L. Moen
—M.C.M.
and to my parents, Reverend Erick I.
and Mrs. Dagmar C. Gustafson
—L.S.G.

Contents

Preface

For centuries, philosophers have posited that religion will fade away in the face of enlightenment. In the Western world, a litany of political thinkers has advanced that thesis; in the Eastern world, many modern regimes have sought to hasten the process, in the name of "scientific socialism." This disdain for religion stems from the view that ignorance and fear are the root causes of religious belief. Thomas Hobbes, the seventeenth-century political philosopher, asserted in the *Leviathan* that the "natural seed of religion" is the "opinion of ghosts, ignorance of second causes, devotion toward what men fear, and taking of things casual for prognostics." Since religion was essentially superstition, the reasoning went, it would atrophy as enlightenment spread.

Philosophers also argued that the emergence of individual freedom would contribute to the demise of religion. They assumed that as people's rights and autonomy increased—in the midst of constitutionalism, modernization, and urbanization—citizens would anxiously and willingly cast off any possible encumbrances. Religion would be a casualty of that process, because it provided a set of beliefs and a code of conduct for the faithful to follow.

The famous French political thinker Alexis de Tocqueville dissented from such maxims. He singled out his secular European predecessors for peddling such views, saying in *Democracy in America* that "eighteenth-century philosophers had a very simple explanation for the gradual weakening of [religious] beliefs. Religious zeal, they said, was bound to die down as enlightenment and freedom spread. It is tiresome that the facts do not fit this theory at all." In Tocqueville's view,

ix

enlightenment and freedom were far from incompatible with religion. In fact, in America, "free and enlightened people" zealously performed their religious duties.

The 1980s provided some support for Tocqueville's view of the compatibility of enlightenment and freedom with religion. Even as scientific discoveries abounded and the Iron Curtain fell, for instance, religion resurged all around the globe. The Islamic Revolution swept across much of the Middle East, Africa, and parts of Asia. The peace movement, with its deep roots in Protestantism, prospered in Western Europe. Across the Atlantic, evangelical Christianity burst onto the American political scene, and Pope John Paul II confronted Latin America's liberation theology with more traditional Catholic positions. Near the end of the decade, the Russian Orthodox church was reawakened in the Soviet Union, as was Catholicism in Eastern Europe, as communist regimes toppled or grew more tolerant of religious expression. Arguably, religion thrived in the 1980s, even as enlightenment and freedom spread.

This volume focuses on the importance of the resurgence of religion for politics in various parts of the world. Its contributors examine the monotheistic religions of Islam, Christianity, and Judaism in the context of the challenge that they presented to competing ideologies and particular regimes. Certainly, no single volume can cover the sweep of religious change around the world, nor the role of religion in political affairs. The daunting task of covering religious/state interaction should not be eschewed, however, because it is difficult; the topic is too important and too central to contemporary times to ignore. It simply must be approached with the realization that long-term study is required. In that sense, this volume is a companion to preceding and subsequent religion and politics books.

This book is primarily intended for scholars interested in questions of religious persistence and resurgence, including social scientists, theologians, and religious historians. They may find the themes elucidated in the volume rewarding, or specific chapters helpful in their own work on particular regimes or religious traditions. The book may also have some utility for policymakers, since the contributors have provided a vast amount of information. Because the approach of the contributors is normative and historical, the volume is accessible to a wide readership.

No book of this nature can be assembled without the support of many people. Thanks are due to the following people for their financial support of a religion and politics conference held at the University of Maine in 1989 that brought many of the contributors together: Dale Lick, president of the University of Maine; John Hitt, vice-president for academic affairs; Greg Brown, vice-president for research and public service; and Julia Watkins, dean of the College of Social and Behavioral Sciences. Professors Ed Collins and Kenneth Hayes, as consecutive chairmen of the Department of Political Science, provided sagacious counsel and invaluable assistance. In a broader sense, colleagues at our home institutions provided encouragement and a positive working environment.

Two active and notable scholars must be thanked for their helpful comments and suggestions on the substance of the chapters: Lonnie Kliever, Department of Religious Studies, Southern Methodist University, and Jerrold Green, Department of Political Science, University of Arizona. Their perspicacious remarks assisted many of the contributors and enhanced the quality of the final product. Naturally, they should not be held responsible for any interpretations or shortcomings.

The folks at Temple University Press have been very helpful throughout the publication process. Their early interest in the project was warmly appreciated, and their professionalism has made working with them both delightful and informative. In particular, Jennifer French has provided excellent advice in the production phase, and Doris Braendel should be singled out for her efforts in bringing this project to fruition. Doris is not only a consummate professional, but also a remarkable person. We also appreciate the professional work done by Elizabeth Shaw and Karen Chatfield in copyediting the book and by David Updike in bringing the project to completion.

Finally, the unending patience and good humor of our wives and families is acknowledged. Throughout the years, they have enriched our lives in many ways, as well as sacrificed to permit us to stay in the "ivory tower." Without their support, our scholarly efforts would be diminished; more importantly, so would our lives.

M. M. & L. G.

The
Religious Challenge
to the State

PART I

Introduction

I.

Challenge and Accommodation in Religion and Politics

LOWELL S. GUSTAFSON and MATTHEW C. MOEN

From the Peace of Westphalia in 1648 through the post–World War II decolonization of Africa and Asia, the state system spread from Europe to the entire world. To the first few states more were added until there are now some 160. Almost the entire land surface of the globe now lies within one of these states.

When the state became the highest unit of political organization, it replaced a localist system in which the highest practical political and economic units were the feudal manors, over which a transnational religious institution theoretically presided. The Roman Catholic church was often thought to provide for what order existed in medieval Europe. The rise of transmanorial merchants and bankers in the late medieval period, however, provided an alternative to local lords or the landed gentry. The rise of towns provided an alternative to the manor. The discovery of the New World provided an alternative to the Old. In Germany, Martin Luther had sparked the great schism within Christendom and provided a religious alternative for Christians to the Catholic church.

Some princes were attracted to Luther's religious ideas because they wanted to determine their subjects' religious loyalties and free themselves from the restrictions of a transnational institution. Other princes, merchants, and Protestants had their own reasons for wanting to free themselves from the old order. The gentry sometimes resisted the rise of the merchant towns and of national kings. Catholics often resisted the rise of Protestantism. Religious cleavage became mixed with other cleavages and sometimes produced violent conflict.

3

The Thirty Years' War, fought between Protestant and Catholic forces largely on the territory of German principalities, was a particularly violent conflict. As much as one-third to one-half of the German population died during the wars, exhausting both sides before either could gain victory. So great was the loss of life that the word *fanaticism* usually came to be modified by *religious,* until secular totalitarians of the twentieth century carried out their unparalleled massacres.

The war removed the premise (which had been dubious for some time anyway) that Catholicism could provide a European political order. The state would henceforth be above religion in providing for what political order would be established by the state system. The result of the Thirty Years' War was the Peace of Westphalia and the origin of the global, sovereign state system. A monumental struggle between Christians led to a system in which religious principles were made secondary to a modern, secular state.

The essential principle claimed by each state was sovereignty, a quality previously attributed to God and God's intermediary to humankind, the pope. This was a basic change in regime. The divine right of kings did not justify monarchs doing whatever they wanted; it had originally demanded that monarchs abide by natural and divine law. The modern sovereign right of kings did justify kings' unlimited power. Each state denied that any other institutions were above it. The Reason of State was understood by enlightened despots and their advisors and was not to be challenged by the mystery of the church. Enlightened despots were not to be like medieval kings, who claimed to be political intermediaries between their people and the religious authority of the pope, who was the intermediary between the ultimate sovereign and humanity.[1]

The state's sovereignty over religion took many forms. In still-Catholic countries, the "sovereign" or the monarchs struggled to control the church's institutional affairs even while they accepted the authority of the pope in matters of faith and morals. Certain Protestant countries developed national churches whose highest authorities were the national monarchs. Others developed the liberal notion of separation.[2] Not only were economics and politics to be separate; religion and those two fields were also to be separate. Religion had nothing to offer to other areas and should stick to the business of saving individual souls through the voluntary acceptance of personal beliefs. Still others viewed some or all religions as a threat to the state's claim to sovereignty and power and sought to eradicate religion even from its liberal, private domain. Marxist states became especially well known for their hostility toward religion, in part because of Marx's famous statement about religion being the opiate of the people.[3] However, the French Revolution was little less opposed to even privately held religious beliefs. Although these approaches differ, in all of them the state challenged the idea that any institutionalized religion should be superior to it, especially in political, but even sometimes in private, affairs.

Religion often tried to transform itself to accommodate these challenges from the state. The Catholic church sometimes allowed Catholic monarchs essentially to appoint church officials and make decisions about church administration within their countries and colonies. Protestant churches sometimes accommodated themselves to their role as almost civic religions. Other times they accepted the role of only saving individual souls and having nothing to say about public affairs. On still other occasions they agreed to spread some states' materialist ideology, cloaked in redefined religious symbolism. Religion sometimes seemed prepared to accommodate itself to the state's hostility to the private belief in transcendence to maintain its institutional survival.

Some thinkers of the French Enlightenment developed the idea of popular sovereignty, in which the state was identified with its people. A people became a nation that often shared a common language, ethnic background, historical myths, symbols, and goals. Religion sometimes became defined as being about people's ultimate concerns rather than about an objective, transcendental divine being. Such a redefined religion could be a possible component of nationalism.[4] Nationalism sometimes became its own secular religion. "State and nation are now linked as servants of Man's highest ambitions," Leonard Tivney writes. "There is a sense in which the state has become a god-substitute; if so, nationalism is the religion substitute."[5] Nations, using religion and other elements to define themselves, claimed the right to national self-determination, or the right to have their own states. The nation-state had been born.

Whether the state was to be organized according to the conservative idea that it was individuals in a democracy who were sovereign, or the progressive idea that the masses' general interest was articulated by a leader, the people were sovereign. Representation of the people, whether through elections or not, established the legitimacy of the state. In electoral democracies, people supposedly used their reason to select their leaders in elections; leaders used their reason to deliberate about and choose between policy options. In authoritarian democracies, individual leaders, parties, or governments claimed to best understand and represent the real interests of the people. Under popular sovereignty, the state was legitimate if it followed the will of the people and served their worldly interests. The state was not to follow the Will of God or help prepare people for the next world; it was to help prepare heaven in this one.

Worldly perfection could take one of two general paths. One was moral. Once the oppression by the unjust ended and the right political conditions were established, people could live in perfect harmony and could voluntarily work for each others' mutual benefit. A happy outcome of this moral bliss would be that everyone's material needs would be met. The other path was directly economic. All individuals' consumer desires could be satisfied in the modern temples called shopping malls. In the first, the state would wither away; in the second it would remain totally outside of economic affairs. Socialism and consumerism were fundamentally utopian, materialist heavens of this world.[6]

Many missionaries from religious groups left Europe to propagate their faiths in the New World. The European imperialists were more effective in spreading the modern belief in state, and sometimes popular, sovereignty. European imperialism gave the continent domination over most of the world. Anticolonial movements were later carried out in the name of achieving independent nation-states. European armies and administrators were ejected from the former colonies, but European ideas established a global state system by the 1960s for the first time in history.

During the centuries-long growth of the sovereign state in world affairs, various religious groups have challenged its ascendancy. This was often thought to be a rearguard counterrevolution that was bothersome but inevitably doomed to failure as modernity replaced traditionalism.[7] However, several seemingly successful challenges to the state began to call this assumption into question.[8] A series of religious movements challenged individual states or groups of states within certain regions, if not the state system as a whole.

Islamic fundamentalism was said to be a potential threat to many Middle Eastern states after the Iranian Revolution of 1979 and the assassination of President Anwar Sadat of Egypt by fundamentalists in 1981. In the United States, various Jewish and Christian groups worked to influence politics. A New Age movement developed ideas about the inherent sacredness of nature, which was sometimes linked to challenges to governmental policies toward the environment. In Latin America, priests who participated in revolution and held office used Liberation Theology as a justification for political action.[9] Religious Jews gained political power within Israel, causing concern among the more secular Israeli Labor party and Zionists everywhere. By supporting the Polish trade union Solidarity, the pope, and the leadership of the Catholic church in general, challenged communist rule in Eastern Europe and even the Soviet Union.

State sovereignty was not exclusively, or in some cases even primarily, challenged by religion. Some forces have worked to replace state sovereignty with international law or organization. Then too, no sooner had the state system been established globally in the 1960s than it was threatened by the historically unprecedented growth of multinational or even transnational corporations. States tried to benefit from direct foreign investment even while they resisted the perceived attempts of multinational corporations to limit national economic sovereignty. When these corporations threatened state sovereignty, many states nationalized them and began to borrow from private, transnational financial institutions instead. These institutions in turn began to represent a threat to national economic sovereignty.

Religious groups were challenging the basic principle of state sovereignty as well as the proposal to replace the state system with transnational materialism. Would they actually succeed in some cases in reintegrating religion and politics, or in making religious institutions superior to the state and religious principles superior to state sovereignty? Would religion successfully challenge the state? Were religious challenges to the state becoming irrelevant as economic actors more effectively challenged the state system? Would religion, the state, or a yet to be established world central bank be the sovereign of the future?

Religious Challenges to Dominant States

The challenge that religion presented to the state came in different contexts, depending upon the nature of the regime and the impediments that it erected for the faithful. For their part, states approached religion in broad terms in one of three ways.[10] The first of those was to co-opt religion, integrating it and making it heavily dependent upon the state. Dominant states in particular employed that approach, because they often sought the legitimacy that religious affiliation conveyed. Association with religion was a way for the state to gain sacramental standing; attempts by religious authorities to lessen this dependence were generally resisted. In such an arrangement, however, ecclesiastical authorities would make sacralization of the state conditional upon independent religious evaluation. That assessment challenged the legitimacy of the state and the principle of state sovereignty. This particular ordering of relations often has been found in various South American, Central American, and Caribbean countries vis-à-vis Catholicism.

In South America, a case of this relationship is found in the state patronage of the church in Argentina. Regimes throughout much of Argentina's history have sought the blessing of the Roman Catholic church, because of its overwhelming presence and importance. In Chapter two, Lowell S. Gustafson carefully traces the history of *patronato* in that country, showing how its early leaders in particular tried to derive legitimacy for their rule from the Catholic church. He then demonstrates how the state gradually weakened that association, so much so that in later time, it even tried to deny the church a legitimate public role. During these machinations, the church often pursued an autonomous role, challenging particular leaders it found unpalatable and laws it found wholly unacceptable. The net result has been a continuous jostling for position between Argentina's government and the Catholic church along a continuum of challenge to legitimation.

Throughout much of its history, Mexico has presented a fairly clear case of a dominant state. At different times, Catholic clergy in the country have been subjected to fines, imprisonment, and even execution for their role in political affairs. Their standing in the judiciary also has been nominal, and in recent times even a papal visit was approached by government officials in a "very secular aura," according to Allan Metz, the author of Chapter five. In that chapter, Metz starts by outlining the various frameworks through which scholars have examined the relationship of the Mexican government to the Catholic church. He finds the "corporatist model," with its emphasis on state regulation of social groups (including the church), a useful heuristic tool for understanding the state's hegemony over the church. He then proceeds with case studies of events in recent times—such as the Chihuahuan elections of July 1986, the beatification of Father Miguel Agustín Pro, and the erection of the Laguna Verde nuclear power plant—to demonstrate how the Catholic church has "soft-pedaled" its role in a constitutionally hostile environment. That approach has led to slightly improved relations, though Metz finds that, at best, an uneasy truce exists between the Mexican government and the Catholic church.

In the case of Cuba, triumphant rebel leader Fidel Castro did not wish to compete with an independent religious institution for the loyalty of the people. In Chapter three, Damián J. Fernández explains how relatively easy it was for Castro to neutralize (if not actually win over) the predominant Catholic church in the period surrounding the Cuban Revolution. Fernández shows that despite its majoritarian presence, Catholicism was actually practiced by few Cubans; coupled with Castro's entreaty to religious leaders to assist the poor, it was possible for Castro temporarily to defuse the Catholic church as a potential source of opposition. In addition, allegiance to Protestantism, *santería* (Afro-Cuban), and *espiritismo* (a type of animism) within a significant minority of the population fragmented religious belief and helped create an environment in which authority was personalized (in Castro) and Marxist-Leninist ideology was ascendant. According to Fernández, the hold of this "political religion" has waned in recent years, though, providing Castro with a potentially serious challenge that is just beginning to surface.

Religious Challenges to Separate States

A second approach of the state has been to limit the political role of religion by demarcating spheres of influence and authority. In regimes with this arrangement, religion is often conceived of, and even lauded, as an intensely personal matter between the believer and God. The "public square" is viewed as a place where overt religious values and rhetoric should not intrude, or should at least be circumscribed to the greatest extent possible. [11] This arrangement originated in Europe; some strands of the Enlightenment facilitated its export around the world, to many different regimes and different faiths. The central challenge for religion in this context is to gain access to the public square, to inject religious beliefs into political decision making. That effort often meets with hostility from confirmed secularists, and with skepticism from religious adherents, who fear that well-intentioned attempts to enter the public square will diminish the purity of the faith.

In Chapter seven, Mark Bartholomew argues that the threat of nuclear war provided the impetus for the Lutheran and Catholic churches to access Germany's public square. The role of religion in Germany historically has been confounded by the existence of large

Protestant and Catholic populations, and more recently by the culpability of the church in the rise of nazism. The confluence of certain developments in the 1980s—the invention of the neutron bomb, the deployment of a new generation of intermediate-range nuclear forces, and the resurrection of debate over the immorality of nuclear deterrence—created an environment for a far-reaching peace movement that was heavily supported within the lay circles of the Lutheran church. Bartholomew traces some of the crosscutting cleavages in religion's role in the peace movement, its relationship with the Social Democratic party of Germany, and then draws some comparisons with the peace movements in other countries of northern Europe.

In the United States, the separation of the religious and the political had been particularly pronounced. The First Amendment to the Constitution, which prohibits the government from establishing a state religion or interfering with religious activities, has eventually come to mean that a "wall of separation" should exist between church and state. In the 1980s, evangelical and fundamentalist Christians challenged that notion, overtly interjecting religious values and biblical rhetoric into the public domain out of concern that secular culture was undermining traditional morality. In Chapter four, Matthew C. Moen chronicles the transformation of the Christian Right in the 1980s as it proffered a challenge to the state. He argues that the Christian Right's structure, strategy, and rhetoric all changed over time; moreover, that those changes were consciously driven by increasingly sophisticated political leaders. In the process of challenging secular policies and principles, though, Moen argues that the Christian Right's leaders were themselves somewhat secularized, gradually mimicking the standards and norms of the secular political world. The net result of all of the changes was a movement that initially challenged the state but ultimately accommodated itself to it.

Some of the newly formed and/or decolonized countries of the Middle East are in the throes of the same conflict exhibited in northern Europe and the United States, namely the attempt by religious forces to gain or maintain access to a public square where religious and political boundaries are cordoned off. Many Muslims and religious Jews view the principles of the modern nation-state with suspicion and protest the separation of the ecclesiastical and political realms. Perhaps nowhere is this relationship more intricate, or more vigorously contested, than in Israel. In Chapter eight, Allan Metz explains the prisms through which scholars examine contemporary religious and political relations in Israel.

He notes that despite widespread agreement that Israel should be a Jewish state, considerable disagreement exists over what it means to be Jewish and over the desirability of religious foundations as the central underpinnings of a modern society. The conflict is found in the Orthodox Jew's call for the state to be based on halakah, or biblical Jewish law; secular Jews seek rule by the Knesset in majoritarian fashion. Metz then studies abortion and autopsy laws, as well as the 1988 election, to develop these themes, finding that religious parties exercised disproportionate influence in those matters given their modest numbers. Israel proves interesting, because instead of the state assuming more responsibility in social areas, as is the norm in most modern societies, the opposite pattern has developed.

Perhaps nowhere have the secular premises of the modern nation-state been more visibly challenged than by Islamic fundamentalists in the Middle East and Islamic Africa. The Islamic Revolution in Iran in 1979 caused Western scholars to reconsider previously held assumptions about the effects of modernization on religion. [12]

In Chapter nine, Ann M. Lesch provides an exegesis of the tactics of the fundamentalist Muslim Brotherhood of Egypt. She documents the emergence of the brotherhood under Hasan al-Banna and proceeds with discussions of its role in the Nasser, Sadat, and Mubarak eras. A major theme is the manner in which the brotherhood and the government have sometimes violently attacked and other times peacefully accommodated each other. In general terms, Lesch finds that following the assassination of Sadat, the trend has been toward accommodation, most recently manifested in the peaceful election of thirty-six Islamists in 1987 to the People's Assembly. What remains unclear, though, is whether those accommodationist tactics by the brotherhood reflect a greater commitment to constitutional government, or a disingenuous short-term ploy to gain greater access to the public square, with the long-range goal of toppling the regime and replacing it with a thoroughly Islamic one. Lesch closes with a discussion of the balancing act that Mubarak must perform, providing the brotherhood a forum to express its views, without allowing that free expression to overwhelm the government in a heavily Islamic society.

In Chapter ten, John O. Voll also discusses Egypt, but in the context of analyzing the principle of the nation-state in all of Africa. He examines four countries where the Muslim percentage of the population varies greatly: Egypt, where Muslims constitute an overwhelming majority; the Sudan, where they are a significant majority; Nigeria, where they are a significant minority; and South Africa, where they are a nominal minority. Voll finds that throughout Africa, Pan-Islamic groups have rejected the principle of the sovereign state and the notion that secular nationalism should command the highest loyalty of Muslims. They accept that religion and politics constitute distinct areas but believe the former is superior to the latter; they reject the contention that religion is a private matter between a believer and Allah. Voll contends that such sentiments have gained greater acceptance in recent times all across Africa, in light of the perceived failure of competing ideologies such as capitalism and Marxism. In fact, he believes the Islamic challenge in Africa is serious enough to call into question the very existence of the nation-state model for African societies.

In South Asia, the desire to establish an Islamic homeland was one motivation for Pakistan separating from Hindu-dominated India at the time of independence from Britain. In Chapter eleven, Mumtaz Ahmad concentrates on the Islamization of Pakistan as it proceeded over three decades. He focuses in particular on the challenge that Field Marshall Ayub Khan, who ruled Pakistan from 1958 to 1969, offered the ulama, on the grounds that their conflict (over such matters as the Muslim Family Laws Ordinance of 1961) set the stage for subsequent Islamization struggles. Ayub Khan was vitally interested in issues of economic development, national integration, and political stability; accordingly, he tried to reconcile Islam with those objectives, and to entice religious authorities to bestow a mantle of religious legitimacy on his regime. This reformist version of Islam created fierce resistance from the Jamaat-i-Islami in particular, which organized opposition even during the years of martial law. Ahmad then shows how Zulfikar Ali Bhutto, perhaps the most secular of all Pakistani leaders, actually paved the way for the full Islamization that occurred during the reign of General Zia. The chapter closes with a discussion of the role of the military during Zia's rule, as a means of furthering his desire for a strong, centralized state. Looking retrospectively over several decades, Ahmad concludes that Islam challenged the hegemony of the state apparatus during the Ayub Khan and Bhutto eras but became a source of legitimacy during Zia's tenure.

Religious Challenges to Hostile States

A third approach of the state toward religion, in addition to attempts to "use" it as a legitimizing tool or to separate it from the political realm, has been to extirpate it. In regimes with this arrangement, private observance of religious ritual, or even individual acceptance of religious belief, is inherently suspect. Both are considered a form of covert challenge to state sovereignty. The first goal for religion in these types of regimes is simply to remain viable; the second is to gradually and incrementally gain autonomy, without appearing to undermine either state sovereignty or the ideology (such as Marxism) upon which the state rests.

Before Mikhail Gorbachev, Soviet leaders generally tried to excise religion from public affairs and private spheres, or at least manage its institutions so completely that religion served the national interest as it was interpreted by the Communist party. In Chapter twelve, James W. Warhola examines the roots of Soviet hostility toward religion in the aftermath of the 1917 Russian Revolution, and particularly the forced secularization that followed Stalin's "Law on Cults" of 1928. He argues that the secularizing tendencies of the Enlightenment were incorporated with a vengeance in the Soviet Union, because of its leaders' driving desire to modernize and achieve parity with the West. The efforts to squelch religion failed, though, not only because persecution had the effect of solidifying commitment among the faithful, but also because Communist party doctrine did not provide a compelling alternative to religious belief. Warhola states that Gorbachev has assumed a more accommodationist posture vis-à-vis religion since coming to power, particularly since the summer of 1988. In the 1990s, Warhola believes that Gorbachev faces an explosive mix of resurgent religiosity, and nationalistic sentiments in the Baltic countries and in central Asia that are tied to religious belief. The net result is the gravest of threats to Communist party ideological hegemony.

The difficulty that Marxist regimes have experienced with religion, of course, is not restricted to the Soviet Union. In Chapter six, Donald E. Bain demonstrates the role that the transnational Roman Catholic church has played in the communist states of Eastern Europe in the 1980s. He argues that the Catholic church has adopted a relatively accommodationist foreign policy toward the Soviet bloc in the post–World War II era, until the papacy of John Paul II. His symbolic position and substantive leadership, which included a more confrontational posture, threatened communist rule in his native Poland most directly, but also provided a significant challenge elsewhere in Eastern Europe. Accordingly, Bain argues that both Bulgaria and the Soviet Union had ample geopolitical incentive to participate in the 1981 assassination attempt of Pope John Paul II. He further notes that while the "Polish Pope" has driven change in Eastern Europe, his challenge to communism has been neither indiscriminate nor uniform in effect. For instance, the pope conducted a policy of great restraint vis-à-vis Lithuania, a predominantly Catholic republic that declared independence from the Soviet Union in 1990.

Transnational Religion and Geographic States

Christianity, Judaism, and Islam are each said to possess universal truths. As an empirical matter, each religious tradition has adherents all around the globe. In turn, states are political entities that are deemed to be legally sovereign over all of the people who live within their territorial boundaries. The clash of transnational religions with sovereign nation-states is therefore inevitable, and an enduring and important feature of human existence.

The organization of any volume focused on such topics could be based plausibly upon either the transnational character of religion or upon geographic principalities known as nation-states. The former arrangement would entail consecutive chapters on Judaism, Christianity, and Islam, if they are considered in the chronological order in which they appeared in human history; the latter arrangement would entail consecutive chapters grouped according to region. The editors of this volume have opted for the latter scheme on two grounds: (1) state sovereignty over geographically defined boundaries is a key and familiar element of modern life; (2) given the wide range of regimes that have attained status as or within sovereign states, religion probably has challenged or accommodated itself more to the state than vice-versa. Thus discussions about state and religious interaction arguably should accept the territorial principle. The remainder of this volume takes that principle as its point of departure, examining the interaction of Christianity, Judaism, and Islam in South America and the Caribbean, North America, Europe, the Middle East, Africa, and Asia.

Notes

1. Thomas Molnar, *Twin Powers: Politics and the Sacred* (Grand Rapids, Mich.: William B. Eerdman's Publishing, 1988).
2. Eldon J. Eisenach, *Two Worlds of Liberalism* (Chicago: University of Chicago Press, 1981).
3. Marx was not the only one who believed that religion, like other

cultural and political ideas, had an economic base. See Max Weber, *The Sociology of Religion,* trans. Ephraim Fischoff (Boston: Beacon Press, 1963); Bryan S. Turner, *Religion and Social Theory: A Materialist Perspective* (Atlantic Highlands, N.J.: Humanities Press, 1983).

4. The relationship between religion and nationalism is discussed in Peter H. Merkl and Ninian Smart, eds., *Religion and Politics in the Modern World* (New York: New York University Press, 1983). See especially chapters 1–10.

5. Leonard Tivney, "States, Nations and Economies," in *The Nation-State,* ed. Leonard Tivney (New York: St. Martin's Press, 1981), 70.

6. For physical well-being and the kingdom of God as an earthly, political project of modern political philosophy, see James V. Schall, *The Politics of Heaven and Hell: Christian Themes from Classical, Medieval, and Modern Political Philosophy* (Lanham, Md.: University Press of America, 1984), 176–79.

7. The role of religion in the modern period is discussed in Donald E. Smith, ed., *Religion and Political Modernization* (New Haven, Conn.: Yale University Press, 1974).

8. See Richard T. Antoun and Mary E. Hegland, eds., *Religious Resurgence: Contemporary Case Studies in Islam, Christianity, and Judaism* (Syracuse, N.Y.: Syracuse University Press, 1987); Richard L. Rubenstein, *Spirit Matters: The Worldwide Impact of Religion on Contemporary Politics* (New York: Paragon House, 1987).

9. The role of Liberation Theology, and the role of religion in revolution, is discussed in Lonnie D. Kliever, ed., *The Terrible Meek: Essays on Religion and Revolution* (New York: Paragon House, 1987); Guenter Lewy, *Religion and Revolution* (New York: Oxford University Press, 1974); Bruce Lincoln, ed., *Religion, Rebellion, Revolution* (New York: St. Martin's Press, 1985).

10. A discussion of other possible interpretations of state and church relations, such as the direct, disjunctive, unitary or indirect, and subsidiary positions, may be found in John J. Schrems, *Principles of Politics* (Englewood Cliffs, N.J.: Prentice-Hall, 1986), 208–14.

11. The term is borrowed from Richard John Neuhaus, *The Naked Public Square,* 2d ed. (Grand Rapids, Mich.: William B. Eerdman's Publishing, 1984).

12. See Jerrold D. Green, "Religion and Countermobilization in the Iranian Revolution," in *Religion and Politics,* ed. Myron J. Aronoff (New Brunswick: Transaction Books, 1984), 85–104; Nikki R. Keddie, *Religion and Politics in Iran: Shi'ism from Quietism to Revolution* (New Haven, Conn.: Yale University Press, 1983).

PART II

South America
and the Caribbean

2.

Church and State in Argentina

LOWELL S. GUSTAFSON

From the colonial period through the present, the institutions of church and state in Argentina have influenced each other along a continuum from challenge to legitimization. Using state patronage of the church, a wide variety of regimes has tried to manipulate the church's right to influence laws and other political decisions. They have attempted to ensure that religion and the church would support the state's existence, power, and actions. While the church frequently has accommodated itself to this effort, important religious movements during certain periods have also vigorously challenged the state, or, more moderately, have tried to use the institution's independent moral force not to challenge or legitimize the state, but to influence its laws. This chapter will examine that interaction.

Because most Argentine citizens are Catholics, most issues concerning religion and politics focus on the proper role of the Catholic church. However, relations between Catholics and members of minority religions constitute an important secondary set of issues. The year 1492, famous for Columbus's first voyage to the New World, was also famous for the final expulsion of the Moors from the Iberian Peninsula after an eight-hundred-year reconquest and infamous for the expulsion of the Jews from Spain following decades of increasing hostility. Centuries-long association between Moors and Catholics in Spain left its imprint on Argentine social relations, architecture, food, dress, and music.[1]

The large numbers of immigrants in the late nineteenth and early twentieth centuries altered the character of the previously Creole population and led to some nativistic reactions.[2] Ancient hostilities toward the Jews were sometimes revived and revised after the 1880s as Argentina gradually developed Latin America's single-largest Jewish population, which in 1990 stood at about 450,000. This religious group has often challenged authoritarian regimes in Argentina and was important in its support for Law 23.592 of 1988, which outlawed ethnic and religious discrimination.[3] Argentina also developed Latin America's largest population of Arab descent, numbering about 500,000. Some 180,000 of these Arabs are Lebanese Christians. President Carlos Menem, elected in 1989, is of Syrian descent, and some speculate that he "converted" from Islam to Catholicism so he would be constitutionally eligible to run for the presidency.

In Argentina, however, "the church" usually refers to the Roman Catholic church, of which the vast majority of Argentines are members, whether nominal or militant. The presence of the Roman Catholic church in Argentina is pervasive. The church operates 1,384 primary schools, 964 secondary schools, and 10 universities. It has its own news service, the Agencia de Informaciones Católicas (AICA), and eight publishing houses. There are three mass-circulation Catholic newspapers and two Catholic intellectual magazines. Many bus riders and pedestrians on the busy streets of Buenos Aires cross themselves while passing in front of churches.

The Right of *Patronato*

The primary issue in Argentine church-state relations throughout the nation's history has been the *patronato,* or the state's patronage of the Roman Catholic church. That patronage has been an essential element of the legal order from the time of Columbus. In the papal bull of May 4, 1493, Alexander VI gave to the king and queen of Castille and León certain lands in the New World in order to instruct the Indians there in the Catholic faith. On July 28, 1508, Pope Julius II conceded to the king and queen of Castille and León and to their descendants the right to nominate appropriate persons for service in the church of the New World and to give their consent to the erection of new church buildings.[4] Julius's document, "Universalis Ecclesiae," was incorporated into the Law of the Indies, by which the Habsburg kings ruled their empire. King Phillip II would say much later, "The right of ecclesiastical patronage belongs to us in all the Indies, by having discovered and acquired that New World, built in it churches and monasteries at our cost, and from the Catholic kings, our ancestors, having been conceded it by Pontifical Bulls of their own motive."[5]

Protestant rulers struggled to make a clean break with the pope. The Spanish Catholic kings, however, remained religiously subordinate to the faith but politically in control of the church.

Father Gomez Zapiola observed of this period that

> the Spanish crown obtained comprehensive powers extending from the appointment of bishops to setting up a village hospital; from building a cathedral to dictating how a tabernacle should be illuminated; from authorizing or prohibiting missions to setting up a religious fraternity; from withholding a papal bull not approved by the Council of the Indies to granting authorization to preside over the election of the provincial in the chapter of a religious order; from authorizing and presiding over councils and synods to prohibiting bishops from ordering excommunications without careful consideration. The legal organization of this whole mechanism is found in Book I of the 1608 Collection of the Law of the Indies.[6]

The kings enforced the collection of the tithe and used this income to support the church financially. All communication between Rome and the church in Latin America went through the crown. Bishops were invested and consecrated by the pope only after being appointed by the crown. This political control became even more tightly organized under the Bourbons, who brought with them the French Royalist theories of Jean Bodin when they came to power in Spain in 1700.

In an era when almost all conquistadores and colonialists were Catholics, the crown wanted religion to help legitimize empire building. After the *cabildo*'s (town hall's) de facto declaration of independence in 1810, the patriots wanted religion to help challenge imperial rule and legitimize the birth and growth of the new nation. Many in the Buenos Aires *cabildo* who were rebelling against Spain assumed that as citizens of the former capital of the Viceroyalty of the River Plate they would continue to govern the interior and inherit the crown's old right of the *patronato*.

In the confusion of the independence period, when Spain's rule was in decline but no clear national authority had yet exerted itself, the episcopal see of Córdoba was filled by the appointment of Father Orellana without following the procedures set in canon law. When a cathedral seat in Buenos Aires was left vacant by the resignation of Father Magistral, the first Argentine junta, in August of 1810, sent notes to two ecclesiastics in the Cathedral of Córdoba, Gregorio Funes and Juan Luis de Aguirre y Tejeda, asking if the right of *patronato* had been conceded to the sovereign or to the persons who had exercised it. The two, having been well chosen, responded the next month that the right had been conceded to the sovereign, not the persons. Since the junta was now acting on behalf of the sovereign king, who had been temporarily dethroned, this gave the right of *patronato* to the junta.[7] From then until now, the Argentine government has claimed this right.

The church did not formally concede the right to the new national governments, as it had to the Spanish crown.[8] Bowing to the de facto limitations it faced, it reached a *modus vivendi* with the new governments. Because of the new, informal rules, the church could claim independence and the state could claim the right of *patronato*. The state would nominate men to fill high church offices after confidential negotiations; the pope would appoint those people without mentioning the state's nomination. The same procedure would be used in the creation of a new archdiocese.[9] Nonetheless, tensions rose whenever the state attempted to formalize the nationally administered *patronato* or when the church actually tried to act independently or to influence the state autonomously.

Enlightenment versus Tradition

The balance of power between the state and the church depended on the outcome of the contest between Buenos Aires and the Argentine interior for leadership of the new nation. Between 1810 and 1880, the provinces of Argentina struggled over the question of whether the majority of provinces should rule themselves in a confederation or Buenos Aires should rule the nation under a more centralized system. Buenos Aires strove to dominate the interior; the interior fought to retain its newfound freedoms from Spain and from the crown's viceroy in Buenos Aires.

One of the differences between the cosmopolitan port and the agricultural interior was often thought to be the port's "enlightened" liberalism, anticlericalism, or even Jacobinism, and the interior's continued devotion to traditional Catholicism. The conservatism of the provinces was well known. Although the *cabildo* of Tucumán supported the movement of independence from Spain, for example, it proclaimed that "this people will not recognize nor will it permit any religion but one, that which is Catholic, Apostolic, Roman."[10] After independence, "the Church continued to control education and maintained its influence over society in all the interior towns, for even the bitter independence struggle could not destroy the customs and heritage of two and a half centuries."[11]

The cosmopolitan unitarists, on the other hand, most often found in Buenos Aires, supported national and global integration based not on Catholic religious belief but on trade with Britain. When Mariano Moreno, a major independence leader, translated and published Rousseau's *Social Contract,* he left out Rousseau's criticism of religion because the topic was too controversial in Argentina. The ploy did not deceive many in the interior, who believed that Moreno and the other self-proclaimed "decent people" (*la gente decente*) of the Buenos Aires aristocracy were fanatical secularists. They feared that, as lawyer for British commercial interests before 1810, Moreno had picked up not just England's notions about free trade but also its hostility to Catholicism. Federico Ibarguren argued much later that Moreno's advocacy of French Enlightenment rationalism had made him an antireligious Jacobin. [12] José Luis Romero wrote that "in essence, Moreno was a Jacobin like the other men of his group such as Chiclana and Castelli and the later heirs of his policies such as Monteagudo and Alvear." He added that "their principles were derived from the deep seated conviction among the enlightened *porteños* [the people of the port city of Buenos Aires] that America offered optimal conditions for a republican system. It would be possible to establish on new bases a social compact like that ideally conceived by Rousseau."[13]

Some of the ideas that the self-styled Argentine Jacobins had acquired were the replacement of heaven with historical fame, goodness with the general will, sin with self-interest, and hell with infamy. In 1813, *El redactor de la asamblea* stated that

> all those who have been faithful to their high duties shall enter the temple of fame and receive public tributes of admiration and gratitude, but if there is anyone who, by confusing the goals of the popular will with his own self-interest, has degraded the principal offices of civil authority, he shall be delivered up to the remorse of his conscience and forever reside in the shadows where crime dwells. [14]

Moreno was not alone in trying to overcome the traditional religion of the interior. Other important leaders of the independence movement joined him, although they tried to be discreet. In 1814, Manuel Belgrano, a general and political leader during the independence period, advised San Martín, the liberator of Argentina, Chile, and Peru, to repress any blatant criticisms of religion:

> The concerns of the people are worthy of much respect, and many of their beliefs, limited though they may be, have a basis in religion. I certainly hope that you will keep this in mind, and that you will see to it that liberal opinions are not spread too widely, especially among the towns of the interior. You will be obliged to wage war there, not only with weapons but also with ideas. You should always appeal to the natural virtues, Christian and religious, since our enemies have made themselves our enemies by calling us heretics. By proclaiming that we have attacked religion, they have been able to summon their barbarian followers to arms. Perhaps some people will laugh at these ideas, but you must not let yourself be swayed by foreign opinions, or by men who do not know the land in which they walk. [15]

These were not the words of a devout Catholic, but of a practical man of affairs who did not want to fight religious provincials while there was still a war to be fought against the Spanish.

The mercantile class of *porteños* considered themselves urbane, cosmopolitan, Europeanized, civilized, and progressive. They also considered themselves to be a minority enclave in a population whose majority was rural, more barbaric than reactionary, receptive to mysticism and demagoguery, dogmatic, fanatical, unrealistic, irrational, and unfit for a constitutional republic. They considered it natural for themselves to inherit the Bourbon control of the inferior interior. [16] They wanted to achieve independence from the Spanish and assert their control over the interior in the name of enlightened principles.

Two groups that worked toward these ends were the *Sociedad Patriótica* (Patriotic Society) and the Lautaro Lodge. Bernardo de Monteagudo was president of the society, and San Martín one of its most distinguished members. According to Ibarguren, San Martín joined the group out of a simple patriotic desire to see the cause of independence furthered. Monteagudo, however, was a member of Moreno's group and was identified with all of Moreno's agenda. He sought to "break with the Hispanic tradition and create in our country the New Humanity heralded by the masonic encyclopaedists and intellectuals of the jacobin dictatorship."[17] According to José Luis Romero, Monteagudo picked up the Jacobin style of terrorism. Monteagudo wrote in April 1812 that leniency was a crime and advised the establishment of a dictatorship to consolidate the revolution.[18]

Many of the society's members also belonged to the Lautaro Lodge. An Araucanian Indian who died in the wars against the Spanish conquistadores, Lautaro had become a symbol of patriotism, valor, and independence, although the members of the lodge were not so romantic as to consider him a symbol of a return to Indian control of Argentina or any other place in Latin America. Monteagudo, Carlos de Alvear, Ramón Anchoris, San Martín, and others formed the so-called secret society in August of 1812 in a house across from the Santo Domingo convent on what is now called Balcarce Street in Buenos Aires.[19] (Secret, even conspiratorial opposition is the only type that is prudently possible under an authoritarian government, and Argentina has had its share of both.) When San Martín left Buenos Aires to retake the field of battle against the Spanish, according to Ibarguren, Monteagudo and his ally Alvear turned the lodge into the antithesis of San Martín's ideas.

Bernardino Rivadavia, first as a secretary for one of the juntas and then as president, brought some of these concerns to the policy level. Rivadavia worked to create a more modern, rational Argentina. He secularized the cemeteries and abolished the ecclesiastical *fuero* (special courts and law for clerics). His project of creating a university of Buenos Aires was inspired by his dedication to an institution of teaching and study free of church control. In 1822 he confiscated the possessions of the church in Buenos Aires and of most religious orders to reduce the amount of its economic power. (The church, for example, owned a quarter of the city of Córdoba's real estate.) He confiscated the Recoleta cemetery, the Casa de la Moneda, Avellaneda Park, Chacabuco Park, many large estates in the rural area of the province, and the land around the Buenos Aires cathedral, which is now the site of many government buildings.[20] The state would henceforth use the wealth from this confiscation to support the church and keep it dependent, and could thus afford to abolish the tithe.

The Church, Dictatorship, and Constitutions

After each stage in the struggle between the interior traditionalists and liberal *porteños,* assemblies and diplomatic representatives of the provinces attempted to codify the nation's political relations. One of the issues they had to confront was the relationship of church and state. The Assembly of 1813 passed a number of laws exercising the right of *patronato* independent of the king of Spain. On June 26, 1813, it stated that the United Provinces were no longer under the jurisdiction of the papal nuncio in Spain.[21] On June 12, it declared that all European Spanish ecclesiastics who had not become citizens should be deprived of employment.[22]

In all the constitutions of Argentina, the Roman Catholic religion was adopted as the religion of the state. Even the proposed constitution of the *Sociedad Patriótica* (1813) was prudent enough to state that the "Catholic religion is and will always be that of the State." The state was obligated to support the church. Its liberalism consisted of its concession that, although every inhabitant of the country would be required to respect the public cult, "no man will be persecuted for his private opinions in matters of religion."[23] The statute of 1815 obligated the director of the state to protect the religion of the state, ensuring its defense and happiness,[24] as did the Congress of Tucumán in 1816.[25] The 1819 constitution reiterated that the government would give the church its most efficacious and powerful protection and that all inhabitants would respect the church, whatever their private opinions.

The Congress of Tucumán in 1816 also stated in Article 24 that the supreme director would exercise the right of *patronato*. It gave the executive the power to name the bishops and archbishops and decide on any new church building.[26] The Constitution of 1826 stated that the executive would have these same powers (Art. 95), and that the Supreme Court would examine all pontifical briefs and bulls and dictate whether the executive should admit or retain them (Art. 125).[27] These articles represented the new national government's attempt to take for itself the crown's old right of *patronato*.

The church, for its part, looked for opportunities not to be separated from politics, but to be more independent of and influential over the state. It thought that it had found such an opportunity in 1828 during the political chaos following Argentina's humiliating loss of Uruguay, which had been a part of the old viceroyalty and ruled from Buenos Aires, and the continuing civil war between unitarists and federalists. Seizing the day in 1832 Pope Gregory XVI named the bishop of Buenos Aires without consulting the Argentine government.

The government accepted the nomination but reserved its claim to the right of *patronato*. Juan Manuel de Rosas eventually established a heavy-handed but originally popular order, and then made good on "the claim of the Argentine government to be the inheritor of the ecclesiastical patronage previously possessed by the Spanish kings."[28] In 1836 he readmitted the Society of Jesus, or the Jesuits, who had been expelled by the Spanish from the New World in 1767; however, when they refused to place portraits of him and his wife on their altars, he had them expelled again in 1843. The other orders prudently permitted such placement of Rosas's portraits.[29]

After defeating Rosas in 1852 at the battle of Caseros, Justo José de Urquiza, the governor of Santa Fe, summoned another constitutional convention, this time to meet in 1853. The delegates to this convention, whose work remains the nation's fundamental law, came with a well-established history of legal pronouncements on church-state relations. The constitution they wrote was largely based on that of the United States, which had also inspired the influential Argentine thinker Juan Bautista Alberdi. It differed from the U.S. document in some respects though, including its provisions for church-state relations.

After invoking the protection of God, "the source of all reason and justice," the constitution directs the federal government to "sustain" the Apostolic Roman Catholic church (Art. 2), although it leaves undefined whether sustenance means only financial support or extends to legislative support of church teachings.[30] Either way, the delegates showed that they were not interested in declaring a separation between church and state. However, they rejected the proposal in Alberdi's book *The Bases* that the state sustain and adopt the Catholic religion. The 1863 Congress again rejected a proposal for a constitutional reform to adopt Catholicism as the state religion.[31] The delegates unanimously agreed, however, to require that the president and vice-president be Catholic (Art. 73). They could not allow a non-Catholic to appoint high church officers and approve or reject the decrees of the pope. One of the delegates proposed that membership in the church be a condition for any civil employment, on the precedent of the English requirement that one be a Protestant to be in the English government; the proposal failed by a vote of 13–5.

The Constitution assigned the right of *patronato* to the central government. Although the delegates recognized the contradiction between Articles 14 and 64, Paragraph 20, which first guarantee the right to associate for useful ends but then give the Congress the power to admit or reject any new religious orders,[32] the delegates approved both. All foreigners were guaranteed the rights to navigate the nation's rivers and trade throughout the country, whatever their religion (Art. 20), but

Congress received the power to approve or reject any concordats with the church and to arrange the exercise of *patronato* in the confederation (Art. 64, Para. 19), and the president was given the power to exercise *patronato,* nominating the bishops and approving or retaining church declarations, with the approval of the Supreme Court (Art. 83, Paras. 8–9).[33]

In Article 105, the provincial governors were explicitly denied the right to admit new religious orders. Previous provincial constitutions (Córdoba, 1821; Corrientes, 1821; Jujuy, 1839) had claimed the right of *patronato* and there was pressure after 1853 to restore some of these powers. Indeed, in 1855 the national executive decreed that the governors exercised the right of *vice patronato,* but in 1870 the Supreme Court declared this right unconstitutional.[34]

In addition to establishing the constitutional provisions for church-state relations, President Urquiza worked to further codify them. He nominated and had installed the bishops of Salta, San Juan, and Córdoba and set up the diocese of El Litoral. Laws 176 of 1857 and 186 of 1858 set the amounts of money the state would provide to cathedrals, chancery offices, and seminaries. Other laws regulated the jurisdiction, installation, and support of bishops and the creation of other dioceses (Laws 28 and 49 of 1855, 85 and 99 of 1856, 116 of 1864, 597 of 1873, 982 of 1879, 1406 of 1884, 2246 of 1883, and 2302 of 1888).[35] The state would directly support Catholic worship by giving money to seminaries and chancery offices.[36] By 1985, this form of sustenance was costing the state 2.312 million australes, although this represented only 0.27 percent of the national budget. The state also supports private Catholic schools, which number about two thousand and comprise some 80 percent of the private schools in the country. The state also pays the salaries of military, police, and prison chaplains.

Some in the church complained that these laws so tightly connected the hierarchy to the government that church leaders had become more responsive to the nation's political elite than to Rome, church teachings, or church members. Mignone writes that the bishops had become influential in government and politics, but not in religion.[37]

Anticlerical governments like those of General Julio A. Roca tried to use the sustenance clause to pressure the church. The ranching-mercantile elite was economically "conservative" as understood in the United States, but "liberal" as understood in nineteenth-century Argentina. They favored private property, free trade, and little if any government-sponsored redistribution of wealth. They were also liberal in the senses of being areligious, hostile to the former political and economic powers of the church, and sometimes hostile to the doctrines of Catholicism. They were inspired not by religion but by the positivist promise of progress through the application of science to social affairs.

A variety of methods were employed to enforce a domesticated role for the church in Argentine society. Since church money came from the government, cutting off funds left the church without other income. In 1882, Roca first cut off the salary to the vicar general of Córdoba, Jerónimo E. Clara, and then removed him from office.[38] He suspended the bishop of Salta, Risso Patron. In both of these cases, Roca treated high church officials as though they were civil servants, which in a way they were.

In 1884 the government passed the law of public education, which threatened the church's formation of future generations. Arguing that the church was not able to educate all the children in the country, who nonetheless all had the right to be educated, whatever their ability to pay, the legislators provided for "secular, compulsory, and free schools." The government's rationale was that future citizens of a republic had the duty to their country to become educated and able to make reasoned choices. Reasoned choice was not possible without freedom of conscience, speech, and thought, or if there were a dogmatic training. Delfin Gallo said in Congress that

> the church has not forgotten its old theories about its predominance over all temporal authority. I do not believe, Mr. President, that this objective will be achieved, given the state of world civilization; but I do fear that some people, who are not very advanced on the cultural scale—for example, the people of Ecuador, and others of our race who still find themselves submerged in semibarbarism owing to the instability of their institutions and to countless revolutions—may fall into this hidden trap. It seems to me that after all the advances that humanity has made, no one can claim the desirability or the utility for the Argentine Republic to have the spiritual power, from which the popes have derived their secular authority, dominate the temporal power, that is to say, the sovereignty of the people, which today is the basis of all political government.[39]

Alarmed by these policies, some Catholics called a congress of their own in 1884. Professor José Manuel Estrada addressed the gathering:

Gentleman, whether or not there is a conscious conspiracy at the highest level of the government to put into effect a Masonic program of anti-Christian revolution is not a matter of discussion. We would not be here if the apostasy of those who govern us had not aroused popular indignation! Whether or not this has been a premeditated, dictatorial usurpation of the rights of God, and of the nation, I can tell you the tale of a year in which an unfeeling government has trampled simultaneously upon the immunity of the Church, the honor and teaching career, freedom of conscience, the faith of their parents, the innocence of children, the freedom of suffrage, and the independence of the provinces—all our rights as Christians and Argentines.[40]

In response, General Roca dismissed Estrada from his teaching posts and, accusing the papal nuncio of agitating for such outbursts of insubordination, expelled the nuncio from the country. Finally, he broke diplomatic relations with the Vatican. These were not renewed until 1900, after Roca's presidency.

In the next presidential administration of Juarez Celman, a proposal to permit civil marriage again caused disturbances. The law was described by Eduardo Wilde, the minister of the interior, as necessary "for the advancement and evolution of our society," and by the minister of justice and religion, Filemon Posse, as a "genuine expression of the holy freedom of conscience, of that freedom, won by civilization, which today makes it impossible for a man to be marched to the stake because he does not believe in Jesus Christ."[41]

The church took the proposal to mean that the laws of the state were not only oblivious but even hostile to its doctrines, that the sovereignty of God had been replaced by the sovereignty of the people. The highest forms of knowledge were no longer mysteriously revealed in Scripture and tradition by God through Christ; they were reasoned out by people and recorded in constitutions. The pope was no longer the final authority in matters of faith and morals because he was infallible; the government was infallible because it was the final authority over which there was no appeal. Instead of all people being members of the body of the church, whose head was the Christ, all citizens belonged to a mechanistic state filled with balances and separations of power.

The church found its powers further reduced after the 1880s, but the state did not yet desire to completely separate the church from politics.[42] The state had benefited from the legitimization a controlled church provided. Even a liberal state saw no benefit in the separation of church and state, as long as the church was under control; as long as many citizens were fervently religious, religion needed to be controlled. But in 1898, Juan Gutierrez presented to the Constitutional Reform Convention a petition signed by twenty-two thousand habitants of Argentina calling for elimination of all the constitutionally mandated responsibilities of the state for religion and a complete separation of church and state. The convention replied that this was not part of the mandate for reform passed by Congress and that they were not allowed by the procedure for constitutional reform to accept other mandates for reform.[43]

Chafing under state control, some in the church challenged the regime of the liberal oligarchy, calling for its replacement with a more democratic one. Most of the immigrants of the late nineteenth century were from Spain or Italy. Some were Socialists or anarchists who had little regard for Catholicism, but the majority were Catholics. And much of the oligarchy was either secular liberal or positivist. The church might have little to fear if a government freely elected by all-male, mostly Catholic citizens came to power. The electoral reform of 1912 was a response to the growing power of many who had been excluded from power by the liberal oligarchy.

Each of these various groups had its own reasons for opposing the liberals, and they did not all agree with the idea that the church should autonomously exercise more influence over the state. Nevertheless, after the election of the middle-class Radical party presidential candidate Hipolito Yrigoyen in 1916, and the loss of political power by the liberal oligarchy, the church thought that its support of democracy could lead to more independence from government control and more influence over politics.

In 1923 the archbishop of Buenos Aires died. The man named by the government as his successor was rejected by the pope, who appointed an "apostolic administrator." This position was given all the responsibilities the archbishop had exercised, but the action looked to the president like intervention and a violation of *patronato,* and he refused to accept the administrator. The Supreme Court agreed that the position was unconstitutional. In 1926, President Alvear nominated another person, who this time was named as archbishop by the pope. The right of *patronato* was thereby reestablished under the democratic government.[44] Democracy had not led to church independence.

Catholic Nationalism, Peronism, and Militarism

While the Radical governments were freely elected, the Argentine political economy remained the same in many other respects. The landed oligarchy continued to possess most economic resources. Trade with Britain was the backbone of the economy. The liberal system had developed; it had not gone through a fundamental transformation. The traditionalist criticism of oligarchical dependence on British, liberal ideas and institutions also developed. Corporatist nationalists believed that political liberalism, constitutional democracy, and mechanistic checks and balances were unnatural, foreign implants. They theorized about the need for a head for the body politic, about an organic state where the natural groups of society were represented.

When the old and rather senile Yrigoyen was reelected in 1928, his advisors were accused of corruption, the military complained that he interfered politically in otherwise professional decisions about promotions, the unions complained that he allowed the police to abuse strikers, and provinces complained that the central government was unconstitutionally dominating the entire country. When the Great Depression hit in 1930, the oligarchy worried that the newly unemployed might follow foreign revolutionary examples. The Catholic Nationalist general José F. Uriburu met little resistance in conducting the coup in 1930 that led to a half century of military predominance in Argentine politics.

The split in the rest of the country between liberalism and antiliberalism was mirrored in the military. The liberal general Augustín P. Justo carried out a counter coup in 1932, and the following year he concluded the Roca-Runciman pact, which reestablished a firm economic relationship with Great Britain. The military tried to restore many of the old policies of the liberal oligarchy, including its fraudulent elections, but Argentina in the thirties was far more urban and industrialized and had better organized labor unions than it had had during the golden age of liberalism. Electoral fraud, ties with Britain, and then Britain's precarious position at the beginning of World War II discredited the liberal military.

Part of the justification for the coup of 1943 was to restore patriotism, which mandated loyalty to the national culture as opposed to slavish imitation of British liberalism. For those who were influenced by the French writer Charles Maurras, the church was part of the nation's historical character, whether or not God existed. Like Maurras, many Argentine Catholic Nationalists were agnostics but still revered the influence of the institutional church. Influenced by European integralism, they supported the coup of 1943 and were rewarded with a number of jobs in the new government. For example, Martínez Zuviría, whose many novels, written under the pen name Hugo Wast, propounded Catholic Nationalist themes, became the minister of education.[45] In October 1943 he restored religious education to public schools, which had been absent since Roca's reforms.

Among those who courted the church and the Catholic Nationalists as worthwhile allies was Juan Perón, who had been at first a minor participant in the coup and subsequent government. Perón, at heart a politician concerned with building supportive coalitions, never intended to empower the church or allow its teachings to restrict his own amorous activities. Instead, Perón used his allies in the church along with those in the military and the unions to work his way to the top of Argentine politics. As secretary of labor and social welfare, he negotiated labor disputes in favor of labor and raised money to help victims of natural disasters such as the earthquake in San Juan. He then used his popularity among the country's many "shirtless ones" to maneuver his way to the top of the military. When elections were called for 1946, the new patron of the poor and of the Catholic Nationalists was freely elected president.

The niceties of democracy usually took second place in the estimation of both Perón and his followers. Peronism had been based on the exchange of labor's support of Perón in return for material benefits from the government for labor. Having inherited foreign reserves accumulated during the Second World War, Perón could hand out benefits at the beginning of his administration. Demand in Europe for Argentine products was high immediately after the war. The monopsonistic Argentine government paid low prices for grain and beef from domestic producers and earned profits by selling to foreign markets. The earnings were put into popular wage increases and social benefits for the urban poor. The landed oligarchy preferred this arrangement to expropriation of their land by the government. By the early fifties, however, when the reserves were exhausted and the European Common Market was overseeing the recovery of Europe and the growing demand by European farmers for protection, Perón could no longer deliver on his end of the bargain. When he tried to do so by printing money, inflation merely caused a decline in real salaries. Labor support for Perón dropped accordingly.

Perón also acquired other adversaries. After the death of his famous wife, Evita, in 1952, he seemed to lose much of his old skill. Those in the military who had been surpassed and suppressed by Perón, those in the universities who had been unwilling to repeat the Peronist ideology (which Perón found more useful than strictly Catholic doctrine) and had been expelled from their jobs, and those landowners who had grudgingly paid for Perón's policies, now shared labor's skepticism of Perón.

The church became an umbrella under which many of these groups came to criticize the once popular leader. Perón's alleged sexual immorality (he was living with a fourteen-year-old girl), his support of the legalization of divorce and prostitution, and his caving in to multinational corporations (strapped for cash by March 1955, Perón announced a deal with his old nemesis, Rockefeller's Standard Oil) gave Catholic Nationalists something to criticize. Perón lashed out at his enemies and escalated the hostilities between himself and the church. He removed all religious education from public schools and ended state subsidies to church schools. In May he proposed to separate church and state constitutionally and began to imprison priests who opposed the plan. In June the church organized its annual parade celebrating Corpus Christi, and 100,000 marchers, chanting "Death to Evita," watched as the Argentine flag was pulled down from the National Congress and the papal flag run up the flagpole. The next day, still-loyal Peronists attacked the national cathedral, and Perón went on nationwide radio to denounce the clergy. On June 14, he expelled two bishops from the country. They fled to Rome, and Perón was promptly excommunicated. Loyal Peronists filled the Plaza de Mayo in support of their leader on June 16. Navy planes bombed the demonstrators, leaving at least two hundred dead. That night, Peronists responded by burning at least twelve churches and the headquarters of the archdiocese.[46] Army units still loyal to Perón restored order, and Perón survived for three more months until overthrown by the "Liberating Revolution" of General Eduardo Lonardi. Perón's "critical mistake," David Rock concludes, "was to have attacked the Church."[47]

The Catholic nationalism of Lonardi lasted only the sixty days that Lonardi did. His successor, General Pedro Aramburu, also rescinded Perón's attacks on the church, but as when General Justo replaced General Uriburu in 1930, a more liberal militarism replaced the Catholic Nationalists who had led the antidemocratic revolutions. The anti-Peronist military factions now in power outlawed the Peronist party and limited opposition to the Radical party. Arturo Frondizi and Arturo Illia, from different wings of the Radical party, won the elections of

1958 and 1963. Neither was able to govern effectively without Peronist support, and their own democratic impulses led them to legalize Peronist electoral participation. This twice led to expectations of imminent Peronist victories.

In exile, Perón was remembered for the benefits he had provided in the late forties and for being the first major leader to include labor's concerns in the government. His successors were blamed for the declining economy that he had bequeathed them. Also, those who were concerned by Perón's implied excommunication were relieved when in 1963 the church clarified that he was a member in good standing. The church said it had only threatened him with excommunication. Perón's popularity was restored in some sectors of Argentine society, but not in the anti-Peronist military factions, which in 1962 and 1966 successfully carried out coups.

While still in office, Frondizi and Illia wanted to move in the direction of greater separation between church and state. Neither wanted to suggest a controversial reform of the Constitution, so Frondizi proposed, and Illia negotiated with the church, to reduce the role of the state in church appointments. Illia was ready to sign an agreement the day he was thrown out of office.

President and General Onganía signed the agreement with the Holy See on October 10, 1966, but for different reasons than the Radicals had.[48] The archbishop had been at Onganía's side during his swearing-in ceremony, which occurred just twenty-eight hours after Illia's ouster. The general wanted to show his loyalty to the church by codifying the practice of giving the church more power in making its own appointments. The goal was not to separate church and state or religion and politics, but to permit a more autonomous church to influence government indirectly. The church would henceforth communicate in advance to the government its intention to name a bishop, who was to be a citizen of Argentina, to see if the government had any objection to that person. Silence would be considered approval. The agreement also recognized the church's right to communicate freely with its bishops, clergy, and members.

Some objected that these new arrangements violated specific provisions of the Constitution, and that a reform of the Constitution would be necessary to make such changes. The government argued that it was merely following the procedures (Art. 67, Para. 19, and Art. 86, Para. 14) that provided for the executive to arrange concordats with foreign powers and send them to Congress for approval.

The church to which Onganía wanted to give more independence was the one that sponsored the weekend religious retreats on traditional spiritual development that he attended. This was not the only church he got. The church in Argentina was known as one of the more conservative churches in Latin America, and even the world. The church outside Argentina was undergoing significant change.

The Vatican II Council of the early 1960s had produced a number of controversial papers, including "The Church in the Modern World." This paper stressed the importance of liberation in this as well as the next life. It condemned atheistic socialism, but also liberal capitalism, and denounced the victimization of underdeveloped countries.[49] Priests and bishops throughout Latin America were reevaluating what it meant to be a Catholic. Bishops who met at Medellín, Colombia, in 1968, and priests like Gustavo Gutiérrez, who wrote *A Theology of Liberation,* gave old religious symbols new political meanings. Sin was no longer just a matter of individual shortcomings or individuals' separation from God; sin could also be social in nature, the domination and exploitation of one group by another. Salvation from sin did not mean only an invisible change in relations between God and humanity because of the atonement made possible by the crucifixion, but also liberation from a situation of exploitation through political action and, if necessary, through the up-dated and collective crucifixion of revolution. A small group of people with a single leader two thousand years before had gone on to conquer the hearts and minds of an empire. Tightly organized cells of the committed in the modern world could repel neo-imperialism. The Third World Priest movement and Liberation Theology had been born.

As teachers in Catholic schools developed these positions, they inspired a number of students to act on them. One group in Argentina that took the new teachings seriously was Catholic Action, out of which came many members of the montoneros,[50] who were named after the armed, horseback-riding gauchos who had supported the provincial caudillos of the early nineteenth century. The term *montón* (mass or crowd) also fit neatly with the usual leftist emphasis on the importance of the masses. The montoneros saw themselves as the modern fighters for freedom from an authoritarian, centralized regime. They were fighting not for provincial independence from Buenos Aires, but for national independence from an enclave in Buenos Aires who were ruling Argentina in the interests of themselves and the World Capitalist System.

The montoneros' symbol was Perón. The youth of the mid-1950s had condemned Perón's heavy-handed treatment of the universities, but the montoneros were not primarily concerned with secondary rights of the bourgeoisie like free speech. Besides, Perón had been out of the country since 1955, and much of the military was determined not to let him or his followers back in. He was not likely to become more than a convenient figurehead.

Moreover, Perón was a symbol that justified the use of force. He was a military man willing to come to power through a coup who had used his power to help the working class. This corresponded to the new radical interpretation of religious violence. God's angel had killed the first-born children of the Egyptians to liberate the chosen people from oppression and poverty. Jesus was born not in Rome, but in a faraway province of the Roman Empire on the periphery of the ancient world. God had required the shedding of blood by Christ to permit a reconciliation with the world. Passover preceded exodus and flight to a promised land of milk and honey; crucifixion preceded the possibility of salvation. The Book of Revelation predicted a period of awful violence before the second coming of Christ. The real meaning of the Bible from Old to New Testament was that a period of violence and bloodshed was necessary to destroy a previous period of imperial oppression and to enable followers to receive their just reward. Only liberals could turn Christianity into a passivity bolstering oppression. Moses and Jesus denounced sin and oppression. Perón had denounced capitalism; U.S. imperialism; the local financial, country-selling oligarchy; and big landowners. Left-wing Nationalists had a symbol in Perón, who was unlikely to return and meddle in current affairs. In radical theology, they had a way to integrate Peronism, radical socialism, and left-wing nationalism.

The military was alarmed by the 1969 riots beginning in Córdoba, initiated by labor but quickly joined by university students. Further unrest convinced them no one but their old nemesis could have a chance of controlling the violent chaos. They allowed Perón to return to power and to become president in 1973. This surprised the montoneros and other radical Peronists, but they at first tried to work with him and even to define his presidency. Perón intended rather to use them in a new coalition. They finally split, and the montoneros and Peronists declared war on each other. After Perón's death in 1974, his wife Isabel, the new president, was widely perceived as ineffective in this struggle. She fell from power in the coup of March 24, 1976.

A Captive Church

The role of the church during 1976–83 has underscored for some the problems of *patronato,* especially during a military government. The military had developed its own version of *patronato* since the turn of the century. Emilio Mignone, an Argentine author whose daughter disappeared during the "dirty war" of the late 1970s, argues that the basic problem in Argentine church-state relations is that "the institutions that make up, or depend on, the official church have no autonomy."[51] This took on particular significance for church-military relations, especially after 1905, when laws 4,031 and 4,707 incorporated into the Argentine system much of the professionalism of the Prussian model. The system for officer training, promotions, retirement, and obligatory military service were to create for Argentina the benefits of discipline and professionalism that characterized the best army in the world. The Prussian model called for total control over the individual soldier. Every aspect of his life while in the military should be under the control of the military.

One of these aspects was religion; so the laws established a permanent body of military chaplains who were given military rank and were under military regulations. They at first reported to the bishop in whose diocese they served, although their pay, promotions, and privileges came from the military. But in 1957, General and President Aramburu and the Holy See agreed to form a military vicarate. The vicar would be appointed by the pope after nomination by the president. The vicarate would be similar to a diocese, with all priests and parishioners in the military under the military vicar.

In 1968, Archbishop Adolfo Tortolo of Parana, president of the Argentine Episcopal Conference, became the military vicar. On December 29, 1975, Tortolo told a luncheon group of the Argentine Chamber of Advertisers at the Plaza Hotel that a "process of purification" was drawing near.[52] The provicar for the military, Bishop Victorio Bonamin, said in a homily that General Jorge Rafael Videla attended on September 23, 1975, that the military was being "purified in the Jordan of blood so that they could place themselves at the head of the whole country. The army is expiating the impurity of our country. May not Christ some day want the armed forces to go beyond their normal function?" The night before the March 24, 1976, coup, two of its leaders, Videla and Admiral Emilio Massera, met with two of the leaders from the episcopate. On March 24, all three members of the new junta met with Tortolo.[53] He publicly urged Argentines to "cooperate in a positive way" with the new government.

Some ten thousand who did not cooperate in a positive way disappeared after 1976. They did not reappear until their skeletons were dug up from no-name graves during the post-1983 democratic government of Raúl Alfonsín. The church's position on the "dirty war" of the late 1970s has been particularly controversial. In testimony before the National Commission on Disappeared Persons (CONADEP), established by Alfonsín after his election, Ernesto Reynaldo Saman (file 4841) stated, "When I was in prison in Villa Gorriti, Jujuy, Bishop Medina said mass, and in the sermon he said that he knew what we were going through, but that it was for the good of the country, and that the military were working for good and we ought to tell everything we knew. For that purpose, he offered to hear confessions."[54] Another detainee of that center, Eulogia Cordero de Garnica, also testified that Medina had visited her and encouraged her to tell her captors all she knew. She was eventually released, but her son and brother have never been seen since their disappearances in 1976. Another testified that a Father Cacabello had attended his torture sessions in Caseros Prison in March 1980. A military chaplain, Marcial Castro Castillo, published a book justifying the techniques used in the war against subversion.[55] Chaplains in the Superior War College warned their students that "democracy based on universal suffrage or popular sovereignty is an effective means for encouraging legal subversion."[56] Mignone concludes that these men had been ordained to serve Christ but had ended up obeying Mars.

Not only was the military vicarate justifying the antisubversive war; most of the church hierarchy was, too. Of the eighty prelates, heads of dioceses, auxiliary bishops, and military bishops in the episcopate, only four openly denounced the human rights violations of the military government from 1976 to 1983. The episcopate did proclaim in general that kidnapping and torture were wrong and even sinful. Their pastoral letter of May 15, 1976, however, supported the government's activities:

> We must keep in mind that it would be easy to err with good intentions against the common good, if one were to insist that the security forces must act with chemical purity of peacetime, while blood is being shed every day; that the kinds of disorders, whose depth we all know quite well, were to be straightened out without the drastic kinds of measures that the situation demands; or that

we should be unwilling to accept for the sake of the common good
the sacrifice of the measure of freedom that this moment requires;
or that with justification allegedly based on the gospel, there
should be an attempt to impose Marxist solutions.[57]

In other words, the necessities of wartime justified drastic measures and
the surrendering of a measure of freedom in order to straighten out deep
disorders and prevent Marxism from being imposed on the nation. In
their report, *Nunca Más* (*Never Again*), CONADEP concluded that "there
were members of the clergy who committed or supported with their
presence, with their silence, and even with justifying words these same
acts which had been condemned by the episcopate."[58]

The convergence of radical Peronism and Liberation Theology was
opposed in a variety of ways by traditional church leaders and by the
military. The Argentine delegates to the Puebla, Mexico, conference of
Latin American bishops in 1979 unsuccessfully tried to bar the use of
the word *liberation* from the documents. Conservative priests wrote
extensively to refute the modern "heresy" of Liberation Theology.[59] In
addition to academic refutations, there were violent attacks on propo-
nents of the new doctrines. Two bishops died in "accidents." A leading
radical priest was shot after leaving mass. Several other priests, and
dozens of other clerical leaders, "disappeared." Many of the top church
leaders in the country either remained quiet about these actions or
publicly supported them.

The Church and the Consolidation of Democracy

After the economic failures of the late seventies and early eighties,
the controversial "dirty war" of the same period, and the military failure
in the 1982 Malvinas war, the military fell from power. The incoming
democratic government was concerned with how the church and democracy could best be related. Paul Sigmund argues that a significant part of
the Catholic tradition indeed favors democratic regimes.[60] In Argentina
specifically, there is some support for this position. For example, the
episcopate in 1981 published a letter, "The Church and National Community," in which for the first time it supported republican, representative government.[61]

The new president was Raúl Alfonsín, who had been a critic of the
military while it had been in power. During the 1983 electoral campaign, he outmaneuvered other Radicals who had been less publicly

critical of the military regime, and then the Peronists, who for the first time during an election were without Juan Perón and had decades of controversy weighing them down.

Alfonsín remained silent during the 1983 campaign on issues concerning the church: constitutional reform of church-state articles, the legalization of divorce, equal rights for women in the family, and reduced censorship at the cost of increased pornography. There was no reason to create needless problems for himself before the election. He and Italo Luder, the Peronist candidate, avoided any anticlerical statements in their campaigns. Both campaigned as respectable family men, in contrast to Perón and Galtieri, whose extramarital affairs were well known.

With neither candidate attacking the church, however, most of the church remained officially neutral. The bishops' conference endorsed no candidate. It criticized only the Communist party, a negligible force in the country anyway. There were individual exceptions, however. Bishop Antonio Palaza of La Plata, for example, endorsed the conservative, gun-toting, and unsuccessful Peronist candidate for governor of Buenos Aires, Herminio Iglesias. The Peronist leanings of some bishops who hoped for a return to Perón's earlier Catholic nationalism were reinforced by their suspicion that the Radicals were the party for Freemasons, liberal Catholics, and Jews. And the bishops did favor "reconciliation," understood to mean the amnesty law decreed by the military government for itself. In spite of all this, the church remained largely out of the 1983 campaign.

Alfonsín returned the favor, initially avoiding conflict with the church. For the first year, he opposed the introduction of legislation aimed at legalizing divorce or liberalizing abortion laws, which prohibited abortion except in cases of rape, incest, or severe deformation of the fetus. No mention was made of separating church and state constitutionally.

His initial lack of aggressiveness in making the church self-financing, as Felipe Gonzalez had done in Spain, may have been because Alfonsín wanted the church's cooperation on the Beagle Channel dispute with Chile.[62] The Holy See was mediating the dispute for the two nations, eventually producing a treaty in which Argentina renounced its claims to the islands. This issue, which had been a point of controversy for a century, had nearly brought the two nations to war in 1978. The church's involvement in the resolution of the dispute, and its implied support for the treaty, was of value for the Alfonsín administration's effort to settle the dispute peacefully. Alfonsín successfully submitted the treaty to a nationwide plebiscite in 1985.

As we have seen, however, mutual suspicions between the church and the administration were present from the beginning. Many in the church were concerned about what they interpreted as the government's toleration or even sponsorship of pornography and Marxism. Lay groups such as the League of Decency or Fatherland, Family, and Tradition were run mainly by Catholics. In April 1985, Jujuy bishop Arsenio Casado proclaimed that "we declare ourselves to be faithful to a Western and Christian civilization, but in practice liberalism and Marxism are collaborating with each other in suffocating Christianity and in undermining morality, which in turn threatens our national identity."[63]

The archbishop of San Juan criticized young Argentines who, with the support of some in the government, were going to Nicaragua in 1985 to help with the coffee harvest.[64] *Cabildo,* a Catholic nationalist journal, accordingly represented Alfonsín on one of its covers as the "Great Satan." Father Manuel Beltran at a mass on August 2, 1986, accused government leaders of being "responsible for and accomplices of the unleashing of anticlericalism. They know about and are quite familiar with the increase of drugs, delinquency, and pornography."[65]

The old theme of Western, Christian, Catholic, Argentine national civilization versus liberal, Marxist, antinational threats was still important to many in the church. During the annual march near the presidential palace in 1985 in honor of the Corpus Christi, the vicar general of the archdiocese of Buenos Aires told the marchers that the state-owned-and-operated mass media was "distorting and degrading love, sex, and the family," as well as running a campaign against the church in general.[66] The AICA regularly reported that the state-run media and public education were permitting or promoting a moral crisis in the country by allowing secularists and Marxists free reign.

Anticlerics were not above inflammatory rhetoric, either. At a rally sponsored by the Mothers of the Plaza in protest of the allegedly light sentences of the military men convicted of human rights abuses, one slogan read, "Let's hang the last capitalist with the guts of a fat priest."[67] The leader of the group deplored such statements. Members of the Right were equally enthusiastic after the sentences. Wives of military men from the "processo" emerged from a mass after the sentences calling press photographers "Jews, blacks, and Marxists."[68]

This type of rhetoric ultimately persuaded Alfonsín to pursue a separation of church and state. He established the Council for the

Consolidation of Democracy, one of whose purposes was to suggest constitutional reforms. The council argued that Argentina now had a pluralist society that supported the free choice of religious beliefs and recognized the diversity of races, religion, and customs. This society was consistent with the new attitude of the Catholic church, which in the conclusions of Vatican II had opposed any pressures on the individual to profess religious beliefs against her or his conscience and had supported freedom of religious conviction. As Pius XII had said, a free church and a free state do not intervene in each other's spheres of activity.

The council recommended many changes in the Constitution, including the removal of all provisions concerning religion in the current Constitution.[69] Except for the mention of God in the preamble, the Constitution should concern itself with religion only by including a new article guaranteeing freedom of religion, without any other mention.

The call for the end of *patronato* and the separation of church and state in Argentina found some support. Mignone, for example, contended that "the next reform of the constitution will have to bring about the separation of church and state." He argued for the elimination of the independent military vicarate, placing all chaplains under the control of dioceses, whose officials would be appointed and nominated by the church without previous consultation or approval by the government. Without government financing, and with greater openness in church financial records, Argentines would be willing to sustain the church voluntarily themselves. The church would become more responsive to the members. But the proposal to reform the Constitution, including its provisions about church-state relations, was opposed by a majority in Congress, and the entire project went nowhere.

This was not the end of Alfonsín's attempts to change the role of religion in politics. Constitutional reform was only one of the church's concerns about Alfonsín. Church criticism of the government intensified when the government proposed a series of laws on family issues. The first was the proposed repeal of the *patria potestad* law, a civil law that helped the state sustain the basic teachings of the church's view of a hierarchical society modeled after its religious hierarchy. This law gave the father complete control over decisions about his offsprings' education, travel, and finances until they became legally independent. The new legislation would give the mother equal rights in these decisions and would extend inheritance rights to illegitimate children. The church maintained the traditional views of sexual roles based on its theology. God the Father had sent God the Son to select twelve male disciples to build His church in the world; the reverence due to Christ's Mother, the Virgin Mary, assured women an important role in Catholicism. Priests, bishops, popes, and church leaders in general were to be male, as was the head of the church (Christ), and as were the heads of families. Feminists and other liberal groups argued that religious symbols may have been manipulated by male authors in ancient times, that when the angel of God announced to Mary that she had been chosen for a role that of course she would be honored to fulfill, she was not being asked to make an autonomous decision about what she wanted. This criticism implied that the Bible was man-made, culture bound, and not the eternal revealed word of God, and that the *patria potestad* was representative of male domination of women and a violation of the principle of equality. Both houses of Congress eventually agreed with the criticism of the law and passed the repeal.

The government was now prepared to take on the even thornier issue of divorce.[70] Current legislation provided for separation but not for nullification of marriage, nor for remarriage. A million Argentines described themselves as separated, and many of them de facto had remarried but were officially only living together. The five hundred thousand children who had been born to these couples were considered illegitimate. The law reflected the position of the church, in which Christ was likened to the bridegroom and His church to the bride, both of whom were to be faithful to each other. This religious symbolism was to be placed upon society by legislating faithfulness in marriage. The mystery and eternity of Christ's relation with His church was to be mirrored in human marriage. All this mystery did not advance Alfonsín's major goal of making Argentine political culture more "rational."[71] Such legal sustenance of the church's teachings seemed anachronistic to many in this more secular age.

The church remained opposed to the changes in the divorce laws. As Alfonsín was well aware, it was around this issue that many in the military and the unions had mobilized in 1955 when Perón had proposed the legalization of divorce and had let inflation bite into real salaries. Because of the broad, intense opposition to the military still evident in 1986, Alfonsín did not expect the successful coup of 1955 to be repeated because of this issue, although he was cautious.

The proposal facing Congress was debated throughout the country for months. Monsignor Emilio Ognenovich, appointed by the Episcopal Conference to formulate church policy toward the divorce bill, stated before the vote in Congress that "the divorce bill is part of a generalized attack on the family, and is supported by groups linked to foreign ideologies and drug traffickers." *Esquiu,* a Catholic weekly, opined after the success of the bill in Congress that "after divorce we can expect the legalization of abortion, drugs, euthanasia, and homosexuality."[72] The *Coordinadora Nacional de Defensa de la Familia* (National Coordinator of the Defense of the Family) took out a full-page ad in *La Nación* to express opposition to a plan to use the public schools to teach the innocuousness of masturbation.[73] The church decided it had to take a stand; it denied communion to lawmakers who had voted for the divorce bill.

There was always the lingering concern that the church might come to legitimize a renewed hostility toward not only the Alfonsín government but also the democratic regime. As had been true with previous presidents, Alfonsín faced declining popularity due in large part to the country's economic difficulties. Would this lead to a rehabilitated image for the military? Would the church play a role in such a rehabilitation? Various statements by members of the military added to this concern. For example, General Justo Jacobo Rojas Alcorta, of the Fifth Infantry Brigade of Tucumán, said in July 1986 that the theory of liberal democracy is "false, because it supports popular sovereignty when, according to Christian doctrine, it is God who confers power."[74] Military disturbances and de facto coup attempts occurred during Easter week of 1987 and during January and December 1988. Left-wing guerrillas, including one priest, Fr. Juan Antonio Puigjane, attacked a military barracks at La Tablada in March 1989. They tried to make the attack look like a right-wing military uprising in order to begin a civil war between actual right-wingers and loyalist troops, after which they would take power.

However, all these disturbances were defeated by the government, and Alfonsín in 1989 became the first democratically elected president in Argentina since Perón to finish his term. Since Perón did not behave very democratically while in power, one could say that Alfonsín was the first *democratic* president to finish his term since 1928. In either case, the fear that a church-supported military government might return to rule the nation was not realized.

The administration of President Carlos Menem has inherited a complex historical debate about *patronato,* liberal reforms of church-state relations, and governmental policies toward areas of interest to the church. Menem and Cardinal Juan Carlos Aramburu met on October 23, 1989, to exchange pleasantries. Menem said that Peronists "are loyal and faithful to the work of Pope John Paul II because we are enrolled in the social doctrine of the church," and Aramburu said that there existed a "state of tranquility" in church relations with the state.[75] In spite of such loyalty and tranquility, however, the state and the church will continue trying to influence each other along the continuum of challenge and legitimization.

Notes

Acknowledgments: The author wishes to acknowledge the financial support from the National Endowment for the Humanities and Villanova University that made the research and writing of this chapter possible.

1. See, for example, Robert D. Crassweller, *Perón and the Enigmas of Argentina* (New York: W. W. Norton, 1987), 27, 28, 31, 43, 46, 81.

2. For example, see Sandra McGee Deutsch, *Counterrevolution in Argentina, 1900–1932: The Argentine Patriotic League* (Lincoln: University of Nebraska, 1986); Natan Lerner, "Anti-Semitism and the Nationalist Ideology in Argentina," *Dispersion and Unity* 17–18 (1973): 131–39; Hector Ruiz Nuñez and Marcelo Figueras, "Los judíos: Los pueblos trágicos," parts 1, 2, *El periodista de Buenos Aires,* August 8–14, August 15–21, 1986; Leonardo Senkman, *El antisemitismo en la Argentina,* 2 vols. (Buenos Aires: Biblioteca Política Argentina, 1986); Jacobo Timerman, *Prisoner without a Name, Cell without a Number,* trans. Toby Talbot (New York: Vintage Books, 1982); "Alertan sobre el antisemitismo," *Clarín,* September 13, 1983:8.

3. See Leonardo Senkman, ed., *El antisemitismo en la Argentina,* 2d ed. (Buenos Aires: Centro Editor de América Latina, 1989); "Ley contra la discriminación," editorial, *La Nación,* August 18, 1988; "No a la discriminación," editorial, *Clarín,* August 6, 1988.

4. Pablo A. Ramella, *Derecho constitucional,* 2d ed. (Buenos Aires: Ediciones Depalma, 1982), 185.

5. Ibid., 186.

6. Quoted in Juan Carlos Zuretti, *Nueva historia eclesiástica argentina—Desde el concilio de Trento al Vaticano II* (Buenos Aires: Itinerarium, 1972), 40; also see Antonio O. Donini, *Religión y sociedad* (Buenos Aires: Editorial Docencia, 1985), 22.

7. Ramella, *Derecho constitucional,* 186.

8. Donini, *Religión y sociedad,* 27.

9. See Ramella, *Derecho constitucional,* 197.

10. Anibal A. Rottjer, *La masonería en la Argentina y en el mundo,* 6th ed. (Buenos Aires: Editorial Nuevo Orden, 1983), 255, 271.

11. James R. Scobie, *Argentina: A City and a Nation,* 2d ed. (New York: Oxford University Press, 1971), 102.

12. Federico Ibarguren, *Así fue Mayo* (Buenos Aires: Ediciones Theoría, 1956), 25.

13. Quoted in José Luis Romero, *A History of Argentine Political Thought,* trans. Thomas F. Morgan (Stanford: Stanford University Press, 1963), 70, 71.

14. Quoted in Romero, *Argentine Political Thought,* 73.

15. From letter quoted in José Luis Romero, *Las ideas políticas en Argentina* (Buenos Aires: Fondo de Cultura Económica, 1975), 100.

16. For the inheritance by Buenos Aires of Spain's claim to rule the interior, see Mario Quadri Castillo, *La Argentina descentralizada* (Buenos Aires: Editorial Universitaria de Buenos Aires, 1986), 42, 43; also see Felix Luna, "Introducción histórica," in *Federalism* (Buenos Aires: Consejo Federal de Inversiones, 1982), 15.

17. Ibarguren, *Así fue Mayo,* 111, 117, 130.

18. Romero, *Argentine Political Thought,* 71.

19. See Frederick Alexander Kirkpatrick, *A History of the Argentine Republic* (Cambridge: Cambridge University Press, 1931), 95.

20. Enrique Udaondo, *Antecedentes del presupuesto de culto en la república Argentina* (Buenos Aires, 1949), 144.

21. Arturo Enrique Sampay, ed., *Las constituciones de la Argentina— (1810–1972)* (Buenos Aires: Editorial Universitaria de Buenos Aires, 1975), 155, 156.

22. Asamblea de 1813, "Privación de los empleos eclesiásticos a los Españoles europeos," in Sampay, *Constituciones,* 136.

23. "Proyecto de constitución de la sociedad patriótica," in Sampay, *Constituciones,* p. 178.

24. "Estatuto provisional para la dirección y administración del estado, dado por la junta de observación (1815)," in Sampay, *Constituciones,* 214.

25. Ibid., 233, 238.

26. "Constitución de las provincias unidas en Sud América sancionada por el congreso constituyente de 1819, seguida del manifiesto que dicho congreso dio con motivo de esa sanción," articles 86, 87 in Sampay, *Constituciones,* 274.

27. "Constitución sancionada por el congreso general constituyente el 24 de diciembre de 1826 . . .," in Sampay, *Constituciones,* 316, 317.

28. Kirkpatrick, *A History of the Argentine Republic,* 157.

29. John Lynch, *Argentine Dictator Juan Manuel de Rosas, 1829–1852* (Oxford: Clarendon Press, 1981), 183.

30. Donini, *Religión y sociedad,* 49.

31. Carlos Sanchez Viamonte, *Manual de derecho constitucional,* 4th ed. (Buenos Aires: Editorial Kapelusz, 1959), 108, 109. Neither would they separate the church from the state. The doctrine of separation of the two was still condemned by the church, as in proposition 55 of the "Syllabus" of Pope Pius IX in 1864.

32. Ramella, *Derecho constitucional*, 191.

33. Given all of these provisions, which are still part of the existing constitution, it is not true that like other intermediate organizations, the "church lie[s] entirely outside of the president's constitutional authority." Daniel Poneman, *Argentina: Democracy on Trial* (New York: Paragon House, 1987), 67.

34. Ramella, *Derecho constitucional*, 201.

35. See Emilio F. Mignone, *Witness to the Truth: The Complicity of Church and Dictatorship in Argentina, 1976–1983*, trans. Phillip Berryman (Maryknoll, N.Y.: Orbis Books, 1988), 79.

36. Faustino J. Legon, *Doctrina y ejercicio del patronato nacional* (Buenos Aires: J. Lajouane Editores, 1920), 584.

37. Mignone, *Witness to the Truth*, 96.

38. Ramella, *Derecho constitucional*, 198, 199.

39. Quoted in Romero, *Argentine Political Thought*, 198. Concerning the criticism of Ecuador, it is worthwhile to remember that Bolivar called Venezuela a military garrison, Colombia a debating society, and Ecuador a convent.

40. Quoted in ibid., 197.

41. Quoted in ibid., 199.

42. See Scobie, *Argentina*, 153, 154, 207; also see David Rock, *Argentina, 1516–1982: From Spanish Colonization to the Falklands War* (Berkeley: University of California Press, 1985), 155.

43. Viamonte, *Manual de derecho constitucional*, 109.

44. See Austin F. Macdonald, *Government of the Argentine Republic* (New York: Thomas Y. Crowell Company, 1942), 199, 200.

45. For example, Hugo Wast, *El Kahal-Oro* (Buenos Aires: Editorial AOCRA, 1975).

46. See Crassweller, *Perón*, 276–79.

47. David Rock, *Argentina, 1516–1982: From Spanish Colonization to the Falklands War* (Berkeley: University of California Press, 1985), 317.

48. "Acuerdo con la Santa Sede: Regimen de concordato," *Ley* 17.032, (November 23, 1966), reprinted in Cesar Enrique Romero, *Derecho constitucional: Realidad política y ordenamiento jurídico*, vol. 2 (Buenos Aires: Victor P. De Zavilia, 1976), 372, 373.

49. Robert McGeagh, "Catholicism and Sociopolitical Change in Argentina: 1943–1973" (Ph.D. diss., University of New Mexico, 1974), 312–13.

50. For a literary treatment of the effects of revolutionary Catholicism on the young Peronists of the 1960s and 1970s, see Tomás Eloy Martínez, *The Perón Novel*, trans. Asa Zatz (New York: Pantheon Books, 1988), 59, 60, 168, 346, 347; for a discussion of how members of Catholic Action helped develop the montoneros, see Poneman, *Argentina*, 73, and Richard Gillespie, *Soldiers of Perón: Argentina's Montoneros* (New York: Oxford University Press, 1982).

51. Mignone, *Witness to the Truth*, 119.

52. Quoted in ibid., 3.

53. See Jimmy Burns, *The Land That Lost Its Heroes: The Falklands, the Post-War, and Alfonsín* (London: Bloomsbury, 1987), 21–24, also see 18, 68–73, 95–100.

54. Quoted in Mignone, *Witness to the Truth,* 8.

55. Marcial Castro Castillo, *Fuerzas armadas—Ética y represión* (Buenos Aires: Editorial Nuevo Orden, 1979).

56. Quoted in Mignone, *Witness to the Truth,* 16.

57. Quoted in ibid., 20.

58. Comisión Nacional sobre la Desaparición de Personas, *Nunca más: Informe de la Comisión nacional sobre la desaparición de personas* (Buenos Aires: Eudeba, 1987), 247–59.

59. For example, see Jordan B. Genta, *Acerca de la libertad de enseñar y de la enseñanza de la libertad; Libre examen y comunismo; Guerra contrarrevolucionaria* (Buenos Aires: Ediciones Dictio, 1976); Mario Enrique Sacchi, *Aristoteles, Santo Tomás de Aquino, y el orden militar* (Buenos Aires: Cruz y Fierro Editores, 1982).

60. Paul Sigmund, "The Catholic Tradition and Modern Democracy," *Review of Politics* 49, no. 4 (Fall 1987): 530–48; also see Alejandro F. Diaz, *El Cristiano y la política* (Buenos Aires: Ediciones Castañeda, 1983), 51, 52.

61. Conferencia Episcopal Argentina, "Iglesia y comunidad nacional," (Buenos Aires: Editorial Claretiana, 1981).

62. See Burns, *Falklands,* 185.

63. Quoted in ibid., 186.

64. Monsignor Italo Di Stefano, quoted in Poneman, *Argentina,* 112.

65. Quoted in Mignone, *Witness to the Truth,* 95, 96.

66. Quoted in ibid., 186.

67. "The Aftermath of the Sentences," *Buenos Aires Herald,* December 15, 1985, 2.

68. Ibid.

69. Consejo para la Consolidación de la Democracia y la Reforma Constitucional, *Reforma constitucional dictamen preliminar del consejo para la consolidación de la democracia* (Buenos Aires: Eudeba, 1986), 44–48, 196–202.

70. There was also the view that the government believed divorce was merely a convenient distraction from the far more pressing economic problems that were besetting the country. From this view, arguing about divorce was a pleasurable change for the radicals. See "Divorce Becomes an Issue—But Not for Gov't," *Buenos Aires Herald,* March 2, 1986, 3.

71. On "reason" as a basis for the new democratic regime, see, for example, Pablo Giussani, *¿Por qué, Dr. Alfonsín?* (Buenos Aires: Sudamericana/Planeta, 1987), 11, 41, 141–45, 204; also see Fundación Plural, *Raúl Alfonsín: El poder de la democracia* (Buenos Aires: Ediciones Fundación Plural, 1987), 24, 25, 42, 47, 91, 94, 96, 101, 121, 128, 208.

72. Quoted in Burns, *Falklands,* 189.

73. "¿Enseñar la inocuidad de la masturbación?" *La Nación,* August 12, 1986, 6.

74. Quoted in Mignone, *Witness to the Truth,* 108.

75. "La iglesia dió su apoyo al gobierno, por la pacificación," *La Nación,* international ed., October 30, 1989, 1.

3.

Revolution and Political Religion in Cuba

DAMIÁN J. FERNÁNDEZ

January 1959, the new year begins in Cuba with the flight of dictator Fulgencio Batista and the triumph of the revolutionary movement led by Fidel Castro. The archbishop of Santiago, Enrique Pérez Serantes, who years earlier had convinced Batista to spare the rebel leader's life, writes a pastoral letter entitled "*Vida Nueva*" ("New Life"), in which he claims that "the commitment of a man of exceptional qualities, backed enthusiastically by almost all of his coprovincials and a considerable portion of the Cuban people, and supported by the unwavering effort of his courageous followers . . . have been the letters with which the Divine Providence has written on Cuba's sky the word TRIUMPH."[1] As the *barbudo* (bearded) revolutionaries come down from the Sierra Maestra mountains, where they have fought the Batista forces, they stop at churches and shrines on their way to Havana. Women in towns and villages give them flowers and rosaries. Who would expect that less than two years later church and state relations would be on a collision course, resulting in the expulsion of priests from the island and the crippling of the church as a social institution.

Religion and politics in revolutionary Cuba have been studied from one main political/historical perspective. The paradigm has focused on competing power structures (the Catholic church vis-à-vis the state) and the different stages of their interaction since 1959.[2] Although the political/historical perspective is useful, it does not address the phenomenon of religion and revolution either in its complexity or in its sociocultural context. The traditional approach is incomplete insofar as it emphasizes the Catholic church while neglecting other, arguably more important, manifestations of religion on the island. Moreover, the scholarship has not tied church-state relations to the questions of author-ity, legitimacy, ideology, and popular mobilization in revolutionary Cuba. As a result, the political/historical approach has failed to see that popular religiosity, not institutional religion, played a crucial role in the consolidation of the Revolution and the creation of the new society.

Popular Religiosity and Political Religion

Rather than focusing on the reasons behind the confrontation between the Catholic church and the revolutionary state, this chapter examines how popular religiosity facilitated the neutralization of the Catholic church during the first two years of the Revolution and thus helped to consolidate the Revolution. Popular religiosity is a concept that can illuminate the connection between nation (the people), state (the leaders), and church (the Catholic church) during the initial years of the Revolution.

Religious life in Cuba during the Revolution was not dominated by the Catholic church, although around 80 percent of the population considered themselves Catholics.[3] The Cuban church was a weak in-stitution in comparison to its counterpart influence in most Latin American countries. According to a 1954 survey, only 24 percent of Catholics attended mass regularly.[4] Other scholars estimate the number of practicing Catholics at 4 to 6 percent.[5] Anticlericalism, a residue of French writers and the French Revolution, was common. Few Cubans, especially among the rural majority, had contact with priests and/or the church.[6]

This does not mean, however, that the Cuban people were not religious. On the contrary, Cubans have always manifested a preoccupa-tion with the spiritual and the transcendental (a concern that would be reflected in the new revolutionary ideology). The Catholic church was a small but significant piece of the puzzle of religion in Cuba. Catholicism coexisted and was practiced syncretically with several other religions: Protestantism (around 6 percent of the population), *santería* (Afro-Cuban religions), *espiritismo* (a type of animism), *brujería* (witchcraft), and "superstitions." A 1954 survey conducted by an organization of Catholic university students revealed that although 96.5 percent of the Cubans polled believed in the existence of God, only 17 percent at-tended religious services regularly.[7] Religion for the majority of the population was personal rather than institutional, and syncretic rather than purist. This cultural expression of religion in Cuba is popular religion. Popular religiosity allowed seemingly incompatible beliefs to be meshed together in one eclectic worldview.

Popular religiosity facilitated the consolidation of the Revolution not only because it countervailed the influence of the Catholic church but also because it provided a fertile source for revolutionary myths and symbols. It laid the foundations for what David E. Apter has called political religion:

> An ideological position is put forward by government that identifies the individual with the state. Modern political leaders come to recognize quickly, however, that no ordinary ideology can prevail for long in the face of obvious discrepancies between theory and practice. A more powerful symbolic force, less rational, although it may include rational ends, seems necessary to them. This force is what I call political religion. It feeds its own categorical imperatives into authoritarian political structure on the one hand. On the other . . . it affects the most fundamental needs of individuals by specifying through the state religion the permissible definitions of individual continuity, meaning, and identity.[8]

Popular religiosity and political religion help define the narrow issue of church and state as well as broader issues of revolutionary life. These two concepts open the doors to understanding how the Cuban Revolution faced the challenges of authority, legitimacy, ideology, and social mobilization and control.

The revolutionary regime confronted the challenges posed by the conservative elements in the Catholic church by emphasizing in the official discourse values, symbols, and myths associated with noninstitutional, popular religions on the island. A new mystique or political religion was born, both as a conscious political decision by the top leaders and as an unconscious cultural reaction by leaders and mass alike, to the events of the times. Political religion married the political and religious values of Cubans. The new state thereby filled the institutional political and religious vacuum in the island. But the political religion associated with Castroism and Marxism-Leninism would fail in the long run, for it did not bridge the gap between theory and practice. Political religion was unable to deliver the spiritual and material rewards it promised. Disenchantment with political religion in the 1980s paved the way for the rebirth of traditional religions in Cuba.

The Catholic Church and the Revolution, 1959–1961

Despite division within the hierarchy, the attitude of the Catholic church toward the 26 July movement, the armed revolutionary group struggling to overthrow the Batista dictatorship, was one of cautious support. The church's official position rejected violence as a way to solve the political problems of the island and supported national reconciliation. A declaration issued by the Cuban bishops during Batista's last months in power exhorted "all who today form part of the opposing camps to cease their hate and violence and to set their sight only and exclusively on the common good . . . with the purpose of achieving the establishment of a Government of National Unity."[9]

Several members of the hierarchy (among them Archbishop Evelio Díaz and Monsignor Enrique Pérez Serantes) sympathized with and aided the rebels. Priests ministered to the *barbudos* in the Sierra Maestra and the Escambray mountains. The most famous of these, Fr. Guillermo Sardiñas, later became known as the Priest Commander.[10]

Church sympathy for the revolutionaries was the result of three factors: first, the atrocities committed by Batista (who a Catholic leader referred to as satanic); second, the participation of Catholics and Catholic organizations in the revolutionary movement; and, third, the apparently reformist agenda of the 26 July movement. That most of the rebels were Catholics was a source of reassurance for the church. The leader himself, Fidel Castro, had studied with the Jesuits in the most prestigious high school of the island, Belen. Organizations such as the *Juventud de Acción Católica* (Catholic Youth Action or JAC), the *Juventud Obrera Católica* (Catholic Working Youth or JOC), and *Acción Católica Universitaria* (Catholic University Action or ACU) were engaged in the struggle against Batista, specifically in the urban areas. Although none of these groups had a broad national following, they were important heralds of a new trend of sociopolitical consciousness and reformism among the younger generation of Catholics on the island.

The agenda of the 26 July movement was reformist, nationalist, democratic, and middle class. It called for the reinstitution of the progressive Constitution of 1940, social justice, economic diversification, agrarian reform, political honesty, elections, and national sovereignty. The reforms reminded the church of the papal encyclicals "Rerum Novarum" and "Quadrajessimo Anno":

We can summarize by saying that the socio-economic program of the Revolutionary government, and the social thought of Fidel Castro, are very far from the utopic and unnatural postulations outlined by the theoreticians of marxism-communism, and are close to without reaching them fully, the social and economic principles presented in the pontifical encyclicals "Rerum Novarum" and "Quadrajessimo Anno."[11]

Once the Revolution reached power in 1959, the church endorsed its *líder máximo* (top leader) and the revolutionary laws. One of the priests who served the rebels in 1959, Fr. Lucas Iruretagoyana, answered "De Comunismo nada," in response to those who spread the rumor that the Revolution was a product of a Communist conspiracy. "As a priest I only found assistance for my ministry, high morale in the troops and a Christian spirit in all."[12] Fr. Ángel Silvas, another priest who ministered to the rebels, reached the same conclusion: "The immense majority of the members of the troops were Catholic. We did not find one that was communist or atheist."[13] After mid-1959 the position of the church would become increasingly critical, foreshadowing the eventual clash between church and state.

The triumph of the revolutionary forces generated much enthusiasm and high expectations by the majority of Catholics, causing a liberal Catholic leader to proclaim that "it is possible that in Latin America there is no other case of such collaboration of Catholics with a revolutionary movement." He commented further that "the collaboration was not the result of plot organized hierarchically; it was a spontaneous reaction against very serious violations of human dignity and human rights."[14] According to the writer, "This whole process of participation by practicing Catholics has culminated in the naming of distinguished Catholics to public posts in the new free Republic."[15] During 1959, the church endorsed the revolutionary laws, at times more enthusiastically than others. The Catholic church supported the agrarian and urban reforms, but educational reform caused friction between church and state because the proposed reform would eliminate private (read Catholic) education, something that the law eventually did. The goodwill of the more progressive sector of the church (associated with *La Quincena* magazine) toward the new government was manifested in another thorny issue: the execution of Batista's collaborators. Although the official policy did not approve death by firing squad, the *La Quincena* group recognized the right of the state to execute officials of the ancien régime.

During this period the church treated Castro with respect. Some high-ranking members of the priesthood almost deified Fidel. Monsignor Serantes's pastoral letter "New Life," for instance, established a direct link between God and Castro. *La Quincena,* the Catholic magazine with the largest circulation, depicted Fidel Castro and Camilo Cienfuegos, another popular guerrilla leader, as divine. The March 6, 1959, front cover of *La Quincena* was a close-up photograph of Cienfuegos, striking in its resemblance to Jesus Christ. [16] The magazine portrayed the revolutionary struggle as a conflict in which good conquered evil, redeeming the Cuban people.

Some sectors of the church shielded Fidel Castro from the "worrisome developments" of the 1959–60 period. For example, the church took issue with the growing presence of members of the pro-Soviet Partido Socialista Popular (PSP) in government posts. (The PSP, detested by the population for collaborating with Batista, had not joined the revolutionary movement until late 1958.) However, the church did not hold Castro personally accountable until late 1960. Two additional factors that signaled the Revolution's radicalization were also of concern to the church: the campaign against private property and the turn toward Moscow. The segment of the Catholic church that published *La Quincena* (Father Biaín, specifically), an important minority, implied in 1959 and 1960 that the "negative" events were taking place behind Castro's back, a common view among the population at the time. According to the church, the Communists were steering the Revolution off course.

The Biaín group trusted that Fidel Castro, who had saved the Cuban nation from dictatorship, would save the Revolution from the clutches of Marxism once he realized what was happening. This attitude reflects both the personalism of Cuban culture and the island's weak political institutions. In fact, the church enhanced Castro's "otherworldly" aura, an image partly created through a process of myth making by Castro and his followers and partly a result of popular perceptions of a man who defied and conquered great odds. Castro's otherworldliness won him followers, constituting an additional obstacle for the church once the revolutionary state challenged ecclesiastical interests and the institutional supremacy of the Catholics.

In late 1960 the church restated its opposition to communism in Cuba. Several priests joined, or later would join, counterrevolutionary groups. At the same time, the *líder máximo* and his supporters launched a campaign against the church. According to Castro, the church had become an enemy of the people. The institution of the church, elitist and conservative, was part and parcel of the evil that the Revolution set out to uproot. Speaking to a youth group in March 1961, Castro declared that "imperialism and the high hierarchy of the Church are one and the same thing."[17] Two years earlier Castro had praised the Cuban church for having "placed itself in a truly revolutionary position; the Catholic Church is the most revolutionary in the social sphere."[18]

When *La Quincena* shifted its position from one of support to one of criticism of the revolutionary process, the hard-liners associated with the PSP counterattacked in a series of articles published in early 1961 in the newspaper *Hoy*. The author of the series, Blas Roca, argued that "the magazine, *La Quincena,* has become the voice of all the enemies of the Revolution."[19] In another article, entitled "Martí combatió a la jerar-quía católica" ("Martí Fought against the Catholic Hierarchy"), Roca quotes José Martí, the apostle of Cuban independence: "Ni religión católica hay derecho a enseñar en las escuelas, ni religión anti-católica." ("There is no right to teach Catholic or anti-Catholic religion in schools.")[20] Roca aptly meshed communism with patriotism and anti-imperialism while depicting the Catholic hierarchy as pro-Yankee and proimperialist, feeding the anticlerical sentiments of the Cuban people. Castro, on the contrary, was portrayed as the leader of a revolution of, by, and for "*los humildes*" (the poor).

What explains the final showdown between church and state? First, the church's critical posture vis-à-vis the radicalization of the Revolution was a thorn in the side of the regime. The church could become the voice of, and the catalyst for, the opposition. Second, the ideology of the church was in the way of the ideology of the revolution-ary state. As Clifford Geertz has written, political transformations in the Third World are accompanied by "a disorientation in whose face received images of authority, responsibility, and civic purpose seem radically inadequate. The search for a new symbolic framework in terms of which to formulate, think about, and react to political problems is therefore tremendously intense."[21] Third, the "new symbolic framework," the political religion of the regime, combined elements of traditional Cuban culture (including the religions practiced on the island) with new elements introduced by the revolutionary leaders (such as the idea of the creation of a new man, martyrs, mass mobilization, and the Marxist-Leninist official ideology). The church's position was at most reformist and, as such, part of an old tradition in Cuban politics. From Castro's perspective, and that of many other Cubans, including old-time PSP members now in official posts, the old tradition had been inadequate to solve Cuba's problems. Political religion captured the essence of the Revolution through familiar symbols, which in turn mustered the support of the population.

Castro garnered the population's support largely due to the fact that he provided what a religion was supposed to provide: an answer to the questions of personal and collective identity, destiny, morality, and the hereafter. This helps explain why the regime encountered little opposition from the population when it turned against the church. In addition, the regime was delivering material benefits (such as education, housing, and health services) and apparently initiating a spiritual revival on the island.

The Revolution and the Other Religions of Cuba

In Cuba there are dozens of different religions and sects. The Protestants, *santeros,* and *espiritistas* reacted to the Revolution in a way similar to the Catholic church's reaction. They perceived Castro as heaven-sent.

In July 1960 Rafael Cepeda, president of the Cuban Evangelical Council, expressed his assessment of Castro in *Bohemia,* the most popular magazine on the island:

> It is my conviction, which I share here with full responsibility, that Fidel Castro is an instrument in the hands of God to establish His Kingdom among men. This does not have anything to do with the question of whether [Fidel] has or does not have religious faith. Biblical history is full of examples of men who God in his eternal wisdom used to assure his effective control of historical events.[22]

While Cepeda might not have expressed a majority opinion among Protestants, his view reflected those of an undetermined number of faithful. The fact that his interpretation of the revolutionary experience was published in *Bohemia* added relevance to his point of view.

Afro-Cuban religions, commonly called *santería,* were more important in terms of numbers and influence than Protestantism. About one-half of the Cuban population is black or mulatto. The traditional religions of their predecessors, African slaves, were, and still are, widely practiced on the island in a syncretic form. That is, the religious beliefs of different traditions in Africa have been superimposed on, and mixed with, Catholic saints and rituals. African deities have become identified with and have assumed the personality of Catholic saints. In this pantheon, the patron saint of Cuba, the Virgin of Charity, represents Oshum, the goddess of pleasure.

The *santeros* reacted enthusiastically to the advent of the Revolution. In December 1958 they celebrated in Havana the "gran ewo," a religious ritual to commemorate the new year. The celebration was dedicated to Castro. The *santeros,* who had visions of a bloodbath, interceded with the gods to prevent the tragedy and to facilitate Castro's triumph.[23] The reaction had religious, racial, and socioeconomic dimensions. *Santero* priests expected the new government to recognize *santería* as a legitimate religion on an equal footing with Christianity. In predominantly black and lower-class neighborhoods the networks of the *santeros* and their secret societies facilitated the state's penetration of the localities. The establishment of the Committees for the Defense of the Revolution (CDRs) in some neighborhoods is a case in point. The *santero* priests provided a focal point through which the Revolution could transmit its message. The support of the *santeros* constituted an additional source of legitimacy for the new regime.

One of the protagonists in *Four Men: Living the Revolution* by Oscar Lewis et al. claimed that his political work as first president of his neighborhood's CDR and his chairmanship of the committee's education front "was greatly aided by his power as a *santero*. . . . His reputation for working cures gained him entrance to many homes in the barrio and gave him an audience for his political ideas."[24] Another of the protagonists revealed a troubling dimension of the connection between *santería* and Marxism:

> When someone belongs to the Party and is head of a Committee, shouldn't they work to unite the neighborhood and make it prosper? But how can it prosper when Minerva [a neighbor] belongs to such a backward religion? The cult is against science, against modern life in all its aspects. How does being a communist fit in with believing such stuff? It is too great of a contradiction. Yet Minerva thinks she's such an intellectual and she claims to be revolutionary, so fervent a communist. It is true she's been a Party member for years and was active in the early days of the Revolution.[25]

The black population (the majority of which practiced *santería*) supported the Revolution for socioeconomic reasons as well as racial and religious ones. As the lowest income group on the island, they were the ones who stood to gain most by many of the reforms the regime promised. This came to pass, as the blacks during the Revolution have found new opportunities and have received benefits not readily accessible to them in pre-1959 Cuba.

From the beginning, then, revolutionary attitudes in Cuba coexisted in a large segment of the population with what many would consider primitive, or backward, religions. After the Revolution's radicalization and the adoption of Marxism-Leninism, *santería* continued to coexist with the official ideology, but in the closet:

> I know many white people who are believers and have their *santos*. Most of us are believers because we were born in the midst of believers. Perhaps Fidel doesn't like us to believe in religion, but he has never interfered with us. Maybe I am outside the law, but what harm does it do if I believe in saints and put flowers before them?[26]

The title of a book published in 1961 encapsulates the attempt to understand and explain the phenomenon of *santería* and *espiritismo* from a Marxist perspective: *El materialismo explica la santería y el espiritismo* (Materialism explains *santería* and *espiritismo*).[27]

Unlike the Catholic church, the government and the *santeros* did not clash during the first years of the Revolution. The reason is that *santería* is less institutional than the Catholic church for it does not have a strong economic and structural base. The *santeros* did not have their own journals, radio programs, or schools. They had few social links to the upper and upper-middle classes or to the United States, the centers of opposition to Castro. Therefore, *santería* was less of a threat to the regime. It was a religion largely of the poor (who stood to gain from the socioeconomic changes taking place) and practiced in the privacy of homes. Allegedly, several members of the top circle of revolutionary leaders, close associates of Fidel Castro (including Dr. Vallejo, Celia Sánchez, and Pepín Naranjo), were practitioners of *santería*, which helps explain good relations between the state and the believers. According to some observers, Castro himself wore an *ekele* (a *santero* necklace); others claim he wore a gold medal.[28]

According to Nelson Valdés, the regime courted the *santeros* by granting them special favors to practice their religion, including the convergence of revolutionary and *santero* holidays.[29] Carlos Moore, a Cuban anthropologist, argues that the benign policy of the initial years changed to one of repression years later.[30] Other scholars, such as Mercedes Sandoval, claim that the revolutionary government's tolerance of *santería* can be explained by Fidel Castro's foreign policy interests in Africa (which date back to the 1960s).[31] The connection between *santería, espiritismo,* and politics was stronger in certain regions than in others. Is it a coincidence that two of the vital regions of support for the Revolution, Havana and Oriente, were also the stronghold of *santería* and *espiritismo?*

Espiritismo, an influential current of popular religiosity that believes the dead can influence the living world, was fertile ground for revolutionary zeal. As with other manifestations of popular religiosity, *espiritismo* did not escape syncretism with politics.[32] During the initial years of the Revolution, organized *espiritista* groups supported the new regime. Some of them used Marxism to understand both political and spiritual matters: "Soon the esoterics will have the inspiration to demonstrate through the scientific method of dialectical materialism that the science of history and of human knowledge is nothing more than the development of the esoteric method to understand nature established by Hermes Trimegisto, and in our times translated by Frederick Engels to a philosophical code."[33]

According to the *espiritistas,* dialectical materialism was the philosophical tool with which to understand *espiritismo.* In *Jesucristo era comunista* (Jesus Christ was Communist), the author argues that private property is against the law of nature—"Jesus Christ developed social class politics"—and adds that "therefore rank and file Christians should be brought up with people that do not have private property."[34] He concludes that "the God and the Kingdom of Heaven that Jesus Christ preached about were also communist."[35] In another book by the same author, *El materialismo explica el espiritismo y la santería* (Materialism explains *espiritismo* and *santería*), one of the chapters analyzes, through dialectical materialism, the figures of Santa Barbara, a Catholic saint, and her Afro-Cuban counterpart, Shangó.[36]

One of the *espiritista* groups functioning at the time, the *Asociación Espiritista Enrique Carbonell* (Enrique Carbonell *Espiritista* Association), published a newsletter entitled *Boletín* from 1958 to at least 1961. From February 1959 to 1961 the association stood firmly behind the Revolution, offering the president of the Republic their assistance "in the measure of our powers, to [help in] the moral and spiritual healing that our country requires."[37] The association highlighted the role of Castro in the triumph against Batista's tyranny. The association supported democratic ideals including the separation of church and state, and asked that all religious beliefs be respected. In 1959, the association defended the agrarian reform law and advocated the establishment of an "*Espiritista* Fund for Pro-Agrarian Reform."[38] The article ended with "Viva la Revolución Cubana. . . . Viva el Espiritismo en los Seres Libres!" ("Long live the Cuban Revolution. . . . Long live *Espiritismo* in Free Beings!")[39] Reformist nationalism and admiration for Castro were evident throughout the *Boletín.* In the last available newsletter the *espiritistas* reaffirmed their support for the Revolution and requested that *espiritismo* be recognized as a bona fide religion.[40]

Shortly after the advent of the Revolution, Castro became known as "*el caballo*" (the horse). The origin of the term, unknown to most Cubans, is found in the cosmology of the *paleros,* an *espiritista* sect; the horse (*el caballo de Troya*) is the medium through which the spirit talks to the people. The common usage of "*el caballo,*" however, refers to a strong man who knows it all, an indication of the physical power, wisdom, and *machismo* of the *líder máximo.*

Espiritismo was particularly strong in the rural areas of the island and was usually combined with Christianity and *santería.* The hallmark of popular religion in Cuba was its ability to weave together beliefs from different traditions into one fabric. Cuban culture has been described as an *ajiaco* (stew) in which everything and anything can come together and contribute to its color and its taste.

Charisma, Ideology, Mobilization, and Political Religion

The symbols and myths associated with the revolutionaries, as well as the language spoken by them (particularly Ernesto "Che" Guevara and Fidel Castro), were largely religious. Fidel's first message to the Cuban nation, "History Will Absolve Me" (1954), initiated what became one of the hallmarks of revolutionary language, the use of biblical metaphors. Fidel portrayed himself as a man with a mission entrusted to him by history and by the heroes of Cuba's past. He spoke of setting wrongs right, and on several occasions on national television he quoted Jesus Christ's words "My kingdom is not of this world."[41] When he arrived in Havana after Batista's departure he called on Cuba to "purify itself."[42] A 1959 cover of *Bohemia* pictured Castro in the likeness of Jesus Christ.

Reality fertilized the religious myths, symbols, and rhetoric of the Revolution. The official version of the revolutionary war claims that the survivors of Castro's invasion of Cuba in 1956 were twelve, the twelve who formed the embryonic rebel army. Some observers argue that this may have been a misrepresentation for the specific purpose of constructing the mythology of the Revolution. What is not a misrepresentation is that on January 8, 1959, as Castro delivered a nationally televised speech a white dove perched itself on the leader's shoulder. Heaven seemed to send another sign.

It is not surprising, especially when one considers Cuba's weak political institutions, the low educational level of the majority of Cubans, and the personalism enshrined in Cuban culture, that Fidel Castro was perceived as a savior. A 1960 survey of the attitudes of the Cuban people toward the Castro regime indicated that 86 percent of the urban and semiurban population supported the new regime; 43 percent of the population were fervent supporters, bordering "on the fanatic in their expressions of fervor."[43] A housewife, for instance, claimed that "Fidel has the same ideas as Jesus Christ, our protector and guide."[44] Fervent supporters and supporters in general were significantly higher among those with elementary or no schooling, among those living outside Havana, and among the lower socioeconomic group.[45]

Castro's leadership style and the perceptions of his followers fit Max Weber's concept of the charismatic leader. Popular religiosity in Cuba, as well as other cultural, sociopolitical and educational factors, contributed to the emergence of a charismatic leader. Castro, therefore, is a product of Cuban culture. The bond between leaders and mass, as well as Castro's governing strategy, must be seen in this light.

If ideology is defined as a set of beliefs whose function is "to make an autonomous politics possible by providing authoritative concepts that render it meaningful, the suasive images by means of which it can be sensibly grasped,"[46] we can see that Castro and the Revolution used traditional symbols as guideposts for the future, a common tactic in revolutionary situations. The symbols and metaphors rendered "otherwise incomprehensible social functions meaningful, to so construe them as to make it possible to act purposefully within them."[47] The ideology of the Cuban Revolution was based largely on the traditional cultural and religious values of the Cuban people, and new values introduced by the *líder máximo*'s ideology, Castroism, and by the official state ideology, Marxism-Leninism. Political religion merged seemingly incompatible beliefs into one worldview, serving different constituencies and different purposes at the same time. The result was an autonomous and authentic ideology.

Political religion provided a source of legitimate leadership, a messiah, and implied a strategy for political organization, mass mobilization, and centralization of power on the *líder máximo* initially and later on authoritarian structures, the state and the party. Through political religion the state catalyzed mobilization and exerted social control. The state and the party led by Fidel Castro became the only "sacred" source of morality, the new church. The private and public spheres became politicized. The collective will and the national struggle for revolutionary ideals were led by one party and one leader in a harmonious one-class nation. Politics became an ethical phenomenon (a crusade against imperialism, dependency, counterrevolution, illiteracy, exploitation, selfishness). Therefore, nonconformists were made to pay a high price. Faith was to be placed on the leader, on the collectivity, and on man's perfectibility. The ultimate goal was the creation of a utopian society and a new human being who would embody virtue.

The Failure of Political Religion and the Resurgence of Traditional Religions in the 1980s

By late 1961, the year that Castro embraced Marxism-Leninism as the official ideology of the Revolution, the church was a crippled institution. Private schools were nationalized, and hundreds of priests and nuns left the island voluntarily. Over one hundred others were forced to leave. Of the 723 priests in Cuba in 1961 only 220 remained by 1964.[48] Since then, church-state relations have continued to be strained, although less confrontational.

Relations improved after 1968. By then, the church had resigned itself to live within the parameters set by the state, to accept the Revolution, and to pursue ecclesiastical activities as best it could. In 1971 while on a visit to Chile, Castro praised the role of Chilean Catholics in the construction of socialism, reaffirming his conviction that Christianity and Marxism were not mutually exclusive. In 1975, the First Congress of the Communist Party of Cuba (PCC) recognized the right of Cubans to practice any religion.

Improvement in church-state relations in the late 1960s and throughout the 1970s did not entail a greater role for the Catholic church in society. The revolutionary state assigned a minimal living space for religion as a whole. Protestant churches were relegated to the same position as that of the Catholic church, despite the fact that several prominent ministers endorsed the tenets of the revolutionary regime. *Santería* was pushed to the colorful arena of folklore. Religion continued to be discouraged and repressed, although harassment became less frequent once the church no longer threatened the survival of the Revolution. The personal cost of being religious continued to be high, though (i.e., no admission to the PCC and certain professions). Traditional religiosity, by and large, was a departure from the new code of conduct prescribed by the official Marxism-Leninism and by the unofficial political religion of the regime.

Political religion has not been capable of secularizing society nor of eliminating Christianity, *santería*, and the other manifestations of Cuban popular religiosity. In 1986 the National Encounter of the Cuban Church (*Encuentro Nacional Eclesial Cubano* or ENEC) acknowledged that "at present, the phenomenon of popular religiosity is evident in the Cuban people and represents a high degree of diffusion and vitality."[49] According to the ENEC, popular religiosity has played a vital role in instilling religious values in the younger generations of Cubans who have grown under the Revolution: "In spite of its limitations and its weaknesses, we realize that popular religiosity has been the force which has allowed and made possible the transmission of the faith to many Cubans, in particular the youth."[50]

Santería has survived, and maybe thrived since 1959. Although compatible with the political religion of the early years, *santería* is incompatible with Marxism. The state's attempt to relegate it, and other "cults," to the picturesque niche of anthropological folklore has failed. A study of the relationship between scientific materialism, literature, and Afro-Cuban religions concluded that

> abolishing the economic bases of a class society is a relatively easy task; eradicating inclinations and habits stemming from a vigorous tradition is another story. To transform the religious ceremonies of African origin in mere folkloric dances, as it has been attempted in Cuba, is literally a superhuman undertaking. Afro-Cuban religion has constituted a point of ideological resistance much stronger in reality than what can be perceived from outside Cuba.[51]

Political religion would seem to succeed where Marxism-Leninism fails, for it accommodates issues of the soul, life and death, and the supernatural within a specific cultural context. Yet as a political strategy for the long run, political religion fails even in the face of the "institutionalization" of the Revolution. Its failure is the failure of prophecy. Political religion in Cuba has not fared better than theories or ordinary ideologies in resolving "the discrepancy between theory and practice,"[52] or in meeting the challenges of development. As a result, the persuasive power and the legitimacy of the system have suffered from erosion. At this moment of crisis, political religion becomes a poor and discredited substitute for traditional religion.

The 1980s in Cuba witnessed a crisis of confidence in the political religion espoused by the regime and, in turn, a resurgence of traditional religions, particularly Catholicism and *santería*. The failure of political religion was the result of an unbridgeable gap between theory and praxis, an endemic phenomenon in contemporary communism as well. Throughout the island, attendance at Catholic services is rising and there is an increasing demand for Bibles. Over one hundred priests have been ordained since 1970 and approximately forty seminarians are preparing for the priesthood. Although only 38.9 percent of the population considered itself Catholic in 1983 and of these a mere 1–2 percent were practitioners, popular religious ceremonies (such as *la fiesta de San Lázaro*) now attract over one hundred thousand Cubans. Approximately 50 percent of the population request a religious ceremony at the time of burial.[53] To reach out to the flock and to accommodate the renewed interest, the church has manifested an activism unknown since the 1950s, including the establishment of youth groups. During 1989 and the first five months of 1990, the image of the patron saint of Cuba was taken to local parishes in preparation for the pope's visit to the island in 1991. Thousands of Cubans turned out to see the Lady of Charity.

The church has displayed a strong and critical voice in the late 1980s and early 1990s. Monsignor Carlos Manuel de Céspedes's December 1988 homily in memory of Fr. Felix Varela, an early Cuban Nationalist, epitomized the newfound strength: "Cuba . . . is experiencing a very difficult period and the prognosis is not favorable. The apparent socio-political monolithicism does not succeed in reducing tensions, actual and potential pluralism, or frustrations."[54] Céspedes's indictment of Cuban society was surprisingly harsh coming from an institution that had remained relatively silent for almost three decades: "Each day we meet someone who wants to leave [the island] because he does not have any hope of personal fulfillment in Cuba . . . frequently it is the youth. . . . Frequently one accepts externally what one rejects sadly, bitterly and even violently in smaller circles of friends."[55]

These developments cannot be divorced from the socioeconomic and political panorama of the last decade: poor economic performance and increasing economic hardship; renewed militarization; vigorous ideological offensive; repression; war in Angola; bureaucratic inefficiency; natural disasters; the return of affluent Cuban exiles to visit family members on the island; and change throughout the Socialist world. These and other factors have undermined the pillars of political religion. In the words of a Cuban housewife, the result is that "one loses faith in the revolution."[56] Political religion ultimately was unable to fulfill the material and spiritual needs of the population.

Small groups of organized dissent have emerged. Independent organizations, such as human rights committees and art groups, have been established. Youth riots, an increasing crime rate, participation in the black market, defections, and low labor productivity indicate a lack of confidence in the regime and the rejection of its moral code. Some of the disaffected have found refuge in Christianity, *santería,* and *espiritismo.*

The Cuban case is not atypical from other societies in which political religion has been expounded. For instance, Christianity in China has experienced cyclical periods of decline and revival.[57] Moreover, it is not unusual for the church in Communist and Rightist dictatorships to serve as a channel for discontent and opposition—such were the cases of Poland and Chile. The Cuban government is aware and worried because of this.

Resurgence of religion in Cuba has coincided with, and been strengthened by, Castro's interest in Liberation Theology. In *Fidel y la religión,* Frei Betto portrayed Castro as a man who had put into practice the spirit of Christianity through revolutionary deeds.[58] The book was an attempt to place the *líder máximo* among the vanguard of Christian revolutionaries in Latin America. Therefore, it was above all a tool for domestic and foreign propaganda.

The publication of *Fidel y la religión* improved church-state relations by opening a dialogue between both sides, relaxing tensions, and granting Christian sects a larger space in the society. U.S. priests, ministers, and believers since have been allowed to enter the island and worship with their Cuban counterparts. Castro also expressly invited the pope to visit Cuba sometime in 1991. Also in the late 1980s Castro said that it was time to consider allowing Christians to join the PCC. However, in late 1989 and early 1990, church-state relations took a turn for the worse. After Cuban bishops sent him a critical end-of-the-year letter, Castro criticized the ecclesiastical hierarchy for playing into the hands of U.S. imperialism. Another thorny issue was the schedule for the pope's visit. While the church seemed to prefer an early visit (before the PCC's Fourth Congress in early 1991), the government wanted the visit after the Fourth Congress, apparently to avoid any political spill-over from the pope's tour.

The new chapter in church and state relations has coincided with the *líder máximo*'s shift to the formulas of political religion characteristic of 1959 and the early 1960s in an effort to deal with internal and external pressures the regime confronts. Castro's *Por el camino correcto* (Through the correct road) is his new version of the old gospel.[59] It is doubtful, however, that symbols and incantation that were effective in the 1960s can be as effective in the 1990s when the challenges of the Revolution's third decade and the eternal questions of human existence remain unresolved although they continue to be as pressing as ever before.

Conclusions

The Cuban revolutionary government dealt with the challenges posed by the Catholic church—the only national (albeit relatively weak) institution on the island that opposed radical reforms—with a dose of repression and a larger dose of political religion. The government articulated a new political and spiritual mythology based on cultural and religious symbols close to the hearts of many Cubans. The political discourse had all the trademarks of a religion. A number of Christians, *santeros,* and *espiritistas* perceived the Revolution largely through re-ligious lenses.

The relationship between the revolutionary leaders and the fol-lowers was a dynamic and organic one. Political religion not only provided a way to neutralize the Catholic church, but more important it supplied one source of legitimacy for the Revolution and prescribed the controlled mobilization strategy the regime has employed during the past thirty years. In Cuba political religion was a mix and match of traditional Cuban values (including popular religious ones) with Castro-ism and Marxism-Leninism. Political religion synthesized all the cur-rents into one. This eclectic approach to politics and ideology is com-mon to the Cuban experience.

Previous studies on church-state relations in Cuba have neglected the broader cultural context and failed to connect it to the issues of leadership, ideology, legitimacy, and mobilization. The result has been that scholars have missed the relevance of popular religious sentiments to the consolidation of the revolutionary process. Furthermore, we have not realized that traditional values, or so-called primitive beliefs, can serve as nutrients for revolutionary change. The Islamic revival throughout the Middle East has not been the only nor the first example of such phenomena in our times.

In the long run, political religion, like other more orthodox ideologies, fails when it cannot create the heaven on earth it promises. Political religion has not bridged the gap between theory and praxis and, as a consequence, people lose faith, turning to traditional forms of religious expression. This is in fact what has been occurring in Cuba since the 1980s, a renaissance of the Catholic church, other Christian denominations, *santería,* and *espiritismo.* The resurfacing and strengthening of traditional religions point to the resilience of such values, even in a totalitarian context. Increasing numbers of Cubans are seeking answers to the enigmas of life and death outside the officially sanctioned ideology. The challenges posed to the regime by the upsurge of religion on the island are just starting to surface.

Notes

Acknowledgments: An earlier version of this paper was presented at "Religious Challenge to Secular Authority," a conference held at the University of Maine, April 14–15, 1989. I would like to thank Margaret Crahan and Caridad de Moya for valuable comments on the first draft.

1. Enrique Perez Serantes, "La Divina Providencia ha escrito en el cielo de Cuba la palabra triunfo," *La Quincena,* January 1959:18. All translations are my own.

2. See, for instance, Pablo M. Alfonso, *Cuba, Castro y los católicos* (Miami: Hispamerican Books, 1985); Margaret E. Crahan, "Salvation through Christ or Marx: Religion in Revolutionary Cuba," *Journal of Interamerican Studies* 21 (February 1979): 156–84; John M. Kirk, *Between God and the Party: Religion and Politics in Revolutionary Cuba* (Tampa: University of South Florida, 1989); and Manuel Fernández, *Religión y revolución en Cuba: Veinticinco años de lucha ateísta* (Miami: Saeta Ediciones, 1984).

3. Fernández, *Religión y revolución en Cuba,* 22; Kirk, *Between God and the Party,* 176.

4. Fernández, *Religión y revolución en Cuba,* 22.

5. Kirk, *Between God and the Party,* 176.

6. Ibid.

7. Fernández, *Religión y revolución en Cuba,* 22.

8. David E. Apter, "Political Religion in the New Nations," in *Old Societies and New States,* ed. Clifford Geertz (New York: Free Press, 1963), 61.

9. Quoted in Manuel Fernández, "Presencia de los católicos en la revolución triunfante," *La Quincena*, January 1959:15.

10. Yolanda Portuondo, *Guillermo Sardiñas: El sacerdote comandante* (Havana: Editora Cultura Popular, 1987).

11. Rodolfo Riesgo, "15 días en la nación," *La Quincena*, January 1959:8.

12. Manuel Fernández, "El 'barbudo' fraile a quien un ciclón llevó a la Sierra," *La Quincena*, January 1959:4.

13. P. Ángel Rivas, "Con el ejército de los católicos en la revolución triunfante," *La Quincena*, January 1959:10.

14. Fernández, "Presencia de los católicos en la revolución triunfante," *La Quincena*, January 1959:10.

15. Ibid., 12.

16. *La Quincena*, March 6, 1959.

17. Alfonso, *Cuba, Castro y los católicos*, 97.

18. Ibid., 97–98.

19. Blas Roca, *Veneno en la "Quincena": 13 artículos sobre la campaña contrarrevolucionaria de la jerarquía católica* (Havana: n.p., 1961), 3.

20. Ibid., 69.

21. Clifford Geertz, "Ideology as a Cultural System," in *Ideology and Discontent,* ed. David E. Apter (New York: Free Press, 1964), 65.

22. Rafael Cepeda, "Fidel Castro y el reino de Dios," *Bohemia,* July 17, 1960:110

23. Interview with Natividad Torres, Harvard University, June 1989.

24. Oscar Lewis et al., *Four Men: Living the Revolution: An Oral History of Contemporary Cuba* (Urbana: University of Illinois, 1977), xlvii.

25. Ibid., 263.

26. Ibid., 295.

27. Sixto Gastón Aguero, *El materialismo explica la santería y el espiritismo* (Havana: Orbis, 1961).

28. Nelson Valdés, "La Cachita y el Che: Patron Saints of Revolutionary Cuba," *Encounters,* Winter 1989:31; personal conversation with Caridad de Moya, Miami.

29. Valdés, "La Cachita y el Che," 34.

30. Carlos Moore, *Cuba, Castro, and the Blacks* (Los Angeles: University of California, 1989).

31. Telephone conversation with Mercedes Sandoval, Miami, September 1988.

32. For the connection between *espiritismo* and *Fidelísimo,* see Eddu Nitya, *La suprema revelación, precedida de oda a la revolución, una nota liminar y las siete reglas del perfecto espiritista, con Fidel ante la humanidad* (Havana: Tipografía Ideas, 1961).

33. Sixto Gastón Aguero, *Jesucristo era comunista,* vol. 1 (Havana: n.p., n.d.), 5.

34. Ibid., 2:28.

35. Ibid.

36. Sixto Gastón Aguero, *Fundamento de Oshún, virgen de la caridad* (Havana: n.p., 1963).

37. Asociación Espiritista, "Enrique Carbonell," *Boletín,* no. 2 (February 1959).

38. Ibid., no. 3, 5.

39. Ibid.

40. Ibid., nos. 3–4 (August–November 1961).

41. Cepeda, "Fidel Castro y el reino de Dios."

42. "Liberator's Triumphal March through an Ecstatic Island," *Life,* January 1959:28–29.

43. Lloyd Free, *Attitudes of the Cuban People toward the Castro Regime in the Late Spring of 1960* (Princeton: Institute for International Social Research, 1960), 5.

44. Ibid.

45. Ibid.

46. Geertz, "Ideology as a Cultural System," 64.

47. Ibid.

48. Alfonso, *Cuba, Castro y los católicos,* 106.

49. Encuentro Nacional Eclesial Cubano, "Estudio del documento de trabajo del E.N.E.C.," mimeo (Havana: n.p., 1986), 97.

50. Ibid.

51. Julio Matas, "Revolución, literatura y religión afrocubana," *Cuban Studies/Estudios Cubanos* 13 (1): 17.

52. Apter, "Political Religion in the New Nations," 61.

53. Kirk, *Between God and the Party,* 176.

54. Monsignor Carlos Manuel de Céspedes, "Homilía pronunciada por Mons. Carlos Manuel de Céspedes y García Menocal, en la celebración arquidiócesana de clausura del ano bicentenario del nacimiento del Padre Félix Varela," mimeo, Iglesia del Santo Custodio, Havana, November 20, 1988:11.

55. Ibid., 11–12.

56. "Cuba por Dentro," *El Nuevo Herald,* 1988.

57. Frank K. Flinn, "Prophetic Christianity and the Future of China," in *Prophetic Religions and Politics: Religion and Political Order,* vol. 1, ed. Jeffrey K. Hadden and Anson Shupe (New York: Paragon House, 1986), 307–28.

58. Frei Betto, *Fidel and Religion: Castro Talks on Revolution and Religion with Frei Betto* (New York: Simon and Schuster, 1987).

59. Fidel Castro, *Por el camino correcto* (Havana: Editora Politica, 1987).

PART III

North America

4.

The Christian Right in the United States

MATTHEW C. MOEN

In the late 1970s, evangelical and fundamentalist Christians in the United States began organizing to contend in the political arena. They did so out of a concern that traditional American values were waning, and out of a conviction that a secularized government was partly to blame. Reverend Pat Robertson spoke for many conservative Christians at the time: "We used to think that if we stayed home and prayed it would be enough. Well, we are fed up. We think it is time to put God back in government."[1] Toward that end, millions of evangelicals and fundamentalists joined a number of organizations that collectively were labeled the Christian Right. Throughout the 1980s, the Christian Right earnestly challenged both governmental policies and secular principles.

This chapter documents the transformation of the Christian Right during the 1980s, as it proffered a challenge to the state, and focuses specifically on changes in the Christian Right's organizational structure, political strategy, and rhetoric. Elite leaders consciously drove changes in these areas in an attempt to maximize their political influence.

Threaded through the chapter is the argument that the Christian Right's leaders grew more politically sophisticated over time. Many of the movement's early leaders gained political experience and savvy, and some of the less capable people were replaced by those more politically astute. Joseph Conn of Americans United for the Separation of Church and State focused on the latter point in an interview: "Over time, the old guard of the movement has mostly disappeared from the scene. Those early people were strongly motivated by fundamentalist religion, but were not particularly sophisticated in politics. . . . They gradually dropped out or were moved to the sidelines, leaving the political arena to the somewhat less narrowly sectarian, but more sophisticated people."[2] Not surprisingly, Christian Right leaders agreed with the notion of increased sophistication. Gary Jarmin of the American Freedom Coalition flatly asserted that "the sophistication in the Christian Right has clearly increased."[3] Although self-serving, Jarmin's statement was also true, which becomes apparent as the sophistication theme is revisited.

Before proceeding further, though, one caveat should be added: the improved political skills manifested in the leadership did not automatically result in a more powerful movement. In fact, evidence suggests that the Christian Right was a less formidable force at the end of the 1980s than it was at the beginning.[4] Simply put, the movement was better led by the end of the decade, not necessarily a more influential political factor.

This inquiry into changes in the Christian Right is warranted on two counts. First, scholars have failed to examine its changes very thoroughly or systematically. They have focused on the Christian Right's influence in politics through studies of its political action committees, electoral clout, and lobbying activities.[5] With the exception of Lienesch's article, which applies theories of social movements to the Christian Right,[6] there has been virtually no focus on the other side of the causal equation: how has political activism shaped and influenced the Christian Right? It is an equally pertinent and important question.

Second, the inquiry into changes is timely, in the wake of a decade of activity, Rev. Pat Robertson's unsuccessful bid for the 1988 Republican presidential nomination, and the termination of the Moral Majority.[7] The Robertson candidacy and the closure of the Moral Majority, in particular, were substantive and symbolic benchmarks for the Christian Right; before a second full decade of activism is well underway, it is worth pausing to consider the changes that transpired in the first full decade.

Organizational Structure

The Christian Right's structure changed considerably in the 1980s. Ten easily identified national organizations were located in the nation's capital and were active during the decade. Those organizations, along with their major leader(s) and their lifespan, are listed in Table 4.1. An overview of those organizations, and a discussion of the multitude of groups, follows.

TABLE 4.1

Major Organizations of the Christian Right

Group	Leader(s)	Duration
National Christian Action Coalition	Robert Billings William Billings	1978–85
Religious Roundtable	Ed McAteer James Robison	1979–
Christian Voice	Richard Zone Robert Grant	1979–
American Freedom Coalition	Robert Grant Gary Jarmin	1987–
American Coalition for Traditional Values	Tim LaHaye	1984–86
Concerned Women for America	Beverly LaHaye	1979–
Moral Majority	Jerry Falwell Jerry Nims	1979–89
Liberty Federation	Jerry Falwell Jerry Nims	1986–89
Freedom Council	Pat Robertson	1981–87
Family Research Council	James Dobson Gary Bauer	1989–

The National Christian Action Coalition (NCAC) was launched by Robert Billings, a fundamentalist educator from Indiana. In the late 1970s, he spearheaded opposition to Internal Revenue Service regulations aimed at revoking the tax-exempt status of racially discriminatory schools.[8] The NCAC was designed to be the "eyes and ears" of the conservative Christian school network, informing schools of bureaucratic regulations that would affect their operations. Billings bequeathed the NCAC to his son Bill, after the former accepted a position in the 1980 Reagan campaign. Bill subsequently enlarged the NCAC's role by producing materials that taught conservative Christians how to participate effectively in politics, testifying on Capitol Hill for tuition tax credits for private schools, and compiling indexes on the conservatism of members of Congress. All of that activity did not prevent the NCAC from being overshadowed, though, by a budding Moral Majority.

Bill Billings acknowledged that "they [Moral Majority] went up front and we kind of went into the background."[9] By 1985, the position of the NCAC was untenable, and it was terminated.

The Religious Roundtable was formed in 1979 by Ed McAteer, a fundamentalist layperson with deep roots in the Southern Baptist Convention (SBC). He used the roundtable as a forum for training previously apolitical ministers in the art of politics, hoping that they would foment opposition to Carter's 1980 reelection bid. Prior to the election, the roundtable conducted training sessions for an estimated twenty thousand ministers.[10] It also organized the National Affairs Briefing, a forum for Reagan to solicit the support of conservative Christian elites. The Religious Roundtable was disbanded after the 1980 election, other than to serve as a platform for McAteer's political pronouncements. Its headquarters was moved from Washington, D.C., to McAteer's hometown of Memphis, Tennessee. The roundtable is still in existence, but for all practical purposes it is nothing more than a letterhead organization.

Christian Voice was started by Rev. Robert Grant as a California-based, anti–gay rights organization. It received early publicity from Rev. Pat Robertson's Christian Broadcasting Network and from its "moral report cards" on members of Congress. The report cards caught the attention of the national media, partly because they distilled the Christian Right's agenda and partly because they came out so skewed. For example, a Catholic priest in Congress at the time received a zero "moral approval rating," in part because he supported the creation of the Education Department and opposed a balanced-budget amendment.[11] Christian Voice consisted of a lobbying arm, headed by Gary Jarmin; a tax-exempt educational wing, responsible for disseminating information about political candidates; and a political action committee, called the "Moral Government Fund."[12] During Reagan's first term, the lobbying arm was active on behalf of antiabortion and school-prayer legislation, while the tax-exempt wing continued churning out report cards on members of Congress.[13] Near the end of that period, however, the organization's activity waned. A 1984 interviewee noted that the "Christian Voice is largely a letterhead organization these days. They still send out their mailings to raise money, but they do not do much else."

As Reagan's second term opened, Christian Voice's brain trust restructured its operation and channeled its resources away from Capitol Hill, toward the grass roots. It continued to distribute updated report cards, but it effectively suspended its lobbying operation. The moribundity of Christian Voice was evident in June 1989. The organization shared a suite in the Heritage Foundation building with a consulting firm, and the literature was a year old.[14] Gary Jarmin confirmed the dormancy of Christian Voice in an interview, noting that it would only "serve as a door opener to churches" in the future.[15] It was no longer the vehicle outside the church for Christian Voice's leadership.[16] That task was assumed by the American Freedom Coalition (AFC).

According to Jarmin, "Following the 1986 election, Christian Voice had a poll conducted nationwide. We filtered out a group that was conservative, religious, and registered to vote. About 9% of that group was black. We asked them extensive questions about issues and politics."[17] Rev. Robert Grant and Jarmin used that information in 1987 to launch the AFC, which they envisioned as a grass-roots organization. In November 1988, it held its first annual board of governors meeting; today, its leaders are trying to erect "precinct councils" across the United States.[18]

Another organization with connections to Christian Voice was the American Coalition for Traditional Values (ACTV). It was headed by the Reverend Tim LaHaye, a one-time executive officer in the Moral Majority and a member of the executive board of the Christian Voice. ACTV was constructed to register voters for Reagan in 1984, much like the roundtable did in 1980. The quid pro quo for LaHaye's work was an administration promise to appoint religious conservatives to administration positions.[19] According to a 1984 interviewee with intimate knowledge of the organization,

> ACTV began after some discussions among many of the leading television evangelists across the country about the need to set up an organization that would register Christian voters. Of the thirty-two individuals who consented to their involvement in setting up an organization, ten actually contributed their mailing lists. On the basis of those mailing lists, a phone bank was set up that contacted 110,000 evangelical and fundamentalist churches.

ACTV's leaders sought to register two million religious conservatives. Following Reagan's landslide reelection in 1984, ACTV was gradually wound down by Rev. Tim LaHaye, and then terminated in December 1986.[20]

In the same year that LaHaye accepted the vice-presidency of the Moral Majority (1979), his wife, Beverly, created Concerned Women for

America (CWA). According to Laurie Tryfiates, CWA's field director, "CWA started as a response to the stereotype of women brought by the [feminist] National Organization of Women. It really began as a handful of women brought together in neighborhood meetings. . . . From there, the organization mushroomed."[21] For six years CWA was headquartered in San Diego, and then in 1985 it moved to Washington, D.C., "in order to have a greater impact preserving, protecting, and promoting traditional and Judeo-Christian values."[22] It since has lobbied Congress, organized at the grass roots, and marshaled test cases in the courts.[23] Its annual convention was visited by President Reagan in 1987; its current literature contains words from President Bush.[24] Hertzke reports that its membership may exceed the combined total of the three largest feminist groups in America.[25]

The Moral Majority was the most salient and perhaps the most successful Christian Right organization in the 1980s. Initially, it consisted of four divisions: the lobbying and direct-mail operation, called the Moral Majority; the litigation arm, called the Moral Majority Legal Defense Fund; the tax-exempt education division, known as the Moral Majority Foundation; and the political action committee, known as the Moral Majority PAC.[26] Of those divisions, the Moral Majority proper was easily the most important. According to Roy Jones, its legislative director in the mid-1980s, Moral Majority had 250,000 members its first year; that figure doubled the next year, quadrupled the following year, and again doubled, so that Moral Majority had 4,000,000 members by 1983—a figure within the calculations of one scholar.[27] In 1986, Moral Majority was collapsed into the Liberty Federation, ostensibly to facilitate attention to international issues.[28] In reality, its merger with another organization was recognition of the fact that it carried "high negatives" in public opinion polls.[29] Gary Bauer offered an explanation: "The Moral Majority was one of the first groups of what has come to be called the Christian Right. Since it was one of the first groups, it suffered accordingly as people opposed to its agenda attacked it. . . . [Falwell] took the lead to sound the alarm. Having done so, he was the focus of considerable attack. To put it simply, Falwell became damaged goods."[30] Michael Schwartz, of the Free Congress Foundation, echoed that thought, in saying that Falwell was a "lightning rod" for criticism and "humble and intelligent enough" to retreat from politics once he was no longer in a position to advance the Christian Right's agenda.[31] Moral Majority persisted for several more years under new leadership, until Falwell officially nixed it in June 1989.[32]

The Liberty Federation had a vaguely defined purpose and a tenuous existence, attracting very limited attention in 1986 when it engulfed Moral Majority, and virtually none thereafter.[33] By 1989 it was defunct, lacking even a telephone listing for its national headquarters.[34] In retrospect, the Liberty Federation was simply a vehicle for Falwell to divert attention from a dwindling Moral Majority.

The Freedom Council was formed by the Reverend Pat Robertson, who mostly steered his own course in politics in the 1980s. The Freedom Council was designed as a lobbying and grass-roots organization, but according to a 1984 interviewee it never developed a "lobbying presence in Washington, D.C. . . . no lobbying presence at all." Its grass-roots orientation was more apparent. According to Howard Phillips, "The Freedom Council of Dr. Pat Robertson, when it was first formed, was designed to provide some of that grass-roots emphasis [lacking in the movement]. . . . Certainly the Freedom Council had the grass roots in mind when it formed and began operation. What happened over time [though] was that the Freedom Council changed its mission, becoming personally identified with Pat and his political objectives."[35] It was disbanded by Robertson after the IRS questioned its tax-exempt status and after a spate of negative publicity about a confidentiality agreement, which offered every Freedom Council employee one hundred dollars in return for not speaking with reporters about the organization.[36]

Finally, the Family Research Council (FRC) was created in the waning days of the Reagan presidency by the Reverend James Dobson. He recruited Reagan's domestic policy advisor, Gary Bauer, to serve as the FRC's president. Bauer described the role of the FRC in an interview:

> The Council handles only issues somehow touching upon the family. We interpret the family somewhat broadly, leading us to concern ourselves with issues like the tax code's impact on the family in addition to traditional concerns like abortion and pornography. . . . Our hope is to become known as the premier experts on the family and family issues in the Washington, D.C. area. At that point, policymakers can come to us for advice and assistance.[37]

In 1989, the FRC released a major study on the declining state of the traditional family, which garnered national press attention and served as a means of lobbying for tax breaks for nonworking spouses who stay home with children.[38] The FRC is led by a well-connected and respected conservative in Gary Bauer, and is grounded in Dobson's "Focus on the Family" ministry, which gives him the "largest following, budget, and staff" in the present Christian Right.[39]

Multiple Groups and Sophistication

During the 1980s, no fewer than ten national organizations were promulgated. The large number was partly due to rivalries between Christian Right leaders, some of which were well publicized and grounded in theological differences (for example, pentecostal Pat Robertson versus fundamentalist Jerry Falwell). However, the number was mostly a product of conscious design on the part of Christian Right leaders. They had certain incentives to create multiple organizations, one of which was to gain free national publicity. When Falwell appeared on the political scene, for instance, the *New York Times* had twenty-four references to him and forty-six to his Moral Majority.[40] Other groups never matched that amount of attention, but many of them received national publicity when they were first launched. The American Coalition for Traditional Values, for instance, received full-page coverage in *Newsweek;* Christian Voice and the Liberty Federation received coverage on six and three separate occasions, respectively, in the *New York Times* in their first year.[41] The media focused on the rise of new groups, and the Christian Right's leaders obliged that interest by erecting ten different organizations.

The strategy was all the more compelling once it became clear that the demise of organizations went unnoticed. The closure of the NCAC and the virtual dismantling of the roundtable, for instance, were ignored by the press. The encapsulation of the Moral Majority by the Liberty Federation passed by almost without notice, a fact that Hadden and Shupe found "a strange response considering the tens of thousands of column inches that had been printed about the Moral Majority over the previous six years."[42] Perhaps the most revealing episode involved Falwell's announcement, in June 1989, that the Moral Majority was being disbanded. Falwell rationalized that action on the basis that other groups had arisen to take the place of Moral Majority, including the American Coalition for Traditional Values.[43] The newspapers dutifully reported that comment, apparently unaware that ACTV had been dissolved over two-and-one-half years earlier. Given the predilection of the media to cover the rise, but not the demise, of groups, there was every incentive to create new ones. Why not capitalize on such skewed coverage?

A second incentive to add new groups was to insulate the entire Christian Right from the demise of any one organization. A 1984 interviewee explained the point:

> The Christian Right groups have proliferated like the Christian schools did years before. . . . It makes the movement very fragmented in a sense, but it also means the entire movement will not rise or fall with any one group or any one person. If some group or leader falls from grace, then the entire movement does not fall as well. The numerous groups and leaders, in other words, keep the movement strong by diversifying it.

The importance of so cushioning the movement was apparent once the Moral Majority was disbanded. Despite the termination of its flagship organization, the Christian Right remained intact.

The Christian Right's leaders demonstrated their commitment to a multitude of organizations over the course of the 1980s. After the initial surge in the number of organizations in the late 1970s, new groups emerged at fairly regular intervals. The information presented in Table 4.1, and summarized here, demonstrates both the surge and the regularity of additions: the National Christian Action Coalition in 1978; the Moral Majority, Religious Roundtable, Concerned Women for America, and Christian Voice in 1979; the Freedom Council in 1981; the American Coalition for Traditional Values in 1984; the Liberty Federation in 1986; the American Freedom Coalition in 1987; and the Family Research Council in 1989.

Highly interwoven staffing patterns also surfaced. There was remarkable overlap in the various organizations, with leaders creating and servicing one another's groups. Wald noted that phenomenon in the early groups and likened it to an "interlocking directorate."[44] A 1984 interviewee expressed a similar view: "They [Christian Right leaders] organize and reorganize their groups, but maintain the same individuals in the various organizations." Significantly, the pattern of overlapping leadership in the earliest groups carried over to several of the later groups. Table 4.2 shows the extent of collusion by listing select leaders with multiple organizational affiliations in the 1980s.

Without discussing individual cases, it is evident that Christian Right leaders conspired to launch many groups. Their prototype was the

TABLE 4.2

Multiple Membership in Organizations by Select Leaders of the Christian Right

Person	*Affiliations*
Robert Billings	National Christian Action Coalition, Moral Majority, Christian Voice
Colonel Donner	Christian Voice, American Coalition for Traditional Values
Jerry Falwell	Moral Majority, Liberty Federation, American Coalition for Traditional Values
Robert Grant	Christian Voice, American Coalition for Traditional Values, American Freedom Coalition
Gary Jarmin	Christian Voice, American Coalition for Traditional Values, American Freedom Coalition
Tim LaHaye	Moral Majority, Christian Voice, American Coalition for Traditional Values
Pat Robertson	Religious Roundtable, Freedom Council
James Robison	Religious Roundtable, American Coalition for Traditional Values

creation of numerous liberal organizations in the 1970s. Germond and Witcover noted that "by following such an approach [adding groups], the conservatives are essentially following the same strategy that made the liberal coalition in the Democratic Party the dominant force in our politics over the last several decades."[45] Richard Viguerie, the New Right conservative who helped recruit fundamentalist ministers into politics, likewise stated that "all the New Right has done is copy the success of the old left."[46] Moreover, he acknowledged that conservative elites were "constantly looking for new groups to add to the growing New Right coalition . . . [since] family-oriented issues . . . [are] the key issues of the 1980s."[47] Along the same lines, the leader of the National Christian Action Coalition wrote a volume that stressed the need for coalition politics among multiple groups.[48]

Interviews provided still further evidence of the conscious strategy of adding groups. One person interviewed in 1984 stated directly, "What these guys [in the Christian Right] did was to imitate the liberals, and they are perfectly willing to say that." One of them did say it, in another 1984 interview: "The Left has [long] had a multiplicity of groups, and a decision was made [in the Christian Right] to try and follow that example, creating as many groups as possible. The Left invaded the consciousness of people with that strategy, and the Right wants to do the same." Five years later, interviewees said virtually the same thing. Joseph Conn reflected, "Over time, what the Christian Right has done is to create a group when there was not a group in place to meet its needs."[49] Gary Jarmin echoed that comment: "As I have thought about the key to success over the years, I have come to the conclusion that social movements can sustain themselves in one of two ways. First, they can be built around a single charismatic personality. . . . Second, they can develop a variety of organizations, each with its own niche. . . . The Christian Right has gone the way of creating multiple organizations, each with their own niche."[50] The fact that a member of the opposition and a Christian Right leader agreed on the same point suggests its veracity.

Taken together, the evidence overwhelmingly indicates that the sheer number of groups was mostly driven by Christian Right leaders anxious to capitalize on certain incentives and to accommodate the movement's evolving needs. By the end of the 1980s, an almost entirely new set of organizations had replaced those that began the decade. Out were groups like the National Christian Action Coalition, the Freedom Council, Christian Voice, and Moral Majority; in their place were groups like the American Freedom Coalition and the Family Research Council. Along the way, people like Beverly LaHaye, Robert Grant, and Gary Jarmin—all active at the beginning and end of the decade— gained political experience and skills. In addition, people like Gary Bauer (Reagan's domestic policy advisor before joining the Family Research Council) joined the movement. The net result was an overall increase in the level of political sophistication, a point that was affirmed in the pursuit of a new political strategy.

Political Strategy

A second area of change for the Christian Right during the 1980s was in the realm of political strategy. In essence, the Christian Right's leaders changed their strategic focal point. Initially, they focused on Congress. Paul Weyrich stated the rationale for this in 1980: "If you want to change America, you have to change the Congress."[51] Focusing on Congress was a logical move in the early 1980s because of the quick and easy access it afforded, due to decentralization in the 1970s.[52] Concentrating on the legislative branch was also a fine means of raising money, since as a 1984 interviewee noted, "the money is there for the legislative struggles, where they [Christian Right leaders] can whip up enthusiasm."

In both the 97th (1981–82) and 98th (1983–84) Congresses, the Christian Right was very active on Capitol Hill, with its apex occurring in the latter. What Kingdon has termed a "policy window"—an opportunity for agenda action due to a confluence of factors—opened during that period.[53] Behind the opportunity lay the fact that Reagan's tax-and-budget packages were in place and required little action; Reagan faced reelection in 1984 and needed the support of conservative Christians; the Supreme Court had paved the way by upholding the constitutionality of the so-called Hyde Amendments restricting taxpayer funding for abortion, and the equal-access concept permitting student religious groups to use school facilities; and the Conservative Opportunity Society, a group of junior Republicans, had agitated on behalf of the social issues.

In the 98th Congress, the Christian Right helped obtain votes on constitutional amendments permitting school prayer and banning abortion; defeat the Equal Rights Amendment; tack a rider onto an education bill permitting silent prayer in the public schools; pass an equal-access bill to permit high school students to use school facilities for voluntary religious meetings; and pass a bill allowing churches to opt out of the Social Security system (and thereby not be taxed by the secular state). Those successes were supplemented by inroads into the congressional agenda and supplantation of an alternative liberal agenda.[54]

Thereafter, though, the policy window closed abruptly. Once Reagan won reelection, he was no longer beholden politically to the Christian Right. Once the 99th Congress convened (1985–86), members tried to avoid the same divisive social issues that they had passed or defeated in the preceding Congress. Cobb and Elder have shown that once agenda items are considered seriously, as were the Christian Right's issues, they frequently fall off the political agenda.[55] That point was evidenced by the two-thirds drop (from six to two) in the number of congressional hearings on the social issues from the 98th to the 99th Congresses.[56] Then too, by the start of Reagan's second term the nation's budget deficits had caused a recentralization of power in the "money committees" of the Congress. That development diminished the role of the authorizing committees, where the Christian Right's agenda lay. The combination of those circumstances effectively prevented serious congressional action.

Sensing that Congress was no longer a prime target, even as the 98th Congress was winding down, Christian Right leaders began focusing on the grass roots. Gary Jarmin prophesied that "if I had to guess, I would say it is at the local level where our future lies and where our successes will be found."[57] The emphasis on the grass roots as the primary focal point for activism constituted a major strategic shift, away from lobbying on Capitol Hill and generating mail to influence members of Congress.

The organizations that were founded and/or active around the time of the 99th Congress (1985–86) demonstrated the emphasis on the grass roots. The American Coalition for Traditional Values, for instance, was designed as a grass-roots "umbrella" organization. Its primary purpose was to register voters all across the United States and to provide them information through a church network.[58] ACTV consisted of three hundred local chairpersons, located in three hundred cities across America. It was not even headquartered in the nation's capital for much of its existence, but in San Diego. Although ACTV eventually folded, before that time it performed grass-roots work.

The AFC also was launched with the grass roots in mind and was organized around a series of task forces (religious freedom, education, environment, world freedom, economic justice) that were led out of such states as Alaska, Washington, and Maryland.[59] The AFC's booklet asserted that its role was "to unite a vast array of groups, activists, churches, and community organizations in cooperative and effective action."[60] Accordingly, the first two working sessions at the AFC's first annual meeting were on the influence of grass-roots organizations on policymakers, and on the plan for building "local AFC development down from the national level to the local precinct."[61] Even more to the point, AFC political director Gary Jarmin spent over an hour in an interview laying out the plan to organize "precinct councils" across America.[62] His explanation follows:

> The important thing about precinct councils is that they will put a structure in place. It will be a structure composed of local citizens motivated by issues of direct interest to them. . . . [We are operating] on what I call the four *s* principle: that most people are

concerned with sewers, sidewalks, streets, and schools more than
anything else. . . . Only after the local coalitions are in place on
local issues, can they then be used on national issues.[63]

The grass-roots emphasis that began in the mid-1980s was deeply
rooted by the end of the decade. In addition to the AFC, Concerned
Women for America possessed a very tangible grass-roots element.
Hertzke earlier described its constituency-oriented "535 program,"
which keeps local CWA affiliates informed of the activities of their
congressional representatives; CWA also has a corporate program, in
which individual contributions to the organization are matched by
corporate sponsors.[64] More revealing than either of those programs,
though, was the way that Laurie Tryfiates, CWA's field director, described America's ills: "The answer to the problems facing America are
not all solved here in Washington, D.C. For that reason, there is little to
be gained by every group flocking to the capital city. Indeed, we mimic
the liberals if we think only of Washington, D.C. for answers."[65] CWA
has always taken pride in being the outgrowth of local women's prayer
chapters,[66] a grass-roots beginning that was even more firmly en-
trenched at the end of the 1980s.

The Christian Right's reorientation to the grass roots over the
course of the 1980s was so evident by fall 1989, that a schism broke out
in conservative ranks over whose idea it was to focus on the grass roots in
the first place.[67] Perhaps more than anything else, that dispute demonstrated the new strategic focal point.

Quite apart from the nature of organizations, other evidence also
indicates a shift to the grass roots. Beginning in the mid-1980s, religious conservatives started contending for control of the Republican
party in select states. As *Congressional Quarterly* noted in 1986, "In no
modern election year have there been so many primaries in which the
split between evangelicals and the GOP establishment has been a central—if often unspoken—issue."[68] In that year, Christian Right candidates contended for an estimated twenty-three House seats, in such
states as Arizona, North Carolina, South Carolina, Indiana, Tennessee,
and Michigan, as well as for Senate and gubernatorial seats in North
Carolina, Oregon, Nebraska, and Minnesota.[69] In 1988, a conservative
estimate identified four House challengers directly associated with the
Robertson presidential candidacy.[70] The infiltration of the Republican
party is further proof of the reorientation to the grass roots.

Then too, the Robertson candidacy testified to grass-roots activism. It began with his announcement on September 17, 1986, that he would seek the presidency if he received the signatures of three million people on petitions.[71] He subsequently won caucuses in Alaska, Hawaii, Nevada, and Washington; ran second in Minnesota and Iowa; and took second in the South Dakota primary. His strong performance in the caucus states, where organization is paramount because turnout is low, testified to the grass-roots work of his supporters. In fact, journalists coined the phrase "invisible army" to describe the methodical but unobtrusive way in which religious conservatives were mobilized for Robertson.[72]

The switch from heavily lobbying Congress to relying primarily on grass-roots organization was a wise move, reflecting increased political sophistication. The change in tactics represented more than Christian Right leaders recognizing which avenue provided the greatest opportunity and tailoring their efforts accordingly; it also included the realization that inundating Congress with mail might do more harm to the cause than good. After years of lobbying by mail the Christian Right's leadership recognized its mistake, aptly summed up by Gary Jarmin: "Both postcards and petitions do your opponents a favor by giving them a mailing list."[73] Equally significant, the new grass-roots focus provided the Christian Right's leaders with a means to deflect common strains of criticism. For years, opponents had charged that the leaders were too intolerant and judgmental, citing things like moral report cards as evidence. The greater emphasis on grass-roots work muted such criticism by changing the focus of discussion from questions of perceived intolerance toward questions of perceived strength in the grass roots. The emphasis on the grass roots also placed the Christian Right in the midst of a highly valued democratic tradition. What was more integral to democracy than to organize local citizens? The well-conceived strategic shift nudged the Christian Right toward the political mainstream and undercut lines of criticism.

Rhetoric

A third area of change for the Christian Right during the 1980s was its rhetoric. The guiding theme of the Christian Right's language in its early years was morality. Evidence abounds for that proposition, ranging from the anecdotal to the empirical. Hence, the group *Moral* Majority was formed, Christian Voice's leaders named their political action committee the "*Moral* Government Fund," and Christian Right leaders wrote tracts lamenting moral decline.[74] The obsession with morality was reflected in a Moral Majority fund-raising letter: "Moral cancers [are] destroying America and the Moral Majority has been fighting to return America to moral sanity."[75] Substantive empirical evidence of the same point was gathered by Shupe and Stacey, who confirmed that moral themes were a motivating force for the Christian Right's membership; in the same volume, Wuthnow provided a theoretical argument about moral reassertion in the post-Watergate era.[76] Ultimately, of course, one need only look at the Christian Right's political agenda of the early 1980s, which was heavily centered on the issues of prayer in schools, abortion, gay rights, and pornography.

The pervasive morality emphasis motivated hard-core followers, but it also presented problems. More moderate citizens, who were sympathetic to the principles of cultural conservatism, were uneasy with moralistic overtones. It was one thing for moderates to favor school prayer, for instance, but quite another for them to accept the view of Christian Right leaders that the opposition virtually advocated licentiousness in public schools. The morality rhetoric thus caused a slippage in popular support by discouraging those people who subscribed to key tenets of the Christian Right's platform from actually joining its groups.[77]

The morality rhetoric became particularly problematic when it focused on the clergy. Giving a Catholic priest in good standing a zero "moral approval rating" while he was a member of Congress was one manifestation; attacking denominational statements on the basis of dubious biblical interpretations was yet another. For instance, in the early 1980s the Christian Right's leaders claimed that the moral "high ground" was increasing the nation's defense expenditures, while at the same time the Catholic bishops were lamenting the immorality of defense expenditures and nuclear weapons.[78] The Christian Right's position was defensible in secular terms but difficult to justify in scriptural terms. As a general rule, the morality rhetoric placed Christian Right leaders in an awkward position. Neuhaus observed that fact and cautioned religious conservatives that their moral dogmatism would "only drive into the enemy camp the great majority of Christians who do not belong there and who do not want to be there."[79]

Broad themes aside, moral rhetoric was difficult to apply to specific issues. Casting the abortion issue in moral terms, for example, was far from easy. On one hand, it energized the already committed. Moreover, it was a reasonable way to frame the issue: even antiabortion opponents had to concede that the practice of terminating fetuses (particularly those that were viable when aborted) raised profound moral questions. On the other hand, framing abortion in moral terms was not an unequivocal advantage. When presented with abortion as a profoundly moral issue, many people focused on the immorality of forcing women to carry unwanted pregnancies to term. At best, the attempt to cast abortion in moral terms cut both ways.

The issue of tuition tax credits for parents whose children attended private religious schools served as another case in point. The Christian Right advocated such tax credits in moral terms, arguing that they were necessary to get as many children as possible out of the thoroughly secularized public schools. To the faithful, that was a reasonable proposition. To others, however, the immoral element was not the public schools, but the Christian Right's seemingly selfish attempts to draw an advantaged class of students out of the public schools, casually leaving behind a second-rate school system.

The school prayer issue serves as a final example. While Christian Right leaders believed the absence of voluntary prayer in schools was immoral, many others objected to the spectre of forcing children of minority religions or atheists, through peer pressure, to recite public prayers to a Christian God.

As the Christian Right's leadership grew more politically sophisticated, it recognized the problem and jettisoned much of the morality rhetoric. It was replaced with the rhetoric of liberalism, with its emphases on freedom, liberty, rights, and choice. Organizational titles are prima facie evidence of this reorientation. The early groups included the National *Christian* Action Coalition, the *Moral* Majority, *Christian* Voice (and its subdivision, the *Moral* Government Fund), and the *Religious* Roundtable.[80] In contrast, two later organizations were dubbed the *Liberty* Federation and the American *Freedom* Coalition. Even the later groups that did not explicitly incorporate the buzzwords of liberalism, at least eschewed the rhetoric of moralism, with organizational titles like the Family Research Council and the American Coalition for Traditional Values. Largely missing from organizational titles at the end of the 1980s were religious and moral references; in their place was the unmistakable language of liberalism.

The incorporation of liberal rhetoric also occurred with respect to particular issues. Hertzke perceptively pointed out that the issue of voluntary student religious groups meeting in the public schools was framed as one of "equal access."[81] Moreover, his interview with a

legislative director of the Moral Majority uncovered an awareness of the
need to frame the school prayer issue in similar terms: "We pushed
school prayer three years in a row, but we framed the issue in terms of
how prayer in schools is good. But some people feel that prayer in school
is bad. So we learned to frame the issue in terms of 'student's rights,' so
it became a constitutional issue. We are prochoice for students having
the right to pray in schools."[82]

The rhetoric of liberalism was also applied to the abortion issue,
with greater emphasis on the "rights" of the unborn and the need for
"choice" (apart from abortion) for women carrying an unwanted preg-
nancy. In fact, under the rubric "Operation Rescue," antiabortion forces
even took a step beyond rhetoric, actually mimicking the tactics of the
civil rights movement.[83]

Hertzke and Scribner, in their study of the child care issue, noted
how New Right operatives and religious conservatives sought to frame
the issue in terms of "parental choice."[84] That approach appealed both to
the "free marketeers" of the New Right and to Christian Right leaders,
who wanted parents choosing to stay at home with their children to
receive tax deductions along with working parents.[85]

Finally, the Robertson presidential campaign yielded a fascinating
usage of the language of liberalism. Robertson insisted that he was the
"victim" of media "bigotry," because of journalists' proclivity to call him
a "television evangelist," rather than a "Christian businessman."[86] Recently, much has been written about the benefits of attaining "victim
status" in public life.[87] Although his efforts to attain such status and to
recast his role were unsuccessful, Robertson's perspicacity in employing
some of the key words of liberalism reflected the heightened sensitivity
within the movement to framing matters in terms with which average
citizens were accustomed.

Secularization and Accommodation

In the process of challenging secular policies and principles in the
1980s, the Christian Right's organizational structure, strategic locus,
and political rhetoric all changed rather dramatically. What began as
several overtly religious organizations primarily lobbying Congress on a
set of social issues gradually became a different set of organizations,
focused on the grass roots and using liberal rhetoric.

The changes in the Christian Right were advanced by leaders who
became more politically adept over time. In 1984, the legislative

director of a major Christian Right organization wryly commented in an interview, "There is no question that in time the level of political sophistication will increase, but in the meantime, let me say there is still room for improvement." By the end of the decade, improvement had occurred. Organizations had been added or restructured to accommodate needs; resources had been diverted to the grass roots, where they could be used for maximum impact; and issues had been recast in popular and more appealing language. Those changes reflected increased political skills.

If Christian Right leaders were more politically sophisticated at the end of the 1980s, though, their conduct seemed less firmly rooted in religious principles. In the process of challenging the secular state, Christian Right leaders gradually succumbed to its standards and practices, often acting and sounding like their religious principles were less important than their political goals. Put another way, over time Christian Right leaders exhibited conduct that was inconsistent with their religious principles. In that specific sense, they were secularized during the 1980s.

Evidence supporting the notion of secularization abounds. For example, Christian Right leaders exaggerated claims about their organizations. Hadden and his colleagues systematically examined Moral Majority's newsletter and found that claims about the activities of state affiliates were grossly overstated.[88] Scholars scrutinized national data and concluded that organizational membership estimates were similarly inflated.[89] Brozan pointed out that Concerned Women for America inflated its membership by counting every person who was ever a member at any time.[90] The exaggeration of levels of activity and of interest group membership was the prevailing norm in the secular political world, and in that relativistic sense, it was excusable. Nevertheless, these actions were inconsistent with religious precepts.

Along similar lines, Christian Right leaders engaged in hyperbole during the 1980s. The two leading figures of the movement in the decade, Jerry Falwell and Pat Robertson, both provided numerous examples. Falwell, for instance, called Nobel Peace Prize winner Bishop Desmond Tutu a "phony" for purporting to speak for all black South Africans; he also analogized that convicted felon Oliver North, of the Iran-Contra scandal, was like Jesus Christ in that both were "indicted and convicted."[91] Robertson followed suit, particularly in his 1988 presidential campaign, when he claimed that his Christian Broadcasting Network had known the location of the American hostages in the

Middle East; that the Soviet Union had recently placed missiles in Cuba; and that the Bush campaign had leaked information about Reverend Jimmy Swaggart's rendezvous with a prostitute, in order to undercut Robertson's campaign.[92] In addition to those rhetorical flourishes, Robertson circulated a questionable resume. It listed "graduate study" at the University of London, which turned out to be an introductory summer arts course; it also listed membership on a "board of directors," which turned out to be an advisory body for a local bank.[93] Finally, Robertson's resume stated that he was a "combat" veteran. That claim was challenged by a former member of Congress who served in Korea when Robertson served, and who charged that Robertson used the influence of his father (a U.S. senator) to win transfer off a troop ship to a noncombat unit.[94] Robertson subsequently filed a $35 million libel suit, but dropped it when he was ordered to appear in court on Super Tuesday primary day in 1988. Those words and actions demonstrated how low the standards for public discourse had become, which was rather ironic given all of the morality rhetoric early in the movement.

A further example of the erosion of religious principles as a basis of conduct is the acceptance of money by several Christian Right leaders from a highly questionable source. As funds dried up for their organizations, leaders of Christian Voice, the American Coalition for Traditional Values, and the American Freedom Coalition all turned for assistance to Reverend Sun Myung Moon, the Korean capitalist and evangelist, whose claim to be the Second Messiah essentially constitutes blasphemy to conservative Christians.[95] Accepting monetary contributions from a source whose central teaching is contrary to conservative Christianity is virtually irrefutable evidence of the elevation of political goals over religious principles.

Near the end of the 1980s, leaders of two of the major groups essentially conceded their secular orientation to politics. Gary Bauer, of the Family Research Council, said of the movement generally, in the context of framing issues, that "religion may still motivate people, but there is no virtue in quoting Bible verses to policymakers with different value perspectives. The movement has come to see that fact."[96] Gary Jarmin, of the American Freedom Coalition, was more direct: "The AFC has a secular orientation. We found it was easier to attract religious people to work together in a secular context than in a religious context. . . . For that reason, the AFC has been structured to get religious people to cooperate in a secular context."[97]

The secularization that occurred at the elite level also took root within the Christian Right's mass constituency. A recent study of that constituencies' voting behavior concluded that "while the number of people who fit into various definitions of the religious right have generally increased, their political behavior no longer has a unique character to it. . . . Politically speaking, they have become secularized. Their religion no longer transgresses their politics, but is simply part of their political make-up."[98] Further evidence of a secularized mass constituency may be found in the wake of the defeat of the 1984 constitutional amendment for school prayer. Many people sent telegrams to Senator Lowell Weicker, congratulating him on his success in spearheading opposition to the amendment, that were signed "your pal, Satan."[99] It prompted one person, interviewed in 1984, to remark that the fight "was a very nasty thing, as nasty a fight as I have ever been involved in."

The apparent diminution of religious principles during the 1980s, in the process of challenging the state, is consistent with the findings of religious historian Martin Marty for an earlier era. He argued that evangelical Christianity was subtly and gradually secularized in the late 1800s.[100] As in the case of the Christian Right, the secularization was aided and abetted by religious leaders.[101] Just as the Christian Right's leaders adopted the norms of the secular political world, evangelical leaders in the 1800s adjusted religious doctrine to accommodate a changing nation.[102] Against the backdrop of an evangelical faith that was thoroughly modernized and secularized in the 1800s, the Christian Right's own secularization was fairly marginal; however, set against the nature of the movement in its early days, the secularization of the Christian Right by the end of the 1980s was considerable.

At the outset of the 1990s, the Christian Right is a very different movement than it was a decade ago. It consists of new organizations and more skilled but somewhat secularized leaders, who are concentrating on new venues with new rhetoric. The transformation of the Christian Right in these respects dovetails with the pluralist literature in political science, which argues that the American system impels moderation and incorporation into the political system.[103] Lienesch rightly dismissed pluralism as an explanatory framework in the early 1980s, because of the uncompromising moralism of the Christian Right.[104] By the end of the decade, though, it provided a plausible framework for understanding a social movement that adjusted and accommodated itself to the political environment.

The institutionalization of the Christian Right as a political force offers new opportunities and challenges. Its increasingly moderate, secular nature presents greater opportunities to win converts, beyond the relatively narrow strata of fundamentalist and evangelical Christians. However, that same disposition portends a loss of fervor. A 1984 interviewee observed that "if people [in the Christian Right] are only doing their civic duty, rather than their religious duty, they will probably not work as hard." Likewise, the increasingly moderate and secular nature of the Christian Right translates into an erosion of its distinctive character. It was that distinctiveness that captured the attention of opinion leaders and facilitated the high public profile and agenda-setting clout of the movement in its early years. With that distinctiveness somewhat eradicated, its power to influence the national dialogue has been diminished. In all probability, the Christian Right will spend the 1990s "slugging it out" with the other institutionalized political players of the secular state, where its successes will be tangible, but largely invisible to the casual observer.

Notes

Acknowledgments: The author thanks the Faculty Research Funds Committee of the University of Maine for its support of this research.

1. Eileen Ogintz, "Evangelists Seek Political Clout," *Chicago Tribune,* January 13, 1980, 5.

2. Interview with Joseph Conn, June 14, 1989.

3. Interview with Gary Jarmin, June 8, 1989.

4. Steve Bruce, *The Rise and Fall of the New Christian Right* (New York: Oxford University Press, 1988).

5. On the Christian Right's political action committees, see James L. Guth and John C. Green, "Faith and Politics: Religion and Ideology Among Political Contributors," *American Politics Quarterly* 14 (1986): 186–200; James L. Guth and John C. Green, "The Moralizing Minority: Christian Right Support Among Political Contributors," *Social Science Quarterly* 86 (1987): 598–610; Margaret Ann Latus, "Ideological PACS and Political Action," in *The New Christian Right,* ed. Robert C. Liebman and Robert Wuthnow (New York: Aldine, 1983), 75–99; on its electoral impact, see Steven D. Johnson and Joseph B. Tamney, "The Christian Right and the 1980 Presidential Election," *Journal for the Scientific Study of Religion* 21 (1982): 123–31; Arthur H. Miller and Martin P. Wattenberg, "Politics from the Pulpit," *Public Opinion Quarterly* 48 (1984): 301–17; Jeffrey L. Brudney and Gary W. Copeland, "Evangelicals as a Political Force: Reagan and the 1980 Religious Vote," *Social Science Quarterly* 65 (1984): 1072–79; Emmett H. Buell, Jr., and Lee Sigelman, "Popular Support for the Moral Majority in 1980," *Social Science Quarterly* 66 (1985): 426–34; Lee Sigelman, Clyde Wilcox, and Emmett H. Buell, Jr., "An

Unchanging Minority: Popular Support for the Moral Majority, 1980 and 1984," *Social Science Quarterly* 68 (1987): 876–84; Corwin Smidt, "Born Again Politics," in *Religion and Politics in the South,* ed. Tod A. Baker, Robert P. Steed, and Laurence W. Moreland (New York: Praeger, 1983), 27–56; Clyde Wilcox, "Popular Support for the Moral Majority in 1980: A Second Look," *Social Science Quarterly* 68 (1987): 157–66; Ted G. Jelen, "The Effects of Religious Separatism on White Protestants in the 1984 Presidential Election," *Sociological Analysis* 48 (1987): 30–45; Corwin Smidt, "Evangelicals and the 1984 Election," *American Politics Quarterly* 15 (1987): 419–44; Jeffrey L. Brudney and Gary W. Copeland, "Ronald Reagan and the Religious Vote" (Paper delivered at the Annual Meeting of the American Political Science Association, Washington, D.C., September 1988); on its lobbying efforts, see Matthew C. Moen, *The Christian Right and Congress* (Tuscaloosa: University of Alabama Press, 1989); Allen D. Hertzke, *Representing God in Washington* (Knoxville: University of Tennessee Press, 1988).

6. Michael Lienesch, "Christian Conservatism as a Political Movement," *Political Science Quarterly,* Fall 1982: 403–25.

7. The Moral Majority formally closed in June 1989.

8. Jeffrey K. Hadden and Charles Swann, *Prime Time Preachers* (Reading, Mass.: Addison-Wesley, 1981), 135.

9. Bill Keller, "Evangelical Conservatives Move from Pews to Polls, but Can They Sway Congress?" *Congressional Quarterly Weekly Report,* September 6, 1980, 2628.

10. Richard Viguerie, *The New Right* (Falls Church, Va.: Viguerie Co., 1981), 9.

11. Hadden and Swann, *Prime Time Preachers,* 139.

12. James Endersby, "The Cross and the Flag" (Paper delivered at the Annual Meeting of the Southwestern Political Science Association, Fort Worth, Texas, March 21–24, 1984), 3–5.

13. Moen, *The Christian Right and Congress,* 125–32.

14. Based on visit to Christian Voice on June 6, 1989.

15. Jarmin interview.

16. Ibid.

17. Ibid.

18. Dan Fefferman, "The First Annual National AFC Board of Governors Meeting," *American Freedom Journal* 2 (December 1988/January 1989): 6–7.

19. Beth Spring, "Some Christian Leaders Want Further Political Activism," *Christianity Today,* November 9, 1984, 46.

20. Larry Witham, "LeHaye [*sic*] Continues Ministry on Local Level," *Washington Times,* October 20, 1989, F5.

21. Interview with Laurie Tryfiates, June 9, 1989.

22. "Come Help Save America!" (Undated pamphlet distributed by Concerned Women for America, Box 65453, Washington, D.C. 20035).

23. Ibid.

24. Ibid.

25. Hertzke, *Representing God in Washington,* 51.

26. Erling Jorstad, *The Politics of Moralism* (Minneapolis: Augsburg, 1981), 74.

27. Moen, *The Christian Right and Congress,* 77. On the estimate, see Robert C. Liebman, "Mobilizing the Moral Majority," in *The New Christian Right,* ed. Robert C. Liebman and Robert Wuthnow (New York: Aldine, 1983), 54–55.

28. Jeffrey K. Hadden and Anson Shupe, *Televangelism* (New York: Henry Holt, 1988), 172.

29. Ibid.

30. Interview with Gary Bauer, June 14, 1989.

31. Interview with Michael Schwartz, October 16, 1989.

32. Peter Steinfels, "Moral Majority to Dissolve; Says Mission Accomplished," *New York Times,* June 12, 1989, 14.

33. A perusal of the *New York Times Index* revealed that the Liberty Federation had three citations in 1986, and none for 1987–89.

34. Based on an examination of Washington, D.C., Atlanta, and Lynchburg, Virginia, telephone directories, all cities in which Moral Majority was headquartered at one time.

35. Interview with Howard Phillips, June 16, 1989.

36. Jeff Gerth, "Robertson and Confidentiality," *New York Times,* March 19, 1987, 24.

37. Bauer interview.

38. Joyce Price, "Family Group Sees 1990s as Perilous," *Washington Times,* December 15, 1989, 5.

39. Phillips interview.

40. Harvey L. Holmes, ed., *New York Times Index* (New York: New York Times, 1980).

41. Kenneth L. Woodward and Eleanor Clift, "Playing Politics at Church," *Newsweek,* July 9, 1984, 52; based on examination of the *New York Times Index* for 1979 (Christian Voice) and 1986 (Liberty Federation).

42. Hadden and Shupe, *Televangelism,* 173.

43. Laura Sessions Stepp, "Falwell Says Moral Majority to Be Dissolved," *Washington Post,* June 12, 1989, 11.

44. Kenneth Wald, *Religion and Politics in the United States* (New York: St. Martin's Press, 1987), 190.

45. Quoted in Viguerie, *The New Right,* 79.

46. Ibid., 78.

47. Ibid., 55.

48. William Billings, *The Christian's Political Action Manual* (Washington, D.C.: NCAC, 1980).

49. Conn interview.

50. Jarmin interview.

51. Kenneth Briggs, "Evangelical Preachers Gather to Polish Their Politics," *New York Times,* August 21, 1980, B9.

52. Leroy Rieselbach, *Congressional Reform* (Washington, D.C.: CQ Press, 1986), 47–57.

53. John W. Kingdon, *Agendas, Alternatives, and Public Policies* (Boston: Little, Brown & Co., 1984), 176–79.

54. Moen, *The Christian Right and Congress,* 141–42.

55. Roger Cobb and Charles Elder, *Participation in American Politics,* 2d ed. (Baltimore: Johns Hopkins University Press, 1983), 158.

56. Compiled from Congressional Information Service materials.

57. Moen, *The Christian Right and Congress,* 175.

58. "What is ACTV?" (Undated pamphlet distributed during the 1984 campaign season).

59. Based on pamphlets describing each of the task forces, available from AFC national headquarters, 1001 Pennsylvania Avenue NW, Suite 850, Washington, D.C. 20004.

60. "A Promise for Their Future" (Undated booklet available from AFC national headquarters), 3.

61. Fefferman, "The First Annual National AFC Board of Governors Meeting," 6.

62. Jarmin interview.

63. Ibid.

64. Hertzke, *Representing God in Washington,* 52–53; Sara Diamond, *Spiritual Warfare* (Boston: South End Press, 1989), 109.

65. Tryfiates interview.

66. Nadine Brozan, "Politics and a Prayer," *New York Times,* June 15, 1987, 18.

67. See John Elvin, "They Wuz First," *Washington Times,* September 27, 1989, 6.

68. Rob Gurwitt, "1986 Elections Generate GOP Power Struggle," *Congressional Quarterly Weekly Report,* April 12, 1986, 803.

69. Ibid.; Bob Benenson, "Christian Right's Aspirants for Congress . . . Find Their Language, Beliefs Scrutinized," *Congressional Quarterly Weekly Report,* May 14, 1988, 1272.

70. Benenson, "Christian Right's Aspirants for Congress," 1272.

71. Hadden and Shupe, *Televangelism,* 254.

72. Tamar Jacoby, "Is It Time to Take Pat Seriously? The Invisible Army," *Time,* January 4, 1988, 21.

73. Jarmin interview.

74. For example, James Robison, *Attack on the Family* (Wheaton, Ill.: Tyndale, 1982).

75. Moral Majority fund-raising letter, April 30, 1984.

76. Anson Shupe and William Stacey, "The Moral Majority Constituency," in *The New Christian Right,* ed. Robert C. Liebman and Robert Wuthnow (New York: Aldine, 1983), 110; Robert Wuthnow, "The Political Rebirth of American Evangelicals," in *The New Christian Right,* ed. Robert C. Liebman and Robert Wuthnow (New York: Aldine, 1983), 175–77.

77. A good starting point is John H. Simpson, "Moral Issues and Status Politics," in *The New Christian Right,* ed. Robert C. Liebman and Robert Wuthnow (New York: Aldine, 1983), 187–205.

78. Timothy A. Byrnes, "The Silence of the Seamless Garment" (Paper delivered at the Annual Meeting of the American Political Science Association, Atlanta, Georgia, September 1989), 13–16.

79. Richard John Neuhaus, *The Naked Public Square,* 2d ed. (Grand Rapids, Mich.: William B. Eerdmans, 1984), 260–61.

80. The one exception to the early organizational names was Pat Robertson's Freedom Council.

81. Hertzke, *Representing God in Washington,* 195.

82. Ibid.

83. Garry Wills, "Save the Babies," *Time,* May 1, 1989, 26–28.

84. Allen Hertzke and Mary Scribner, "The Politics of Federal Day Care" (Paper presented at the Annual Meeting of the American Political Science Association, Atlanta, September 1989), 30.

85. Ibid.

86. Wayne King, "Robertson Plans an Ad Campaign to Enhance TV Minister's Image," *New York Times,* September 7, 1987, 7; "Pat Robertson Shuns TV Evangelist Label," Associated Press wire story, February 11, 1988.

87. For example, Mike Royko, "Victim Growth Industry," nationally syndicated column reprinted in the *Washington Times,* June 12, 1990, F3; Wesley Pruden, "A Growing Trade in Victimhood," *Washington Times,* June 15, 1990, 4.

88. Jeffrey K. Hadden, Anson Shupe, James Hawdon, and Kenneth Martin, "Why Jerry Falwell Killed the Moral Majority," in *The God Pumpers,* ed. Marshall Fishwick and Ray B. Browne (Bowling Green, Ohio: Bowling Green State University Popular Press, 1987), 101.

89. Sigelman, Wilcox, and Buell, "An Unchanging Minority," 883.

90. Brozan, "Politics and Prayer," 18.

91. Robert Pear, "Falwell Denounces Tutu as a Phony," *New York Times,* August 22, 1985, 10; "North Says Criminal Charges Against Him Are an Honor," *New York Times,* May 3, 1988, B7.

92. Larry Martz, "Day of the Preachers," *Newsweek,* March 7, 1988, 44.

93. "Robertson Blasts Journalists for Exposing Family Skeleton," Knight-Ridder wire story, October 9, 1987.

94. Phil Gailey, "Robertson Used Journalist to Get Data for Libel Suit on War Record," *New York Times,* April 2, 1987, A25.

95. Diamond, *Spiritual Warfare,* 70, 78.

96. Bauer interview.

97. Jarmin interview.

98. Gary W. Copeland and Jeffrey L. Brudney, "Ronald Reagan and the Religious Vote" (Paper delivered at the Annual Meeting of the American Political Science Association, Washington, D.C., September 1988), 19.

99. Steven Roberts, "Fervent Debate on School Prayer," *New York Times,* March 9, 1984, A16.

100. Martin Marty, *The Modern Schism* (New York: Harper & Row, 1969), 95–144.

101. Ibid., 104–8.

102. Ibid., 101.

103. Robert Dahl, *A Preface to Democratic Theory* (Chicago: University of Chicago Press, 1956), 151.

104. Lienesch, "Christian Conservatism as a Political Movement," 422–23.

5.

Church-State Relations in Contemporary Mexico, 1968–1988

ALLAN METZ

The Mexican Roman Catholic church has been studied from a multitude of perspectives: the church and democracy,[1] anticlericalism,[2] legalism,[3] statistics,[4] the church as a pressure group,[5] "religious organizations as political forces of substitution,"[6] the role of religion in economic development,[7] the relationship between religion and nationalism,[8] the Mexican church as historically a force of conservatism,[9] and "a vision of the history of the church in Mexico through church-state relations."[10] While these approaches are all important, this chapter focuses on interpretative frameworks, including viewing church-state relations as a corporatist relationship, church challenges to the state, the political role of the church, and the nature of this relationship on the local level. On the basis of this conceptual framework and historical background, it examines case studies/examples that reflect the nature of church-state relations within the past twenty years. A related theme is to note the provisions regarding religion in the Constitution of 1917 and to see if they are still in effect in the period under study.

Conceptual Frameworks and Historical Background

Karl Schmitt views church-state relations in Mexico as a corporatist relationship[11] and notes, according to the "conventional wisdom," that two divisions took place in Mexico regarding church and state: the first, at the time of the Reforma (1857–61),[12] and the second, the Mexican Revolution (1910–20).[13] These divisions were an outgrowth of increasing "estrangement and hostility" between state and church authorities and ultimately resulted in the Constitution of 1917, which Schmitt describes as "the most anti-clerical and even anti-religious legislation enacted in the hemisphere." While Schmitt acknowledges these historical breaks in church-state relations, he asserts that there have been fundamental continuities in these relations.

Thus, a constant throughout Mexican history is the relationship of the state to the church. Schmitt's thesis is that in Mexico—not withstanding apparent changes in policies, the passage of new laws and constitutions, and sharp shifts from conflict to "peaceful accommodation"—a "corporatist" view of the state has been prevalent in both secular and ecclesiastical circles. This concept of corporatism forms "a mode of political organization and institutional relationships" whose roots are in medieval Europe and even before. Schmitt's purpose is to demonstrate how corporatism has expressed itself in Mexican history from the late eighteenth century to the present. His definition of corporatism is

> A type of political system in which political interests are and should be expressed primarily through groups rather than by individual actions such as voting; in which the state acts as regulator and harmonizer among the groups; and in which the groups themselves are non-competitive, lacking in autonomy, differentiated by function or occupation (not class), and unequal in status. . . . In other words, corporatism postulates a harmonious, organic society of smoothly functioning parts, each performing a necessary and useful task for the general welfare, and regulated by an all-powerful state.[14]

Regarding the state, Mexico's political system has also been described as "corporate," "with its functionally organized official party, legally-mandated business/industrial societies, and constitutionally regulated religious organizations."

According to Schmitt, three stages of church-state relations in Mexico can be discerned from independence through to the present. All of these stages followed the prevailing corporatist pattern (except for brief exceptions in the first two stages). The first stage, 1821–55, marked a continuation of the relationship established in the colonial period. The church had "a degree of freedom and autonomy" in exchange for some state regulation of "ecclesiastical appointments" and "state appropriations of Church property." While the state made other claims regarding the church, neither the regulations nor the claims were ever formalized with Rome or with the bishops in Mexico. Church-state cleavages and disagreements characterized this period regardless of liberal or conservative governments. The liberals favored more control of and less protection and freedom for the church and the conservatives generally agreed with controls but favored more protection and accommodation with the church. An interruption occurred in the first phase in 1833–34 when a "radical regime" advocated substantive changes in the church-state relation.[15] However, its only enduring legacy was the withdrawal of secular authority in collecting tithes.[16]

The second stage, 1855–1910, marked distinctive alterations in practice and increased hostility between church and state. However, the relationship (or in Schmitt's words, "conceptual basis") changed little from the previous stage. Granted, liberal governments of the period spoke of church-state separation and advocated state appointment of church benefices or the right to determine the boundaries of dioceses. All governments made general "claims in law and practice to regulate or to prohibit" various kinds of ecclesiastical activities, however, such as "property ownership, monastic order, lay brotherhoods, the wearing of clerical garb in public and religious services outside of church buildings." The Catholic church's "special legal protection," one of the two major characteristics of the colonial patronate, was abrogated. But the rescinding of protection and the calls for separation of the church and state did not lead to "a laissez-faire state." Instead, the corporatist concept basically remained in effect. Churches (i.e., Catholic and various Protestant denominations) and secular institutions were liable to tight supervision and regulation by the state. Regarding the latter, the new labor associations and mutual aid societies that began to replace the earlier guilds by the middle of the nineteenth century were brought under state control by Presidents Benito Juárez, Sebastian Lerdo de Tejada, and Porfirio Díaz, respectively. Industry and commerce also came under state control, especially via the Chambers Law of 1908. Although the state at that time espoused liberal rhetoric, in practice it continued to perform "a major role as supervisor, regulator and harmonizer of interest group activity, the classical role of the state in a corporate society." As in the first phase, this second stage experienced a temporary exception—the imperial rule of Maximilian, during which an attempt was made to restore a more apparent corporate relationship with the church via a concordat (which never succeeded) with the Vatican.

The third stage (1910 to the present) is characterized by continuity with the second phase but also by a distinct change. Numerous constraints placed on the church by the Reforma were repeated in the Constitution of 1917 in addition to more restrictive measures. The "sharp break" between the two stages occurred in two areas: (1) ministers of all religions lost just about all political rights and a number of civil rights enjoyed by other citizens, and (2) churches according to the Constitution of 1917 had their legal status removed. In addition, clergy cannot possess any property, even church buildings, and they do not have judicial redress to sue against public or private attacks made on them.[17] In essence, churches are legislated "out of existence . . . [and] are declared non-persons." Clearly, "the concept of the state on which these terms are grounded not only" is based on past precedents, but also on "the implicit corporatism of the nineteenth century [which] becomes explicit in the constitution and later legal codes" (for example, creation of corporate villages; the fact that the official party, PRI, established in 1929 is organized on corporatist bases; and the Chambers Law of 1908 has been maintained and broadened). And so Mexico's current political system displays a number of the characteristics of "the corporatist state" vis-à-vis "governmental/political relations with peasants, business organizations, professional organizations, and religious bodies. The fact that religious institutions exist outside the law does not change the fact that they are subject to state control and restrictions, and in many ways are treated as though they were recognized and legitimate parts of the body politic."[18]

In summary, a "great continuity" exists regarding church-state relations from independence to the present in Mexico, according to Schmitt. This continuity does not refer to concordats with Rome, specific rules and regulations determining that relationship, or accommodations between secular and ecclesiastical authorities. In that regard, there have been wide fluctuations. Moreover, "under the harshest legal and constitutional regulations in its history, the Catholic Church [now] enjoys rather" cordial relations with the Mexican state. Government criticism of the church focuses really on the "radicalism" of some church clerics[19] who speak out against poverty and societal injustice. (Since the writing of Schmitt's article, the state has also been critical of the church regarding its support and ties to the National Action Party [PAN], and to protests of elections in 1986 and 1988, which will be discussed later.) The continuity consists "in conceptualizing society as a series of corporate structures or institutions regulated, limited, and harmonized by the state apparatus." This concept was "blurred" due to claims by politicians in the nineteenth and early twentieth centuries that sought the establishment of a "liberal state in which the individual's relation to the political system and to the state superseded group or corporate relationships." The liberal concept was never completely put into effect and most Mexican political leaders, including Benito Juárez himself, essentially thought in terms of a corporate society. The liberals "were never able to free themselves of their history." The revolutionaries of the Mexican Revolution and the reformers in the 1930s under Lázaro Cárdenas "moved Mexico explicitly back to a corporate state without using the term itself. Throughout all three phases of church-state relations, however, Mexican political leaders never abandoned the corporate ideal as a guiding principle in determining their policies toward the Church."[20]

Other observers of Mexican church-state relations such as Dennis M. Hanratty[21] and Claude Pomerleau[22] essentially agree with Schmitt's corporatist interpretation, though both place more emphasis on church-state conflict and its potential in the future. The purpose of Hanratty's article is to discuss the major political issues affecting the Catholic church in Mexico today, which include its relation to the state. Hanratty first presents historical background on the church's position on political and social issues of this century, which is necessary for an understanding of the church due to "a striking continuity of thought" between attitudes held by the church hierarchy early this century and those of today. (Similarities between the corporatist viewpoint of the Mexican state and, historically, the corporatist position of the Catholic church are noteworthy.)

The position of the Catholic church in Mexico regarding the political system is based on "the corporatist framework" outlined in *Rerum Novarum* by Pope Leo XIII in 1891.[23] Pope Leo adapted the "scholastic teachings" of St. Thomas Aquinas to his time (i.e., the church serves to harmonize societal interests reflecting a communitarian position that the church should be above politics). In Leo's view (based on Aquinas), society is composed of "interrelated interests and responsibilities, where the actions of each member constitute a necessary contribution to a well-ordered commonwealth." (In this scheme, for example, the church performs a mediating role between labor and management and should also formulate a church structure that educates and represents various societal groups.) The post–World War II understanding between the church and state[24] enabled the former "to play a more visible role in society." In the late 1950s and 1960s, the Mexican church was characterized by a greater "direct . . . involvement in social issues" in response to the growth of Protestantism in Mexico, but mostly due to the rise to power of Fidel Castro in Cuba, which reflected the church's concern to prevent communism in Mexico. The Tlateloco massacre of 1968 had a "profound impact" on many in the church and the Mexican Social Secretariat, or SSM (which was established in 1920 by the church "as the overseer of ecclesiastical social action policy"). This traumatic event seemed in direct conflict with the harmonizing vision of Pope Leo and led to a more "conflictual" interpretation of society. The then nascent "doctrine of liberation theology fulfilled" this need (i.e., Catholicism via its "social and political dimensions" had "transformative capabilities"). For example, the deep devotion of Mexico's poor to Our Lady of Guadalupe was linked to firm demands for social change. Thus, the Mexican church is divided over such issues as its "appropriate role in Mexican society," increasing challenges to church leadership by church-affiliated groups regarding Liberation Theology, and particularly significant for the purposes of this chapter, the growing "episcopal demands for an abolition of constitutional limitations on political participation." (The specifics of these and other instances reflective of church-state relations will be treated later in the chapter.)

Hanratty concludes that the Catholic church in Mexico reflects sharp conflicts over political and social opinions. The "communitarian consensus" of Pope Leo prior to Tlateloco has since given way to more diversified attitudes and positions. And a new consensus is not very feasible considering deep divisions over Liberation Theology and the role of private property, which are not easily reconcilable. Besides such internal divisions, the hierarchy's wish to be more politically active and visible raises the possibility of direct conflicts with the government in the future. Therefore, the degree of "ecclesiastical contestation" should continue into the future and may even increase.[25]

Claude Pomerleau, while acknowledging the mutuality of interests within a corporatist framework, also points to past and potential sources of church-state discord in a study of the church's challenge to the state. Since the nineteenth century, Mexican history has included many social conflicts ranging from a local to a national scale. "Church-state relations have been closely related to, and affected by, these conflicts." Church-state conflict led to the War of the Reforma (1856) and to the Cristero Rebellion (1926–29).[26] Both of these struggles "were resolved through an improvised and cumulative process that eventually did as much to obscure the causes of conflict as to remedy them." In view of these continuing struggles, the church evolved "into a unique national institution, suspicious of, and eventually isolated from, the political and intellectual mainstream of Mexico. The Mexican state was influenced by these same forces and in reaction hardened its anticlericalism, its authoritarianism, and its paternalism." Despite these reactions, moderate church and state officials (in the late 1930s) began "a process of cautious compromise" leading to restraint on both sides instead of hostility. This compromise resulted "as much in mutual exhaustion as in the emergence of moderate leadership." Pomerleau continues that the "informal compromise produced an equilibrium between the secular and the religious that was based on the complementarity of social ethics and political philosophy." This complementarity was rooted in "the social continuity of the original Spanish institutions which were grafted onto the existing social structures after the Conquest." This led to "a dualistic world of public and private values and concepts which functioned satisfactorily for both church and state" until independence from Spain in 1821. With independence, the concept of monarchy as a basis for the balance between church and state began to erode. As shifts occurred from church to state and then back to church, the conceptualization of the state was variously interpreted from several different political perspectives (i.e., liberal, conservative, positivist, revolutionary). By the mid-twentieth century, "social, economic and political forces (which are noted below) again challenged the precarious equilibrium established earlier. These forces were changing both the church and the state, affecting the delicate balance between the two." Also, at the same time, challenges by "social and religious activists" to the collaboration between church and state were being made. As noted earlier, government repression of the October 1968 student protests drew responses from church activists and political reformers, but they lacked the political organization and wherewithal to sustain their unity. Reforms (i.e., the church's role in the transformation of society—specifically, in dealing with such issues as "justice and violence, peace, family, education, popular religion and innovative ministries" and the establishment of *Comunidades de Base* [CEBs or base communities])[27] prompted by Vatican II, 1962–65, and later by the Second Latin American Episcopal Conference (CELAM II) in 1968,[28] were "slowly and somewhat incompletely introduced into the official documents and pastoral practices of the Mexican church."

Thus, according to commentators such as Pomerleau, the current stabilization of Mexico's political system and the latter's relation to the

church is "more apparent than real," representing a "precarious balance." The maintenance "of the existing social arrangement" relies on
the ability of religious and political leaders to affect "a balance of
conflicting groups and interests and to achieve this within the large
framework of two networks of interests, the public one represented by
the state and the private one represented by nongovernmental interests,
including the church."

Pomerleau utilizes "the theory of minimum institutionalization"
as discussed by Susan Kaufman Purcell and John F. H. Purcell[29] to
explain church-state equilibrium and its fragility. The Purcells assert
that the stability of the Mexican political system relies on the "ability of
the ruling elites to improvise continually and revise the political bargain" that holds Mexico together (i.e., "balancing act"). The church
hierarchy has generally agreed "to play according to the informal rules
of the game." It acknowledges the state's legitimacy despite specific
qualms regarding "the constitutional provisions for the state and its
relationship to society." In exchange, the state permits restricted "institutional autonomy" for those church organizations that are viewed as
"essential for its ministry but are not given juridical personality as a
church organization." There are no formulas for the definition of "the
relationship between the church's institutions and . . . society. Institutional relationships depend as much on precedents and personalities"
regarding specific issues "as on the overall requirements of stability."
(Susan Eckstein's study of Mexican church-state relations on the local
level bears this observation out and will be discussed shortly.)

In sum, Catholicism in contemporary Mexico is a result of conflicts that emerged soon after independence. Church-state accord following 1938 set the stage for "a period of unprecedented growth in religious
institutions until the 1960's when outside forces accelerated a process of
internal transformation of church structures and policies."[30] Pomerleau
characterizes the reaction of church leaders to reformist trends of the
1960s as

> uneven and tenuous but not superficial, involving religious leaders
> in a major reinterpretation of the relationship between religion
> and politics. . . . The reinterpretation and specification of the
> relationship between the individual and the community, the pri-
> vate and the public, the political and the religious will inevitably
> challenge the political ethics on which church and state institu-
> tions are based. The struggle within the Mexican church over the

meaning and application of the new political theology should be measured by the possible effects on the existing equilibrium of church and state, an equilibrium which represents little more than a common law union arranged by two institutional partners whose interests will never completely coincide.[31]

Mexican church-state relations have also been studied from a local and interorganizational perspective. Susan Eckstein[32] discusses relations between church- and state-affiliated groups (i.e., "groups with formal, prescribed ties to Church or state") and groups that are informally or indirectly linked to state institutions. Based on Eckstein's study of "local level church-state relations," an explanation for the decline in "overt church-state conflict after 1940" may not result, as is generally assumed, from each institution respecting one another's autonomy, but in part because "groups affiliated with each are directly and indirectly interlinked and thereby mutually restrained." Such ties are not merely vestiges of Mexico's past. Rather, many have been established in contemporary times. To an extent, the "linkages reflect the failure of the two institutional hierarchies to control their affiliated units" in accordance with the constitution and their own leadership. Eckstein's research indicates that leaders are involved in "extraorganizational" relations besides or instead of within their own organizations "when their positions give them access to little if any effective budgetary or decision-making power . . . and when the organizations with which they are affiliated enjoy a hegemony of influence within their institutional domain." The ties between church- and state-affiliated groups in general ignore "commands of the national institutional hierarchies. They tend to be direct and indirect, formal and informal, legal and illegal." Direct linkages are essentially illegal (such as state or state-affiliated groups subsidizing church and church-sponsored activities and through involvement of priests and government officials in areas that legally are in the other's domain). In violation of the spirit of the Constitution, the state allocates land to the church by not making Catholics buy the land on which they build and it helps finance church-backed social programs (such as parochial schools and literacy programs), even though these schools are illegal and the lay groups sponsoring such programs are not legally sanctioned to do so. Since direct collaboration between church and state is prohibited by law, ties between church and state are generally indirect and may be formal or informal, such as in an overlap of talented personnel (i.e., people with ties and affiliations to both institutions) who wish to extend their power and influence from one sphere to the other. (A number of government officials take leaders of church-linked groups into their formal political and administrative structures.) Also, church and state are "intermeshed through complementary activities sponsored by divisions of the two institutions." For example, supposedly lay *patronatos* (charitable foundations) received parish support for medical services and educational programs where government facilities proved to be lacking. Since the church is constitutionally prohibited from directly engaging in secular matters, priests form "civic groups with lay boards of officers." Therefore, the church offers services to the state while simultaneously extending its own influence. Church and state also cooperate via "inaction." Sometimes, the government allows the church to circumvent laws without directly being involved. Government officials, for example, not only allow, aid, and regulate church-sponsored schools and hospitals, but also permit priests to conduct outdoor religious services in *vecindades* (one- or two-story tenements) and workplaces, thereby violating the Constitution, so long as such events encourage "morality and 'law and order.'" Just as government officials tolerate the church, priests in turn accommodate the government by, for example, not pressuring it to provide more city services to a squatter settlement. "Inaction" by groups also strengthens both the church and the state. Lack of government enforcement of the Constitution allows the church to spread its "secular and religious influence" because Catholic schools are permitted, for example, to supplement official government textbooks with books more in accordance with church views, begin school with prayers, provide classes in ethics and morals, invite priests to occasionally lecture, and encourage student church attendance. Likewise, religious events conducted outside church property, and foreign priests who supplement the shortage of Mexican priests, reinforce and spread the church's influence. In turn, priests who attend government-sponsored events enhance the government's prestige.

Eckstein observes that "Church and state in contemporary Mexico are intertwined and mutually reinforcing, despite the fact that church and state since the 1930s have outwardly established a *modus vivendi* acknowledging each other's 'structural and functional autonomy.'" In spite of "stringent legal, social, economic, political and religious restrictions" on the church, local priests and leaders of lay groups have established ties with local government groups and with the PRI. While lay groups facilitate the church's effort to extend its sociopolitical influence in an officially acceptable form, the church and its leaders are generally subordinate to the state and its representatives. However, if either acts in a manner perceived to seriously challenge the status quo then "such close collusion between church and state is not inevitable." Eckstein concludes that "differentiation of religion and politics is not an inevitable evolutionary process and that such differentiation does not hinge on formal separation of the two institutions. By implication, structural differentiation and formal organizational (or institutional) autonomy in general does not necessarily reflect the degree to which organizations (or institutions) in fact operate autonomously." This article also "can help explain why there is less overt conflict between church and state and greater Catholic religious hegemony in Mexico (when compared, for example, with Brazil), even though historically church-state conflict has been more severe and legal restrictions on Church secular and religious involvements more comprehensive in Mexico."

Case Studies Reflective of Mexican Church-State Relations

The remainder of this chapter provides case studies (and briefer examples) that reflect the nature of church-state relations during the 1970s and, particularly, the mid-to-late 1980s. The discussion of the 1970s focuses on two specific issues: the question of free government textbooks, and the demographic issue (i.e., church opposition to state-sponsored family planning programs initiated under the administration of Luis Echeverría Alvarez beginning in 1972). Catholic education has historically been a sensitive subject in church-state relations,[33] particularly since the establishment of government control over education per Article 3 of the Constitution.[34] While the issue of free textbooks involves a direct conflict between the government and the church, the issue of family planning[35] has been a "latent conflict" that neither institution has "officially confronted."[36]

Some general conclusions may be drawn from these two issues. In Mexico, church-state relations are characterized by the church's distinct disadvantage of lacking a juridical personality. This situation, after the Cristero Rebellion, did not jeopardize the survival of the church in Mexico. Moreover, it can be stated that since 1940, the two entities have coexisted peacefully. One can even speak of "good extraofficial relations and mutual cooperation." However, it is undeniable that legislation "determines, conditions, and restrains church autonomy and its activity" in the country. At any time, the state could use the Constitution to repress the church. As long as this situation exists, the church must carefully avoid a confrontation with the state.

Due to its "structural weakness," the church hierarchy in the 1970s could not "oppose, at least publicly and officially," government policies (as will be discussed later, this situation changed in the 1980s). In addition, the church was compelled to disavow Catholic groups that assumed a view contrary (whether from the Left or the Right) to that of the government. This lack of support lessened the credibility of such groups before public opinion. They also lacked protection from potential government repression, which lessened their potential influence and activity.

Therefore, the Mexican church, for its survival, has had to adapt to government policies. On the other hand, the Mexican church is also linked to another external institution, the Vatican. The Mexican church depends heavily on the Vatican and this dependency can present problems for the church in its relation with the state. Since the Mexican state and the Vatican do not have any fundamental conflicts, this makes for less pressure on the church. In fact, the Mexican church has successfully managed this tension of dual loyalty in such a way that its loyalty to the Vatican does not affect its good relations with the state. This situation allows the church considerable flexibility because it is willing to let the state do what it pleases as long as the issue of loyalty to Rome is not questioned. However, if that loyalty were questioned, then the church would come into conflict with the state because the Vatican is the Mexican church's main loyalty. Therefore, its submission to the state is not absolute and unconditional. Rather, the Mexican church preserves a degree of autonomy "historically managed from a political angle."

It is also in the state's interest to maintain good relations with the Mexican church, since the state recognizes the role that the church plays in social cohesion and as a stabilizing force in view of its considerable influence over the vast majority of Mexicans. However, it is not necessary for the state to modify the Constitution relative to the church, since it has been able to maintain good "extraofficial relations" with the church and, at the same time, exercise control over it.

Pope John Paul II's historic visit to Mexico in 1979 for the Third Latin American Episcopal Conference (CELAM III) held in Puebla brought into focus many issues regarding Mexican church-state relations.[37] In fact, such issues were raised, for example, by Michael Elmer[38] even prior to the pope's arrival in Mexico, for the government had problems regarding exactly how to react due to constitutional restrictions. So while other countries in Latin America accorded the pope with "full honours as both head of the Church and a head of state," in Mexico he was viewed as "a distinguished visitor," and the government had "difficulty in avoiding the token application of some small piece of the country's fairly considerable body of anticlerical legislation." For example, this action could have been manifested in the imposition of a nominal fifty-peso fee for the holding of mass in public, or, more seriously, confiscation of the property where mass was held. In practice, however, Elmer thought it unlikely that such a strict application of law would be enforced; but the government clearly felt constrained to project a very secular aura and to abide by the spirit of the Constitution. Thus, Elmer noted, although President José López Portillo would have a private meeting with the pope, he would not meet him at the airport or go to religious services. The president also stated that there would be no attempt to renew diplomatic relations with the Vatican. In sum, quoting then Minister of the Interior Jesus Reyes Heroles, "Present legislation will be followed in spirit but without excesses from either side. That is, there will be no acts contrary to our church/state separation, but also there will be no excessive severity of the kind that originated in a period of struggle, now happily long past."[39] Thus, up until that time, the state's "biggest concession" to the church was to permit the pope's trip, which marked the first visit of a Vatican leader to Mexico. However, the papal visit also demonstrated that the "fragile church-state truce" could be jeopardized. By donning papal robes in public, by conducting mass, and by not being cognizant of other constitutional restrictions, the pope aggravated a political fallout so great that Heroles (who was in charge of enforcement of the laws) was forced to resign. The pope called for Mexicans to speak up against "attacks on religious liberty and aggression against man." And when several bishops did speak out, Heroles's successor indicated that he was poised "to clamp down" on the bishops and further declared that the pope's visit had "filled the bishops with arrogance and made them forget that the constitution strictly prohibits them from criticizing the government and its policies." So the pope's visit, in a way, placed the Mexican church "at the crossroads in its touchy relations with the state," for the church was "torn between the pope's admonitions and the threat of renewed government suppression." According to Fr. Claude Pomerleau, the church's choice was to either continue "as a quiet defender of the status quo or become a strong voice against political and economic injustices in Mexican society." Either path would be fraught with danger.[40]

The pope's 1979 visit serves as a bridge between the 1970s and 1980s in a discussion of church-state relations in the 1980s via a consideration of several key events that are indicative of that relationship (and some in which the pope was directly involved)—the controversy over elections in the northern state of Chihuahua in July 1986; the electoral reform law passed in reaction to these elections and the church's response; the church's position on AIDS and the Laguna Verde Nuclear Power Plant located in the state of Veracruz; and the beatification on September 25, 1988, of Miguel Agustín Pro, who was executed during the Cristero Rebellion.

In anticipation of government electoral fraud in the Chihuahuan state elections[41] of July 1986, church leaders joined opposition parties (e.g., PAN)[42] and unions to protest. Monsignor Adalberto Almeida y Merino, Roman Catholic archbishop of Chihuahua, publicly denounced as a "sin" what he viewed as the "impending fraud," a charge based largely on the PRI's full control of the state's electoral apparatus. Monsignor Almeida went on to say that "we are with the people against electoral fraud because we consider it to be unjust, because it violates human rights, because it is a mockery of the people and because it takes away the legitimacy of the Government."[43] Several months prior to these elections, a pastoral letter issued in March 1986 by a group of Roman Catholic bishops in the state of Chihuahua asserted their right to question "whether the political activity in Mexico—the exercise of which has become synonymous with corruption in the eyes of many people—would be the same if those lay Catholics who are public servants functioned in accordance with their Christian vocation." Such statements denouncing government corruption and electoral fraud are noteworthy since they came "from a clergy that for decades was silent about Mexican politics and is forbidden by the Mexican Constitution from taking any role in politics."[44] In response to the controversial PRI victory in the Chihuahuan elections, the church broke "all precedent by urging protests against the Government's 'abuse of power.' "[45] Furthermore, Monsignor Almeida announced on July 14, 1986, that he planned to close all churches in the state capital on the following Sunday in a "protest against . . . the 'shameful' electoral fraud on the part of the government." In this call of increased protest, the monsignor in essence "declared the church on strike" in what was viewed "as the most powerful political statement" by the church in over sixty years[46] and as "one of the most significant facts of recent church history" since the refusal to hold mass reminded many Mexicans of the Cristero Rebellion, which was largely initiated by a decision of Mexican bishops to close all churches. And while the Mexican episcopate had denounced electoral fraud in the past, this marked the first time in several decades that direct action was called for in an attempt to reverse the result of the elections. Furthermore, although the church's position was fairly new regarding methods used, church participation in the political arena had been significant for several decades to the degree that the "social context" allowed it.[47]

The archbishop went on to say that the PRI's " 'lies, fraud, blackmail and threats' in elections for governor, mayors and local congressmen were 'incompatible with our Christianity.' "[48] However, in an attempt to avoid a confrontation between church and state in Mexico, Pope John Paul II ordered that churches remain open on the day of the planned shutdown (i.e., Sunday, July 20, 1986). This unexpected papal order was confirmed by the Vatican apostolic delegate to Mexico, Monsignor Jeronimo Prigone—who maintained that the celebration of Roman Catholic mass "can never be an instrument of politically motivated pressure"—and was accepted by Archbishop Almeida. The latter stated that "our denunciation of electoral fraud remains intact, and is supported by the pope as well, because it deals with a very grave violation of human rights of the kind that the pope has continually denounced with great vigor." This "unusual intervention in a local church-state conflict" could be viewed as "a political victory" for the PRI government, which had been the object of "extraordinary direct" church criticism. In addition, a local priest active in left-wing peasant movements had been a favored speaker at anti-PRI protest rallies. Government officials were further angered that the Chihuahuan bishops had joined with business groups in support of protests by the opposition PAN that the election results be voided. As recently as Friday, July 18, the Council of Mexican Bishops in Mexico City had offered its support to the proposed boycott of the Chihuahuan churches. This position represented a shift in the church's traditional policy of averting direct conflict with the state. However, some members of the church hierarchy "were uncomfortable with the unusually public criticism" of the elections by the bishops of Chihuahua, and intervention by the Vatican may have been a reflection of that. (Even though the vast majority of Mexicans are Catholic, Mexico does not have diplomatic relations with the Vatican.) Thus, the church's position in Chihuahua was perceived by the government as being supportive of "the conservative traditionally Catholic PAN." According to "a senior Mexican official" (on July 17) who wished to remain anonymous, such "political activity" on the part of Mexican clergy is "very clearly illegal." "High-level Mexican law enforcement authorities" answered this challenge in Chihuahua by expressing their complaints to the Mexico City Roman Catholic hierarchy, according to this same official, who continued: "In their actions and in their attitudes, the bishops in Chihuahua have overstepped their bounds." In a meeting (held the previous week) with Interior Minister Manuel Bartlett, Bishop Manuel Talamas Camandari of Ciudad Juárez asserted that "Mexican law 'recognizes the rights of priests to express political opinions.'" The Mexican government disputed that claim, citing that the Constitution of 1917, which emerged from the "intensely anticlerical atmosphere" of the Mexican Revolution, clearly prohibits the clergy from participation in what government officials view as partisan politics. Clergy, according to the Constitution, are prohibited from holding office and voting. The state by law is owner of church property, which includes—as pro-PRI supporters were quick to point out—the Chihuahuan churches that were threatened with closure by the bishops. At a conference of Latin American bishops held in early July 1986 in Bogotá, Colombia, "church spokesmen said that the Mexican hierarchy has begun 'taking a more active position' in protesting the 'peculiar' legal restraints on its activities."[49] On a symbolic level, this protest took place in Mexico's largest state, Chihuahua, where seventy-five years ago the Mexican Revolution originated. For the PRI, which has ruled since 1929, "this new stirring" was more than "a national and international embarrassment," for if the "fledgling movement" were to grow, it could potentially challenge the PRI's monopoly over Mexican life and, therefore, Mexico's political structure.[50]

In response to the church's involvement in and public protest of the political process in Chihuahua, the government took measures to quiet such criticism by legislating stiff penalties for clergy who speak out on political issues. Article 343 of the new Electoral Reform Law (effective January 1, 1987) regulating the presidential and congressional elections of July 6, 1988, provided that clergy who "induce the electorate to vote or who act against a candidate or who foment abstention and disorder as a means of pressure" would be liable to a fine of around $4,400, a considerable amount for most Mexicans. The fine was accompanied by a series of restrictions that, according to "religious experts," amounted to "some of the toughest anticlerical laws outside the communist world," originally including a maximum prison sentence of seven years. It remains to be seen if the law will effectively silence "outspoken clergy." Such uncertainty is due, in part, to the fact that neither the state nor the Vatican has been able to furnish "a clear definition of the line between legitimate service to the religious community and inadmissible interference in politics." Charges of fraud have often been made by opposition parties who have been defeated by the PRI since 1929. However, charges of fraud gain added meaning when voiced by "an institution [i.e., the church] whose moral authority is viewed with considerably less skepticism than that of the government."[51] This law is the first to dictate "specific fines for political activism by Mexican clergy—although bans against clerical criticism of the nation's laws, government or officials were written into the 1917 constitution"—and is viewed as an attempt "to silence the growing tendency of churchmen to speak critically during elections."[52]

So while Roman Catholic priest Domingo Arteaga Castaneda of Ciudad Obregón, for example, has had to accept provisions of the 1917 Constitution that prevent him and other members of the Mexican clergy from voting or holding public office, he strongly feels that the government overstepped its limits in promulgating the new electoral code. "Offended" by the legislation, Father Arteaga took then President Miguel de la Madrid, the Mexican legislature, and the minister of the interior to court in June 1988 in an attempt to rescind the provision on the basis that it goes against "constitutional guarantees and various international human rights accords to which Mexico has subscribed." According to Father Arteaga, "This vague law impinges on my liberty to speak and otherwise express myself. . . . The government is trying to suffocate and intimidate me and my fellow clergy." Referring to a history of anticlericalism in Mexico, according to Larry Rohter, Father Arteaga further commented that "There are still a lot of Jacobins out there, and you can see it in our Constitution, which is an anti-clerical and persecutory document. . . . The church does not want to engage in partisan politics, but our right to practice the politics of the common good has been taken away."[53] In addition, Fr. Francisco Ramírez Meza, spokesman for the Mexican bishops' conference, stated that the law will not prevent the bishops from expressing opinions on political issues: "The Mexican Church will not turn back from its determination to point out injustices when it is a moral duty of conscience to do so."[54] Also, the president of the bishops' conference, Bishop Sergio Obeso Rivera of Jalapa, issued "a critical statement" that the law encouraged "personal discrimination, 'impeded liberty of opinion and of expression, discouraged hope in any opening up of democracy, and opened the way to the violation of basic human rights, rights which Mexico supported at an international level.'" The bishop's comments were not aired on the media "for fear of reprisals," but he did place advertisements in the press to note the bishops' position on the law. Fr. Domingo Ortega of the diocese of Ciudad Obregón also filed suit against the government on the grounds that the law violated his civil rights. Until the new law passed, the church had hoped that prior constitutional restrictions (ban on political participation and criticism of the government, for example) "would gradually fall into non-observance." The new law, however, seems to reinforce the provisions regarding religion contained in the Constitution.[55]

Two contemporary issues of international concern also reflect Mexican church-state relations—AIDS and nuclear power. Regarding AIDS, Auxiliary Bishop Genaro Alamilla of Mexico City, president of the Mexican bishops' Commission on Social Communication, was very critical of the Mexican government's promotion of contraceptive use to halt the spread of AIDS, as reported in the London-based international Catholic weekly, *The Tablet*.[56] At a press conference, he stated that this policy would only serve to promote "homosexuality, prostitution, premarital and extramarital sex." He asserted that the "surest way to combat AIDS . . . is by respecting the laws of nature and the commandments of God." However, the bishop did approve of the government's position in shutting down commercial blood banks following a high level of infection found in "some poor professional blood donors" (i.e., those who sold blood for a livelihood).[57]

On another issue of international importance, the church hierarchy seemed divided over the controversy surrounding the country's first nuclear power plant.[58] Archbishop of Mexico City Corripio Ahumada toured the Laguna Verde nuclear plant (located on the Gulf of Mexico coast in the state of Veracruz) and blessed a church under construction in the nearby town of El Farallon, where the plant's managers and technicians live. The cardinal stated that the plant featured "'the most scrupulous safety measures' which would 'avoid any problem of contamination'" and that it posed no threat to humans. The cardinal's position contrasts with two pastoral letters issued by seven local bishops,[59] who pointed out the great risk of deadly accidents and of "genetic consequences" to all forms of life. They went on to state that they empathized with and backed those who were attempting, via demonstrations, to increase the public's awareness of the risks involved. The bishops noted that "accidents have been unavoidable in countries with highly developed technology and regard for safety standards . . . and they are excluding the use of atomic energy because of high risk."[60] They suggested that the Mexican government do likewise by halting construction and converting the plant to harness other forms of energy such as natural gas. The facility (with two reactors of the same kind found in the Three Mile Island, Pennsylvania, plant) was scheduled to go into operation in October 1987 subject to final inspection by the International Atomic Energy Commission. Although construction began in 1969, there were many delays and the final expense was approximately $3.5 billion. Environmental groups maintain that "the plant is unsafe because it is in an earthquake fault zone and construction is unsatisfactory." The bishops share these concerns. Bishop José Guadalupe Padilla Lozano of Veracruz (in whose diocese the plant is located) was with Cardinal Corripio on his visit to the plant, but the former was among those who signed a pastoral letter opposing the facility. He later stated that he and other bishops maintained their position regarding the potential threats posed by the nuclear plant.[61]

An event of great significance and symbolism for Mexican church-state relations took place on Sunday, September 25, 1988. Like the threatened closing of the Chihuahuan churches in July 1986, it evoked memories of the Cristero Rebellion. Pope John Paul II beatified the Mexican priest Miguel Agustín Pro, making him Mexico's "first modern candidate for sainthood." Whereas in other nations this event would be widely celebrated, in Mexico it was downplayed (i.e., "treated gingerly") by both the church and the government. Rev. Felipe Hernández Franco, spokesman for the Mexican Episcopal Conference (the organization that represents Mexico's ninety-seven Roman Catholic bishops), described the event as "a bit of a taboo topic . . . [and] a very delicate matter, and the church itself does not intend to organize any large demonstrations" in Mexico. There was a simple reason for downplaying the ceremony: although dead for sixty years, Father Pro not only represented "religious faith" but was also a political symbol of current significance (i.e., a symbol of past church-state conflict). For both church and state, he symbolized "a disquieting reminder of one of the most violent periods in their long and traditionally uneasy relationship."

On November 23, 1927, Father Pro, a thirty-six-year-old Jesuit priest from the central Mexican state of Zacatecas, was executed by a Mexican army firing squad during the Cristero Rebellion on the grounds that he was indirectly implicated in an assassination attempt on former president Alvaro Obregón. The execution order was given by General Plutarco Elias Calles (who was the president of Mexico at that time),

who in 1929 had laid the groundwork for the founding of the current
PRI. While the incident is generally treated superficially in Mexican
history books, the desire to use the pope's beatification of Father Pro by
"conservative lay Catholics" reflects their goal "to score some political
points." Being against Mexico's "strict separation of church and state
and to official abortion, birth control and AIDS education programs,"
they seek support for their cause by emphasizing the "historical paral-
lels" between 1927 and contemporary Mexico. According to Jorge
Serrano Limón, president of the National Pro-Life Committee, a group
that sponsored commemorative masses and sold Father Pro T-shirts,
"It's the same bunch in power in our time, and we are still fighting for a
Mexico that is sound, Catholic and free. . . . We still have a lay
Government that has distanced itself from the Mexican people, who are
Catholic, and that does not respect freedom of religion and education."

Father Hernández, however, assumes a conciliatory position.
While he hopes for the eventual canonization of Father Pro, he also
hastens to add that should the government's reaction be "negative and
there is conflict, we may leave the matter aside for a few years."
According to church leaders, Father Pro was originally supposed to be
beatified in 1987. However, the Mexican government requested that
the event be postponed until after the 1988 presidential election because
it was concerned that the beatification "would give the right a banner it
could wave during the election campaign," according to an unnamed
cleric.[62] It is generally believed in Mexico that the pope's announcement
(of the beatification), as on previous occasions, was "carefully chosen" on
the heels of the PRI's "unprecedented setbacks" in the July elections,
during which many clergymen, "though formally banned from political
involvement, discretely supported" the policies of opposition leader
Cuauhtemoc Cardenas, who was largely responsible for the electoral
upset. "Whether the reassertiveness presages a new role for the Mexican
church . . . remains to be seen. But the Pope's beatification of Father Pro
could serve as the kind of spark that will bring the Church into the
political arena."[63]

A letter reflecting the extremely sensitive nature of the matter was
sent by an official from the Ministry of the Interior to Mexico's major
television network following a "popular historical soap opera's" brief
treatment of the execution. The letter complained of the negative
portrayal of General Calles and the favorable portrayal of Father Pro. The
official further argued that the television program "could be an instrument used to support current pretensions to canonize him and with that
to denigrate before the people the governments that have emerged from

the revolution." Although the state honors Calles as "a patriot and a reformer," he is viewed by conservative Catholics as a "villain" due to his anticlericalism. September 25th happens to be Calles's birthday, but the hierarchy notes that the decision to beatify Father Pro on that date was not purposeful. According to Father Hernández, "It's just a coincidence, one of God's little jokes."[64]

Conclusion: Improved Relations

Church and state in Mexico "have moved together in recent years toward a dialogue aimed at building bridges and diminishing tensions" and have "sought harmony," although the church hierarchy has criticized, for example, what they perceive as electoral fraud and "institutionalized corruption" by PRI.[65] Leaders in the church, however, note that the "climate" in Mexico has "actually improved" since Pope John Paul's visit in 1979. Relations between political leaders and the church hierarchy are frequently "cordial," and the church is occasionally called upon to assist in state programs such as polio vaccination campaigns. In March 1988, Carlos Salinas de Gortari (at that time presidential candidate of the PRI and the eventual winner of the presidential elections of July 1988) had a meeting with four bishops in Chihuahua. The meeting was of considerable interest and commentary since these bishops were in dispute with the state for having supported public protests against general electoral fraud in 1986 and for sponsoring a series of "democracy workshops." And in "another small sign of detente between church and state," the government had slightly altered the electoral code so offensive to the church. Although clergy are still liable to fines for speaking in politics, the provision for a prison sentence has been deleted.[66] Also, the fact that the church has not pressed for the immediate canonization of Father Pro and is willing to wait a few years may be viewed as another recent example of church-state accommodation.[67] George Getschow thus summarizes the situation: "In recent years, the Church and state have slowly and secretly come to terms. But it is an uneasy truce, based on behind-the-scenes cooperation and compromise between two powerful institutions."[68]

Notes

1. Soledad Loaeza, "La iglesia y la democracia en México," *Revista mexicana de sociología* 47, no. 1 (January–March 1985): 161–68.

2. Emmanuel Ruiz Subiaur, *La vorágine religiosa (El poder contra la fe)* (México, D.F.: Costa-Amic Editores, 1982); and Manuel Buendia, *La Santa Madre,* 1st ed. (México, D.F.: Ediciones Oceano, Fundación Manuel Buendia, 1985).

3. Guillermo F. Margadant S., *La iglesia mexicana y el derecho: Introducción histórica al derecho canónico, los concordatos, el patronato real de la iglesia y el derecho estatal referente a lo eclesiástico* (México: Editorial Porrua, 1984).

4. James W. Wilkie, "Statistical Indicators of the Impact of National Revolution on the Catholic Church in Mexico, 1910–1967," *Journal of Church and State* 12, no. 1 (Winter 1970): 89–106; *Informes de Pro Mundi Vita* (Brussels, Belgium: Pro Mundi Vita) 15(1979): 32–36; and Manuel González Ramirez, *La iglesia mexicana en cifras* (México, D.F.: C.I.A.S., 1972).

5. Otto Granados Roldán, *La iglesia católica mexicana como grupo de presión,* 1st ed., Cuadernos de humanidades, no. 17 (México, D.F.: Universidad Nacional Autonoma de México, 1981).

6. Jean Meyer, "La organizaciones religiosas como fuerzas políticas de substitución: El caso mexicano," *Christus* 41 (December 1976): 30–34.

7. Claude Pomerleau, "Religion and Values in the Formation of Modern Mexico: Some Economic and Political Considerations," in *Global Economics and Religion,* ed. James Finn (New Brunswick, N.J.: Transaction Books, 1983), 143–60.

8. Frederick C. Turner, "The Compatibility of Church and State in Mexico," *Journal of Interamerican Studies and World Affairs* 9, no. 4 (October 1967): 591–602.

9. Jorge H. Portillo, *El problema de las relaciones entre la iglesia y el estado en México,* 2d ed. (México, D.F.: Costa-Amic Editores, 1982).

10. J. Lopez Moctezuma, "Una visión de la historia de la iglesia en México a traves de las relaciones iglesia-estado," *Christus* 38 (September 1973): 24–30.

11. Karl M. Schmitt, "Church and State in Mexico: A Corporatist Relationship," *The Americas* 40, no. 3 (January 1984): 349–76. Unless otherwise noted, all references to Schmitt in the ensuing discussion pertain to this article.

12. For an in-depth study of the Reforma period, see James H. Lee, "Bishop Clemente Munguia and Clerical Resistance to Mexican Reform, 1855–1857," *Catholic Historical Review* 66, no. 3 (1980): 374–91.

13. For more information on church-state relations in the revolutionary period, see Richard Roman, "Church-State Relations and the Mexican Constitutional Congress, 1916–1917," *Journal of Church and State* 20, no. 1 (Winter 1978): 73–80; Robert E. Quirk, *The Mexican Revolution and the Catholic Church, 1910–1929* (Bloomington: Indiana University Press, 1973); and, R. D. Chacon, "Salvador Alvarado and the Roman Catholic Church: Church-State Relations in Revolutionary Yucatán," *Journal of Church and State* 27, no. 2 (Spring 1985): 245–66.

14. Schmitt, "Church and State in Mexico," 350.

15. This brief anticlerical interlude is studied by Anne Staples, "Secularización: Estado y iglesia en tiempos de Gomez Farías," *Estudios de historia moderna y contemporánea de México* 10 (1986): 109–23.

16. For information dealing with the "first stage," see Michael P. Costeloe, *Church and State in Independent Mexico: A Study of the Patronage Debate, 1821–1857* (London: Royal Historical Society, 1978); and Roberto Gomez Ciriza, *México ante la diplomacia vaticana: El período triangular, 1821–1836,* 1st ed. (México, D.F.: Fondo de Cultura Economica, 1977).

17. For details on the provisions of the Constitution that apply to religion, see Granados Roldan, *La iglesia católica mexicana como grupo de presión,* 36–37; Martin de la Rosa, "Iglesia y sociedad en el México de hoy," in *Religión y política en México,* ed. Martin de la Rosa and Charles A. Reilly, 1st ed. (México, D.F.: Siglo Veintiuno Editores, 1985), 268–69; and Luis J. de la Pena, *La legislación mexicana en relación con la iglesia,* Colección canónica de la Universidad de Navarra, Cuadernos (Madrid: Rialp, 1965).

18. Studies of the "third stage" include Harriet Denise Joseph, "Church and State in Mexico from Calles to Cardenas, 1924–1938" (Thesis, North Texas State University, 1976); William R. Ferrell III, "Church and State Relations in Mexico from 1910 to 1940," in *Proceedings of South Carolina Historical Association,* 1981, 79–97; and Alicia Olivera de Bonfil, "La iglesia en México, 1926–1970," in *Contemporary Mexico,* ed. James W. Wilkie, Michael C. Meyer, and Edna Monzón de Wilkie, UCLA Latin American studies, vol. 29 (Berkeley: University of California, 1976).

19. One of the most outspoken of the Mexican clerics is Bishop Sergio Méndez Arceo of the diocese of Cuernavaca. See Gregory Bergman, "Mexico's Socialist Bishop (S. Méndez Arceo; editorial)," *Christian Century* 101 (September 26, 1984): 860–62; and Gabriela Videla, *Sergio Méndez Arceo: Un señor obispo,* 1st ed., Colección religión y política (México, D.F.: Ediciones Nuevomar, 1984).

20. Schmitt, "Church and State in Mexico," 349–76 passim.

21. Dennis M. Hanratty, "The Political Role of the Mexican Catholic Church: Contemporary Issues," *Thought* 59 (June 1984): 164–82.

22. Claude Pomerleau, "The Changing Church in Mexico and Its Challenge to the State," *Review of Politics* 43, no. 4 (October 1981): 540–59. Unless otherwise noted, all references to Pomerleau in the ensuing discussion pertain to this article.

23. Catholic Church, Pope (1878–1903: Leo XIII), *Encyclical Letter of Our Holy Father by Divine Providence Pope Leo XIII: On the Condition of Labour: Official Translation* (London: Westminster Press, 1891) (Translation from the Latin encyclical *Rerum Novarum*).

24. For the events of the 1930s and the *modus vivendi* between church and state in the late 1930s and early 1940s, see A. M. Kirshner, "Setback to Tomas

Garrido Canabal's Desire to Eliminate the Church in Mexico," *Journal of Church and State* 13, no. 3 (Autumn 1971): 479–92; John B. Williman, "Adalberto Tejeda and the Third Phase of the Anticlerical Conflict in the Twentieth Century Mexico," *Journal of Church and State* 15, no. 3 (Autumn 1973): 436–54; and A. L. Michaels, "Modification of the Anti-Clerical Nationalism of the Mexican Revolution by General Lazaro Cardenas and its Relationship to Church-State Detente in Mexico," *The Americas* 26 (July 1969): 35–53.

25. Hanratty, "The Political Role of the Mexican Catholic Church," 164–82 passim.

26. For information on the Cristero Rebellion, see Jean A. Meyer, *La Cristiada*, 3d ed., trans. Aurelio Garzon del Camino, (México, D.F.: Siglo Veintiuno Editores, 1974); Alicia Olivera Sedano, *Aspectos del conflicto religioso de 1926 a 1929: Sus antecedentes y consecuencias* (México, D.F.: Instituto Nacional de Antropología e Historia, 1966); and David C. Bailey, *Viva Cristo Rey! The Cristero Rebellion and the Church-State Conflict in Mexico* (Austin: University of Texas at Austin, 1974).

27. For information on the CEBs, see Miguel Concha Malo et al., *La participación de los cristianos en el proceso popular de liberación en México, 1968–1983*, Biblioteca México: Actualidad y perspectivas, 1st ed. (México, D.F.: Siglo Veintiuno Editores, 1986), 233–92; and Miguel Concha Malo, "Tensiones entre la religión del pueblo y las CEB's en México con sectores de la jerarquía: Implicaciones eclesiológicas," *Ciencia Tomista* 114 (May–August 1987): 287–310.

28. Vatican II, CELAM II and III, and the Mexican Catholic church are discussed in Martin de la Rosa M., "La iglesia católica en México: Del Vaticano II a la CELAM III, 1965–1979," *Cuadernos políticos* 19 (January–March 1979): 88–104; and Enrique D. Dussel, *De Medellín a Puebla,* 1st ed. (México, D.F.: Centro de Estudios Ecuménicos, 1979).

29. Susan Kaufman Purcell and John F. H. Purcell, "State and Society in Mexico: Must a Stable Polity be Institutionalized?" *World Politics* 32, no. 2 (January 1980): 194–227.

30. For information on the institutional structure of the Mexican church, see Manuel González Ramírez, *Aspectos estructurales de la iglesia católica mexicana,* 1st ed. (México, D.F.: C.I.A.S., 1972); and Martin de la Rosa M. and Charles A. Reilly, *Religión y política en México,* part 4, "Analisis institucional," 213–310.

31. Pomerleau, "The Changing Church in Mexico and Its Challenge to the State," 540–59 passim.

32. Susan Eckstein, "Políticos and Priests: The Iron Law of Oligarchy and Interorganizational Relations," *Comparative Politics* 9 (July 1977): 463–81. This article originally appeared in Spanish: "La ley férrea de la oligarquía y las relaciones inter-organizacionales: Los nexos entre la iglesia y el estado en México," *Revista mexicana de sociología* 37, no. 2 (April–June 1975): 327–48.

Unless otherwise noted, all references to Eckstein in the ensuing discussion pertain to this article.

33. For details on the issue of textbooks and church-state relations vis-à-vis education in general, see Guillermo Villaseñor, *Estado e iglesia: El caso de la educación* (México: Edicol, 1978); S. E. Hilton, "Church-State Dispute over Education in Mexico from Carranza to Cardenas," *The Americas* 21 (October 1964): 163–83; Maria Ann Kelly, "Mexican Catholics and Socialist Education of the 1930's," in *Religion in Latin American Life and Literature,* ed. Lyle C. Brown and W. F. Cooper (Waco, Tex.: Markham Press Fund, 1980), 135–48; Judith Friedlander, "The Secularization of the Cargo System: An Example from Postrevolutionary Central Mexico," *Latin American Research Review* 16, no. 2 (1981): 132–43; and María Salinas Suárez del Real, "Aspectos jurídicos de la educación en México," *Logos* 2, no. 5 (May–August 1974): 277–84.

34. Patricia Arias, Alfonso Castillo, and Cecilia López, *Radiografía de la iglesia en México, 1970–1978,* Cuadernos de investigación social, no. 5 (México, D.F.: Instituto de Investigaciones Sociales, Universidad Nacional Autónoma de México, 1981), 63.

35. For details concerning this issue, see Anne Fremantle, "Mexican Confrontation," *The Tablet* 227 (October 13, 1973): 964–56; Frederick C. Turner, *Responsible Parenthood: The Politics of Mexico's New Population Policies,* Foreign Affairs Studies (Washington, D.C.: American Enterprise Institute for Public Policy Research, 1974); and Jorge I. Dominguez, "Planificación familiar: Estado e iglesia," *Christus* 45 (March 1980), 39–45.

36. Arias et al., *Radiografía de la iglesia en México, 1970–1978,* 68, 73, 74. Unless otherwise noted, all references to Arias in the ensuing discussion pertain to these pages.

37. For more information on the pope's 1979 trip to Mexico and the Puebla conference, see Francisco J. Perea, *El Papa en México: Presencia y mensaje de Juan Pablo II* (México, D.F.: Diana, 1979); Soledad Loaeza, "La iglesia católica mexicana y el reformismo autoritario," *Foro internacional* 25, no. 2 (October–December 1984): 138–65; and Manuel Magana Contreras, *Puebla 79: Religión y política* (México, D.F.: Alfa Ediciones, 1979).

38. Michael Elmer, "The Mexican Church," *The Tablet* 233 (January 27, 1979), 76.

39. Ibid.

40. George Getschow, "Mexico's Old Rivalry of Church and State Lingers Despite Truce," *Wall Street Journal,* July 21, 1981, 1, 21.

41. For a detailed study of the Chihuahuan elections, see Victor Quintana, "Mexique: Transformation economique et crise politique au Chihuahua," *Problemes d'Amerique Latine,* no. 86, 4e trimestre: 43–80.

42. For more information on PAN, see Donald J. Mabry, *Mexico's Acción Nacional: A Catholic Alternative to Revolution,* 1st ed. (Syracuse, N.Y.: Syracuse University Press, 1973).

43. John Carlin, "Mexico Rulers Face Fair-Vote Challenge: Fears of Ballot-Rigging," *Times* (London), July 5, 1986.

44. William Stockman, "Mexico Vote: New Voices Join Protest," *New York Times,* July 20, 1986, sec. 1, p. 11.

45. John Carlin, "Mexican Parties in Poll Protest," *Times* (London), July 15, 1986, 12.

46. John Carlin, "Strike Call by Church over Mexican Poll," *Times* (London), July 14, 1986, 5.

47. Roberto Blancarte Pimentel, "La question politique et sociale de l'eglise au Mexique depuis 1929," *Problemes d'Amerique Latine,* no. 86, 4e trimestre: 81–95.

48. Carlin, "Strike Call by Church over Mexican Poll," 5.

49. William A. Orme, Jr., "Papal Order Ends Protest by Chihuahua Bishops," *Washington Post,* July 21, 1986, 1, 10.

50. Stockman, "Mexico Vote," sec. 1, p. 11.

51. "Mexico Moves to Silence Church Critics," *Christian Science Monitor,* January 2, 1987, 15; and Rosalie Beck and David Longfellow, "Notes on Church-State Affairs: Mexico," *Journal of Church and State* 29, no. 2 (Spring 1987): 365.

52. "Mexican Law Seeks to Curb Voting Advice from Pulpit," *National Catholic Register,* January 25, 1987, p. 3.

53. Larry Rohter, "Mexican Priest Seeks to Take Sides: The Silencing of the Church on Politics Is at Issue," *New York Times,* June 16, 1988, 3. On this matter, see also Rosalie Beck and James A. Curry, "Notes on Church-State Affairs: Mexico," *Journal of Church and State* 30, no. 3 (Autumn 1988): 622. For an argument against the statutes regarding religion in the Mexican constitution, see Salvador Abascal, *La Constitución de 1917, destructora de la nación: Estudio histórico-crítico* (México, D.F.: Editorial Tradición, 1982).

54. "Mexican Law Seeks to Curb Voting Advice from Pulpit," 3.

55. "Test Case in Mexico," *The Tablet,* May 30, 1987, 589–90.

56. "Mexican Bishop on AIDS," *The Tablet,* July 4, 1987, 729.

57. Ibid.

58. "Bishops at Odds over Nuclear Plant," *The Tablet,* September 5, 1987, 956.

59. The names of the bishops are Archbishop Sergio Obeso Rivera of Jalapa, president of the Mexican bishops' conference, retired bishop Ignacio Lehonor Arroyo of Tuxpan, Bishop Mario de Gasperín of Tuxpan, Bishop Carlos Talavera Ramírez of Coatzacoalcos, Bishop Lorenzo Cárdenas Aregullín of Papantla, Bishop José Guadalupe Padilla Lozano of Veracruz, and Bishop Guillermo Ranzahuer González of San Andrés Tuxtla.

60. "Bishops Against Nuclear Power," *The Tablet,* January 10, 1987, 45.

61. For more information on and the argument against the plant, see Armando Morones and Javier Esquivel, *Laguna Verde: La contribución de México al*

holocausto pacífico? 1st ed. (Mexico, D.F.: Ediciones El Caballito, 1987); José Arias and Luis Barquera, comps., *¿Laguna Verde nuclear? ¡No, gracias!* 1st ed. (México, D.F.: Claves Latinoamericanas, 1988); Hugo García Michel, *Más allá de Laguna Verde* (México, D.F.: Editorial Posada, 1988); "A-Plant Start-up Ordered," *Facts on File* 48, no. 2500 (October 21, 1988): 782; and Errol D. Jones, "The Mexican Electrical Industry: Conflicts and Issues," *Journal of the West* 27, no. 4 (October 1988): 75–84. According to the *Wall Street Journal* (William Mathewson, comp., "World Wire: Environmentalists' Victory," *Wall Street Journal,* November 2, 1990, A10), although the state finally licensed the plant's operation in August 1990 following numerous delays, Mexican environmentalists succeeded in blocking its start-up through a federal court decision. For the background and events leading up to this staying motion, see Octavio Miramontes, "Wooing Mexico to Nuclear Power," *Bulletin of the Atomic Scientists* 45, no. 6 (July–August 1989): 36–38; and Alva Senzek, "Mexico Considers More Nuclear Plants," *Journal of Commerce,* July 13, 1990, A10.

62. Larry Rohter, "State Power vs. God's Glory: Of Saints and the Not So Saintly," *New York Times,* September 24, 1988, 4. Unless otherwise noted, all references to Rohter in the ensuing discussion pertain to this article.

63. Carlin, "Strike Call by Church over Mexican Poll," 12.

64. Rohter, "State Power vs. God's Glory," 4.

65. Ibid.

66. Rohter, "Mexican Priest Seeks to Take Sides," 3.

67. Rohter, "State Power vs. God's Glory," 4.

68. George Getschow, "Mexico's Old Rivalry of Church and State Lingers Despite Truce," 1.

PART IV

Europe

6.

Miter Against Missiles: The Papal Challenge to Soviet Regimes in Eastern Europe

DONALD E. BAIN

The collapse of Communist governments across Eastern Europe by 1990 was the culmination of a long, tortured struggle between the ideology of Soviet Marxism and the desire for liberation among its captive nationalities.

These developments punctuated a five-year peace offensive launched by Mikhail Gorbachev aimed at redirecting Soviet military expenditures into domestic spending supportive of perestroika. Gorbachev's decisions unleashed powerful forces of ethnic and religious nationalism that, with gathering strength, challenged the authority of Moscow from the Baltic to the Balkans. In addition, glasnost prompted debate over the role of NATO and Warsaw Pact forces in the security of Europe.

Amidst this change, Pope John Paul II stands as a unique symbol of the history of Western determination to withstand Communist suppression. With his potential for fanning the flames of Pan-Slavic nationalism, he was once considered by the Kremlin as a threat to its East European empire. In May of 1981 this almost cost the pope his life. However, his influence on groups such as the Polish labor union Solidarity has earned him respect as a moderator rather than instigator. As prelate of global Catholicism, he is instinctively aligned with the West. Yet as a Pole, he possesses a unique sensitivity to the ideological and policy consequences of living in a Communist state.

As the first significant test site of a serious challenge to Communist authority, the papal-inspired religious nationalism of Eastern Europe offers a unique and useful case study. This chapter examines the nature of Catholic/Communist relationships as they have developed in the *Ostpolitik* (Eastern Policy) of the Vatican and suggests what implications this struggle has had on East-West relations.

Background

In an explosion of anti-Marxist sentiment, Pope Pius XII issued a decree on July 1, 1949, that excommunicated any member, supporter, or follower of a Communist party. His hope was to steady the hierarchies of Eastern Europe and to draw a strong canonical line across which compromising priests and sympathetic laypersons would not dare to tread. [1] Of course he failed to accomplish either objective and, except for those few souls seeking immediate martyrdom, quite the opposite effect took place as church leaders in the East scrambled to salvage what precious little goodwill remained between themselves and the Communist regimes under which they labored. Yet, the behavior of Pius XII was not atypical in the difficult chronicle of East European Catholic and Communist relations. [2]

Catholicism did not worry Bolsheviks in 1917. In fact, the Vatican contributed to the Russian famine relief of 1921–22. By 1923, however, Moscow increasingly perceived the Holy See as an agent of international imperialism, an ideological rival for the loyalties of Russian ethnic minorities, and as a universal religion an opponent in the Leninist plan for a worldwide revolution. At the conclusion of World War II, with much of Eastern Europe under Soviet domination, the strong Catholic tradition in many areas of the region was further cause for the Kremlin to suspect Vatican complicity in the bellicose anti-Russian crusade embraced by the Western democracies. The great fear of popular uprisings along the European border of its empire was sufficient impulse for Moscow to encourage the violent suppression of church activities in Eastern bloc countries.

Destruction of the Russian Uniate church and Russification of the Russian Orthodox hierarchy continued during the early 1950s, as did the attack on Roman Catholicism. Flushed with the enthusiasm of the cold war atmosphere, the church itself joined strenuously the chorus of damnation against the Soviets and their satellite states.

By 1958, however, Khrushchev's efforts of de-Stalinization, coupled with the ascent of Pope John XXIII, introduced a new era of papal-Communist relations. Thinking of John as a "peasant like myself,"

Khrushchev believed he could influence several world leaders—Adenauer and Kennedy for openers—in addition to assisting in the control of East European populations if a *modus vivendi* could be found with Rome. That he sought an opening with Rome was evidenced by his having allowed representatives of the Russian Orthodox church to attend the Vatican Council proceedings in 1962. This gesture found its counterpart in John's 1963 encyclical *Pacem in Terris,* which hinted strongly at the welcome a rapprochement would receive.[3]

John's death in 1963 witnessed the ascent of Pope Paul VI and the emergence of Msgr. Agostino Casaroli as the chief architect of the new Eastern policy. Several factors motivated Casaroli to pursue accommodation while at the same time maintaining resistance to Communist authority. First, he believed then that however unpalatable, Soviet-supported regimes in the East were secure for the immediate future. Continued conflict, he reasoned, would only damage the church's position. Also, as an intellectual, he thought that the fundamental hostility of Christianity and Marxism could at the very least be made manageable in diplomatic relations by establishing a dialogue on the subject. The Vatican knew the attraction of Marxism in many Third World nations and judged that some effort to understand its relation to social issues would further the church's standing among the world's disadvantaged. The new Eastern policy allowed the Vatican to distance itself from the strong identification with the United States and its NATO allies. The hope was to forge a more independent image as an autonomous international force, while at the same time cultivating a foreign policy responsive to the First, Second, and Third Worlds. Eastern Europe was the test site for the initiative and ironically, an East European the inheritor of the legacy.[4]

The View from Rome

The Vatican has always been keenly aware of its role in East-West relations. The Holy See, especially in the person of Pope John Paul II, recognized after his election in 1978 that a new relationship—a Slavic connection really—would henceforth exist between Rome and Eastern Europe. This point was driven home with stunning force during the events of 1980 and 1981 in Poland.

The consequences of these developments have been dramatic. Investigations into Bulgarian and Turkish involvement in the assassination attempt on John Paul in May 1981 suggest a case in point. In

October 1984, Italian state prosecutor Antonio Albano wrote a report to the presiding judge in the case, Ilario Martella, recommending that a new case be brought to trial. Albano based his argument on the belief that Bulgarian complicity in the event would not have occurred without Soviet approval. The Bulgarian motive was borne out of the entire Eastern bloc's concern with the rise of Poland's Solidarity trade union movement. Albano contended that Eastern European Communist leaders perceived the Polish crisis as a "mortal danger" caused principally by the "fervent religious character" of the people and aggravated to an extreme by the election and mere fact of a Slavic pope. Killing the pope would have had the effect of deflecting attention and deflating the enthusiasm for dissidence. However valid the theory, the idea from the Soviet point of view is not without logic. And if, indeed, there is some plausibility to the notion, then the implications are enormous for assessing the importance attached by the Kremlin to papal affairs. That a successful assassination attempt may have had the opposite effect, producing for instance a general Catholic upheaval in the East, was apparently not considered.[5]

Additionally, the Soviet Union had penetrated the church physically and doctrinally. Especially in Eastern Europe, financial support for church activities, including priest's salaries, was provided by the regimes. Poland and the GDR were exceptions, as was Albania. But in the rest of the states involved, even the Vatican's bishopric appointments were made on the basis of candidates submitted to Rome by the regime in question. In Rome and within the hierarchies themselves, the church became a target of repression, violence, espionage, and co-optation.[6]

In the murky, mainly secret give-and-take that existed between the Vatican and Soviet-supported regimes, a *modus vivendi* was established. From the Vatican perspective these policies had one overarching aim: *salus animarum suprema lex* (salvation of the individual soul as the supreme law). To achieve this end, the Vatican maintained as its chief responsibility the assurance of the church's survival, a task that, by its nature, required relations with those powers under which the church was attempting to exist. Rising out of the need for the church to keep its hierarchies intact was leverage possessed by regimes to gain concessions and, at times, cooperation. For their part, the Communists were more than willing to accommodate Vatican initiatives to the extent that these served specific and more generally Communist needs in European affairs.

The goal of the Kremlin in Europe was clear: to weaken the

Atlantic Alliance and reduce the effectiveness of the NATO defense coalition. Cooperation between the Vatican and a Communist regime not only gave legitimacy to the regime itself (Tito, for example, was extremely aware of this, as was General Wojciech Jaruzelski in his January 1987 visit to the Vatican) but also loosened the coherence of a united Western resistance to Soviet ideological influence and geopolitical advances. The emergence of the Peace Priests movement combined with the increasingly popular European antinuclear campaign to play directly into the hands of Soviet policymakers, who sought to establish an antimilitaristic theme to Gorbachev's peace offensive. At least prior to Gorbachev's reforms, the goal was to neutralize (Finlandize) Western Europe to the point of rendering untenable a system of Euro-American collective security. The degree to which the Vatican was aware of these possibilities is cause for considerable debate, but at the center of these discussions is an interesting point regarding how church officials weighed ecclesiastic requirements against political outcomes.

A final note concerns Moscow's belief that the Roman Catholic church could be of assistance in maintaining order in the Soviet Empire of Eastern Europe. Within its own frontiers, the Soviets had to confront resistance from Catholic Nationalists in Lithuania, Latvia, Belorussian SSR, the Ukraine, Poland, Czechoslovakia, Hungary, and Yugoslavia. In seeking an accommodation with Rome, however, Communists were realists, and it is no coincidence that the most threatening social upheavals in the Soviet Empire since 1945 have occurred in Hungary, Czechoslovakia, and Poland. This point was not wasted on Moscow, which of course feared such events, nor on Rome, which saw in them (and to a certain extent exploited as leverage) the potential of Catholic nationalism and papal influence.[7]

View from the Kremlin

From the very beginning of the Vatican's *Ostpolitik,* efforts were made to include the Soviet Union in Rome's rapprochement with the East. From the Russian point of view, there was little to be lost and much to be gained through the relaxation of tensions with the Holy See. The Soviets justified accommodation on the basis of the overall aims of detente and then glasnost, as well as the more immediate results of political expediency. Moscow was also aware of the Vatican's efforts to distance itself from the identification it had with NATO and especially American foreign policy. In addition, Soviet-generated fears associated in Europe with the Reagan administration were enough to convince some members of the Curia that for the church to maintain its perceived neutrality, not to mention its emphasis on nuclear disarmament, it would have to develop a position that did not offend Western allies, discourage Gorbachev's reforms, or provide provocation to the anti-nuclear European Left. In short, Rome would continue to seek a middle course.

The Kremlin, moreover, responded to what it considered encouragement from the church in other areas. Certainly, the nonrecognition of Israel served Soviet diplomatic efforts. In the international community the Russians pointed to their own justification for nonrecognition and compared it to that of the Catholic hierarchy. Papal efforts in the *Ostpolitik* to establish a dialogue with Communists suggested an easing of Catholic hostility to socialism and provided a certain legitimacy to Left-leaning governments, who often received direct Soviet aid, and also to Third World movements that adopted the rhetoric and tactics of the Marxist-Leninist doctrine. Further, papal pronouncements condemning in muscular prose the excesses of Western consumerism and denouncing the inequities of the world's distribution of wealth played pleasingly into Soviet propaganda campaigns. And of course, the homilies of Pope John Paul II bristle with reference to the spiritual wasteland created by Western affluence.[8]

Soviet efforts to capitalize on these trends have been manifested in numerous ways, especially in the Soviets' dealings with Third World states. But a more insidious goal was to isolate even more demonstrably the advanced industrial nations, particularly the United States, as exploiters of natural resources and as dangerous forces threatening world survival. Finding a common ground on this point with the world's single-most respected religious authority, the Russians made obvious efforts at accommodation with Rome and appeasement with Karol Wojtyla. Furthermore, American deployment of missiles to Europe and the response of Catholic bishops there and in the United States facilitated to a considerable degree Soviet efforts to portray the Reagan administration as a warmongering horde bent on thermonuclear Armageddon. Moreover, considering its influence in its Eastern Empire as a bridge to Catholic-dominated Third World countries, and as a partner in denouncing the nuclear militarization of Western Europe, the Kremlin had nothing to lose in its relationship with Rome.[9]

Moscow's greatest anxiety concerning the Vatican was the potential the church has for political destabilization in Eastern Europe and the

Baltic. Poland proved this point. The question must be asked, If it had not been for a Polish pope, would the Warsaw regime have allowed trade unions to reach the levels of organization they had achieved by December 1981? Or, even more pointedly, Would Solidarity itself have found the political coherence and purpose it developed without the spiritual force of Karol Wojtyla as Pope?

Pope John Paul II's abhorrence of violence has proven that his influence has been confined to containing rather than inciting anti-government activities. His absorption in Polish affairs during the crisis of 1980–81 demonstrated that personal intervention was directed toward avoiding bloodshed among his fellow countrymen: a more indifferent pontiff may have allowed events to develop beyond the control of any single actor, but in this case, it seems reasonable to assume that the pope's close attention to Polish events worked to prevent explosive issues from becoming explosive developments. Certainly, the murder of Fr. Jerzy Popieluszko in October 1984 is a case in point. The state-run Italian radio said that the pope received word of the murder with "dismay and great worry" and that he followed news reports late into the night. "We pray God" the pope said, "for peace and order in our country, our Fatherland." Lech Walesa echoed these sentiments when he stated, "We won't let anyone pull us into brawls in which we will lose. We simply cannot let anyone manipulate us into any situation. If somebody assumed it would be a revolution, I won't give him a bloody revolution. I am for peaceful evolution." Walesa's sentiments paralleled exactly those of the pope himself. Whether an undirected fluke (which is unlikely), an effort to route hard-liners from the Interior Ministry (which is possible), or a test of papal patience and response, the Jaruzelski government and Moscow established new boundaries for anticipating Rome's reaction to potentially destabilizing events.

Yet the Kremlin faced a paradox because, ironically, insufficient papal authority held the prospect of disallowing the pope the type of control over events that he had enjoyed in Poland. In other words, the Vatican's ability to restrain social upheaval was diminished proportionately by the degree to which the church was not permitted to culture its relations with Rome and proselytize the faith. If political stability was to be abetted by the church, then the church, especially in the person of the pope, had to be given the freedom to pursue its theological mission. Communists realized this paradox and future dealings with local hierarchies and Pope John Paul II were shaped around this reality. Curiously, both sides wanted it both ways: in the cat-and-mouse game of giving a little and taking a little, both sought to maintain their authority, prevent social instability, and in the process undermine the influence of their adversary. [10]

This relationship was remonstrated in March 1990 amidst the upheaval in Lithuania. In a population of 3.6 million people, 3 million are Roman Catholics. While many expected the Slavic pope to place himself directly in events, he limited his involvement to appeals for sincere dialogue and a just and peaceful solution. A Vatican official summarized the situation when he announced that "Gorbachev knows that this is not a subversive Pope and the Catholic Church is not a subversive church." [11]

Security Implications

Estimates concerning the role of the pope in East-West military doctrine are difficult to discern. Indications, however, are provided by two key issues related to papal influence. The first is the obvious, worldwide credibility that Pope John Paul II enjoys. The gigantic crowds and emotional response to his several international journeys certainly place him among the few most influential people on earth. He is, beyond question, a transnational actor. But popularity does not necessarily translate into authority, and there is considerable debate as to whether his moral and theological dicta are adhered to as enthusiastically as his public appearances are attended. Tom Harpur, a Canadian religious writer, noted during the pope's September 1984 visit to Canada "that Catholics are increasingly ignoring John Paul's authority while continuing to applaud his pop-star image." This star status, however, does not detract from his ability to command the attention and arouse the interest of his audience. When the pope speaks, people listen. [12]

The second issue related to papal influence in strategic matters illustrates the above point. In December 1980, as Soviet and East German armored divisions gathered near the Polish borders, an invasion appeared imminent. Realizing the gravity of the situation, Pope John Paul sent a personal message to Leonid Brezhnev that virtually guaranteed church cooperation in bringing order to the Polish crisis. As examined by Bogdan Szajkowski, the letter was probably delivered by Cardinal Franz Konig of Vienna, who is a papal diplomat well known for his part in secret Vatican relations with the Soviet and East European regimes. [13] Initial press reports incorrectly speculated that the pope threatened to directly intervene by returning to Poland to assist his fellow countrymen. Dismissing this as Hollywood melodrama, Szajkowski asserts that nevertheless, a letter was sent urging Soviet prudence and that this was confirmed in an address delivered by Cardinal Wyszynski to the Senate of the Academy of Theology in Warsaw in March 1981.

The advantage for the Russians, should they choose to exercise restraint, was enormous, for not only did they prefer to avoid military intervention but also the political leverage gained from withdrawal of an invasion order might well indebt the Holy See to similar measures of future conciliation. The October 1984 Popieluszko assassination may well support this point. The role of the pope, therefore, in calculating the political outcome of a volatile situation must be considered in any country, but especially in those states where Roman Catholicism represents a significant percentage of the population.[14]

The military outcome of a NATO/Warsaw Pact confrontation may also have been linked to papal interdiction. The high concentration of Roman Catholic populations in the East European central region suggests qualitative differences that may have affected combat motivation and reliability. Inflexible field command and control systems coupled with restive troops would have made marginal the strike capability of Warsaw Pact forces. Furthermore, securing rear areas from partisan guerrilla attacks would be exceptionally difficult under the political and economic conditions that would precede an actual outbreak of war. One of the best studies of the question suggests that Warsaw Pact armed forces could not be relied upon for suppressing internal upheavals, would offer limited support for strikes on fellow Warsaw Pact states, and would probably not participate in full-scale invasions outside of their respective national boundaries. Russian forces are currently thought to be the only troops reliable in such instances, and even here some doubt exists.[15]

Conclusions

The goal of the Vatican in Eastern Europe since 1945 has been the ministry of souls. This is most effectively accomplished through efforts to worship in peace, administer the sacraments, and instruct its membership. Maintaining a church hierarchy in the East was essential to this purpose, and the appointment of bishops was the single most important aim of the *Ostpolitik* as it sought to strengthen the bond between Rome and local congregations.

The Kremlin has tried to manipulate the Vatican in an effort to secure the boundaries of Eastern Europe and maintain social stability (and political legitimacy) within the Soviet Empire. Aware of the high concentration of Roman Catholics in Eastern Europe, Moscow realized that the area was particularly vulnerable to the influence—after 1978— of a Slavic pope.

Beyond its post-1945 empire, Moscow hoped to undermine the cohesion of the Atlantic Alliance and erode the unity of the NATO defense coalition. In accommodating Rome in the East by allowing calculated degrees of church activity, the Soviets hoped to gain leverage for Vatican acquiescence to their initiatives in the West.

The pope always viewed relations with Moscow as the key in establishing working relations with Communist regimes in Eastern Europe. Conversely, Soviet policymakers realized Rome's potential for destabilization yet understood Pope John Paul II's ability to act as a steadying influence in times of crisis. In challenging each other in Eastern Europe, both Rome and Moscow sought to maintain their credibility and constituencies through a process of measured—albeit grudging—accommodation.

Finally, in pitting themselves against the colossus of Soviet ideological and military authority, East European Catholic Nationalists— and the pastoral leadership that inspired them—contributed to the bankruptcy of atheism, the collapse of communism, and the liberation of captive people everywhere behind the Iron Curtain. Gorbachev himself offered the most fitting epilogue when during his December 1989 visit to the Vatican he acknowledged in a speech that the Soviet Union had been wrong in rejecting religion. Viewing the church as an ally in encouraging the work ethic and stable family life, he stated that the moral values it has provided to the rest of the world, now "can help in the renewal of our country."[16]

Notes

1. For a review of literature dealing with the subject of East European religious nationalism see Donald E. Bain, "Iron Curtain/Steel Cross: The Politics of East European Religious Nationalism," in *East European Quarterly* 24, no. 1 (1990): 113–24. See also Pedro Ramet, *Cross and Commissar: The Politics of Religion in Eastern Europe and the USSR* (Bloomington: Indiana University Press, 1987); Dennis J. Dunn, *Religion and Nationalism in Eastern Europe and the Soviet Union* (Boulder, Colo.: Lynne Rienner, 1987); and Paul Mojzes, *Church and State in Postwar Eastern Europe: A Bibliographic Survey* (London:

Greenwood Press, 1987). For general background material related to this chapter see Paul Johnson, *Pope John Paul II and the Catholic Restoration* (New York: St. Martin's Press, 1981). Few good studies have been directed specifically toward the subject of papal relations with Eastern Europe. Some of the best efforts are represented by Hansjakob Stehle, *Eastern Politics of the Vatican: 1917–1979* (Athens: Ohio University Press, 1981); Bogdan Szajkowski, *Next to God . . . Poland: Politics and Religion in Contemporary Poland* (London: Francis Pinter Publishers, 1983); Dennis Dunn, *Detente and Papal-Communist Relations, 1962–1978* (Boulder, Colo.: Westview Press, 1979); and Trevor Beeson, *Discretion and Valour: Religious Conditions in Russia and Eastern Europe,* rev. ed. (Philadelphia: Fortress Press, 1982). In periodical literature a review of *Journal of Church and State, Religion in Communist Lands,* and the *Journal of International Affairs* reveals occasional selections. See, for example, John Kramer, "The Vatican's Ostpolitik," *Review of Politics* 42 (1980): 283–308; Pedro Ramet, "Catholicism and Politics in Socialist Yugoslavia," *Religion in Communist Lands,* Winter 1982:256–74; Jacques Rupnik, "The Vatican's New Ostpolitik and Church-State Relations in Eastern Europe," *World Today* 35 (July 1979): 286–94. See also George Bull's *Inside the Vatican* (New York: St. Martin's Press, 1982); and Peter Nichols, *The Pope's Divisions* (New York: Holt, Rinehart, and Winston, 1981).

General treatment of the life of Karol Wojtyla may be found in George Blazynski, *John Paul II: A Man from Krakow* (London: Wiedenfield, 1979); Mary Craig, *Man from a Far Country* (London: Hodder and Stoughton, 1979); Mieczyslaw Malinski, *Pope John Paul II: The Life of Karol Wojtyla* (New York: Seabury Press, 1979); and George Williams, *The Mind of John Paul II* (New York: Seabury Press, 1981). For a thorough bibliography of Karol Wojtyla's life up to 1979, see "Gaude Mater Polonia," *Polish Review* 24, no. 2 (1979): 95–106. See also "From Poland to Rome," *L'Osservatore Romano,* October 26, 1978, 2. There were, for instance, three secret bishops in Romania not listed in *Annuario Pontifico* yet known to authorities. They are Joan Ploscaru, Alexandru Todea, and Joan Chertes (cited in Stehle, 422n4). For additional discussion see Gerhard Simon, "The Catholic Church and the Communist State in the Soviet Union and Eastern Europe," in B. R. Bociurkiw and J. W. Strong, eds., *Religion and Atheism in the USSR and Eastern Europe* (Toronto: University of Toronto Press, 1975), 190–301. See also "Dossiers Two and Three" of Erich Weingartner's *Church within Socialism* (Rome: IDOC, 1976), especially 35–48.

2. *Acta apostolicae sedis* (Rome: Citta del Vaticano) 41 (1949): 74. The spirit of the new *Ostpolitik* has been captured in the news media as demonstrated in "Ranking Vatican Official Holds Friendly Talks with Gorbachev," *New York Times,* June 14, 1988, 8; and "Vatican Must Deal Even for Small Gains" *New York Times,* January 18, 1987, 3. For a still excellent study of the subject, see Robert A. Graham, SJ, *Vatican Diplomacy: A Study of Church and State on the International Plane* (Princeton, N.J.: Princeton University Press, 1959).

3. Significant changes were brought about during John XXIII's pontifi-

cate, not the least of which was the initiation of the Vatican Council II. For background see *Acta synodalia sacrosancti concilii oecumenici vaticani II* (Vatican City: Polyglot Press), 1970–78. See also *The Pope Speaks* 27, no. 1 (1982): 335.

4. The historical context is discussed in Dunn, *Detente and Papal-Communist Relations,* 1–18; and Stehle, *Eastern Politics of the Vatican,* 263–314.

5. A fine study is Ronald C. Monticone, *The Catholic Church in Communist Poland, 1945–1985: Forty Years of Church-State Relations* (Boulder, Colo.: East European Monographs, 1986). See also *New York Times,* October 26, 1984, 1.

6. For an interesting examination of the problem see a paper given by Robert Chapman at the Georgetown University Center for Strategic and International Studies Colloquium on Clandestine Collection, October 30–31, 1981, titled "Collection in More Open Regions," and published in Roy Godson's *Intelligence Requirements for the 1980's: Clandestine Collection* (Washington, D.C.: National Strategy Information Center, 1982), 41–62.

7. Peter Hebblethwaite, "The Vatican Power Game," *The Observer* (London), December 22, 1974, 9; and Francis Murphy, "Vatican Politics: Structure and Function," *World Politics,* July 1974:542–59. Also, according to Dennis Dunn in *Detente and Papal-Communist Relations,* 47n12, classified handbooks of the KGB-dominated Russian Council on Religious Affairs designate the Vatican as a dangerous and powerful foe.

8. A full statement may be found in the Papal encyclical *Laborem exercens* (Washington, D.C.: National Catholic News Service) 11, no. 15 (1981): 227–44. See also George H. Williams, *The Mind of John Paul II,* 11, 139, 150, 167, 251.

9. For treatment of the Soviet Union see Albert Boiter, *Religion in the Soviet Union,* Washington Papers 8, no. 78 (Beverly Hills, Calif.: Sage, 1980); and Dennis Dunn, *The Catholic Church and the Soviet Government* (Boulder, Colo.: Westview Press, 1977).

10. See, for example, A. Farrante, "Free behind the Iron Curtain, a New Pope," *McLeans,* October 30, 1978, 30–32; and F. Broadhead and E. S. Herman, "The Press, the KGB, and the Pope," *Nation,* June 2, 1983, 1.

11. *New York Times,* March 26, 1990, 9.

12. E. J. Dionne, Jr., "Reporter's Notebook: Pope as Star," *New York Times,* September 23, 1984, 3.

13. Szajkowski, *Next to God . . . Poland,* 111–12.

14. See Edmund Walendowski, *Combat Motivation and Reliability of the Polish Forces* (New York: St. Martin's Press, 1988), especially 90–106; and Richard Staar, *Communist Regimes in Eastern Europe* (Stanford, Calif.: Hoover Institution Press, 1982), 293.

15. Specific data and general treatment may be found throughout *Soviet Military Power* (Washington, D.C.: Government Printing Office, 1990); and Barry Blechman and Edward Luttwak, eds., *International Security Yearbook* (New York: Georgetown University Center for Strategic and International Studies, St. Martin's Press, 1983–84), particularly for Warsaw Pact and NATO information.

16. *New York Times,* March 26, 1990, 9.

7.

The Church, the Peace Movement, and the Social Democratic Party of Germany

MARK BARTHOLOMEW

The conflict between religious and secular authority was one of the structuring characteristics of modern European society. In northern Europe the centuries-long struggle between church and state was often made even more bitter and complex by the fact that the Catholic church tended to find itself at loggerheads with the state, whereas the Protestant churches tended to be more supportive of state power. This was the case for many reasons, but the fact that Protestant churches could envision themselves as national churches, whereas within the Catholic church there has always been an important ultramontane dimension that encourages allegiance to the Vatican, deserves special note.

In Germany, the church-versus-state struggle was made much more complex by crosscutting cleavage of Catholic-versus-Protestant authority. The fact that Martin Luther sparked the Protestant Reformation in Germany is certainly significant, as is the fact that the German states played host to the Thirty Years War and in so doing lost between one-third and one-half of their population to the Catholic-versus-Protestant as well as interdynastic savagery.

While the principle of *Culus regio lius religio* (whoever rules chooses the religion) served as part of the religious settlements of the sixteenth and seventeenth centuries, it had a more dramatic significance at the interelite level than at the mass level. The masses were expected to conform to the religion of their monarch. This was no real solution to Germany's problems, for by the early eighteenth century the overwhelmingly Protestant state of Prussia began to rise and expand, incorporating the German states of the West. By the end of the nineteenth century, Kaiser Wilhelm I's *Kulturkampf* was taking shape and German Catholicism was under siege as Catholic schools were closed, priests were expelled from government positions, and bishops were imprisoned or forced to flee the country.

The legacy of the *Kulturkampf* was intense enough that by the Weimar era the Catholic church had decided to create its own political party, the *Zentrum*. In many respects the current Christian Democratic Union (CDU) is the inheritor of the *Zentrum* tradition. However, the CDU appeals to, and draws support from, a smaller number of Protestants, as well.

What was until 1990 East Germany occupies the territorial heartland of historic Prussia and is overwhelmingly Lutheran. West Germany, which occupied the territory of the historic German states, was composed of a small Protestant—mostly Lutheran—majority and a large Catholic minority. Therefore, in West Germany and in reunified Germany there are at least two major lines of religious cleavage: church versus state, and Catholic versus Protestant. Church-state relations have been uniquely structured in the Bonn republic so as to give both the Catholic church and the German Evangelical church (the federation of Protestant—mostly Lutheran—churches) routine access to state authority. Germany's corporatist method of policy-making and implementation is conducive to systematic church input into the national and land policy process. If the churches support government policy, the result is increased governmental and policy legitimacy. If the churches oppose the government, they possess an unusual capacity to modify, check, or subvert state policy.

By the last half of the twentieth century, the religious challenge to state authority had waned to the point of becoming a nonissue in most of northern Europe. However, the cluster of defense issues that captured widespread public interest in northern Europe in the late 1970s and early 1980s—the neutron bomb, the new intermediate-range nuclear forces (INF), and the renewed question as to the morality of nuclear deterrence—reopened the church-state issue as the church itself and allied organizations began to question state security policy and thereby question governmental legitimacy. Nowhere was this felt more intensely than in Germany and the Netherlands. Belgium and Britain experienced a very similar, although less intense, phenomenon.

While in no case did a major church in Western Europe express no confidence in a government, in many cases the churches, and more commonly their lay organizations, questioned or expressed no confidence in government security policy. Perhaps ironically the challenge was expressed most vociferously by the Protestant churches. This was particularly true in Germany, where the Protestant umbrella organization, the *Evangelische Kirche in Deutschland* (EKD) served as a leading forum, and at times actor, in the campaign against nuclear modernization. Typically, the challenge came in the form of peace movements composed of informal alliances between church lay organizations, socially active clergy, grass-roots citizens groups, and activists within the Social Democratic and Labor parties of northern Europe. No single organization—church, party, or grass-roots group—dominated the peace movement. Rather, it was the ensemble of such differing groups, informally organized, each with a slightly different agenda, that made the peace movement so extensive, so flexible, and so challenging to state authority.

The Church, the Peace Movement, and the Social Democratic Party

The first half of the 1980s was a time of profound disquietude in Western Europe. The NATO decision to counter the Soviet intermediate nuclear force buildup with a similar Western capability rocked the "defense consensus" within NATO, seriously split several of the European Social Democratic parties, and catapulted the church into the political fray as it defined its role in the reemergent peace movement. While the Euromissile crisis appears to be over due to both the signing of the INF treaty in 1987 and the rapidly changing security environment initiated by President Gorbachev's "new thinking," several European Socialist parties are still grappling with the political hangover from the INF controversy, and the European churches—particularly Protestant denominations—are once again casting for a proper role in European society.

In comparing the peace movement of the 1980s with that of the 1950s, Nils Ørvik notes that thirty years ago the European peace movements were poorly organized, ran across party lines, and lacked routine access to the regular political process. In the 1980s the peace movements were much better coordinated and tended to find a rather systematic voice in the Social Democratic parties.[1] Whereas in the 1950s the European churches had a supporting role in the peace movement, that role tended to be played by individuals peripheral to the church hierarchy. In the 1980s the churches—particularly the lay associations—played a central and organizing role in much of the peace movement.

The support of the church and the peace movement's influence within the Social Democratic parties allowed the peace movement of the 1980s what Jürgen Habermas calls a "disciplined aggressiveness" that it did not have thirty years earlier.[2] Such institutional support provided the movement with far greater national success and transnational mobility.[3] The Dutch Interchurch Peace Council, for example, was instrumental in helping organize anti–neutron bomb and anti–intermediate nuclear force demonstrations in the Netherlands, Belgium, West Germany, and France.[4] This international linkage and operation is primarily a northern European phenomenon that does not extend to the south. For example, it has been argued that in Italy, a major handicap borne by the peace movement is the suspicion that it might have been "imported from abroad."[5]

The special relationship that exists between the church and the peace movement must be singled out for particular attention. In Germany and the Netherlands, the countries in which the movement has been most active and influential, a sizable gap exists between the orientation and behavior of the Protestant and Catholic churches and between their members. One researcher notes that religious orientation has little effect upon *attitudes* toward the peace movement, but it has a marked impact upon the degree of *activism*.[6] Protestants are much more likely to participate in the peace movement. Another researcher observes that Protestant churches "provide the battalions of nuclear demonstrators in West Germany and the Netherlands."[7]

The difference in the degree of activism of Protestants and Catholics is probably due to a number of variables. However, in what was West Germany the case can be made that Catholic and Evangelical Lutheran churches play very different roles because they are reacting to fundamentally different perceptions of their own recent history. Specifically, while neither church may claim high honors for its struggle against nazism, the Catholic church has been far less willing to accept guilt for tolerating the Hitler regime than has the Lutheran church.[8] It has been argued that Martin Luther's "two kingdom thesis"—namely, that God's kingdom on earth can be harsh, cruel, violent (and therefore, one should be prepared to accept this earthly travail), whereas God's kingdom of heaven is ruled with love and mercy—provided the backdrop for German acceptance of nazism and the policies it entailed.[9] As a result, the postwar Lutheran church carries a heavier psychological burden of guilt and its support for the peace movement of the 1980s is, at least partially, in atonement for past misdeeds. Perhaps the Protestant (Confessing church) pastor Martin Niemuller was the most outspoken critic of Erastian subservience to state policy, but since the war the Evangelical Lutheran bishops have encouraged Protestants to participate actively in political affairs.[10] One sees the call to action throughout the Protestant denominations but particularly in the Brethren and Confessing churches. The Brethren have systematically opposed German rearmament, conscription, and nuclearization, and their "Ten Theses" (1958) implore Christians to refuse military service and to refuse to prepare for war.

In the Netherlands too, the Protestant churches have been more actively supportive of the peace movement. While the Dutch Interchurch Peace Council draws membership, financial support, and staff from Catholic and Protestant churches, it draws most activists from the Protestant and nonsecular portions of society.

The Social Democratic parties of northern Europe also have a special link to the peace movement. While in almost all cases the movement arose outside of the party, in almost every case it presented a special challenge to, but also opportunity for, the Social Democrats. First, the peace movement presented a challenge in that it raised a series of foreign policy questions to a new height of public awareness. Consideration of NATO and Warsaw Pact nuclear strategy and weapons systems became a topic for discussion and judgment in church lay organizations, student organizations, peace movement assemblies, and peace research institutes.

Ingemar Dorfer has noted that "an informed and sophisticated counter-elite has emerged in the nordic countries and has entered the security debate."[11] In West Germany, the various foreign policy and peace research institutes played a similar role.[12] As the peace movement became better organized, more articulate, and better financed, the Social Democrats could ignore them only at their own electoral peril. Conversely, if the Social Democrats worked with the peace movement they stood an excellent chance of gaining electoral support while cutting into would-be Green and Far Left votes. If managed wisely, the nuclear issue could even win previously centrist and conservative voters to the Social Democratic fold.

Second, within the northern Social Democratic parties there existed a left wing that was often open to and supportive of many principles expounded by the leading edge of the peace movement: a with-drawal of INF weapons, a denuclearized corridor in central Europe, nuclear free–zoning, et cetera. Perhaps the Palme Commission's study, *Common Security,* is most representative of this approach,[13] but Alva Myrdal's *Game of Disarmament* illustrates a very similar strategy.[14] Not only was the left wing open to such principles but in many cases it actively promoted their acceptance.

As a result, many of the leading ideas of the peace movement have found their way into Social Democratic party manifestos. Perhaps this is most notable in the case of Britain's Labour party, which until the 1990 Brighton Conference called for unilateral nuclear disarmament, the expulsion of U.S. nuclear weapons from British soil, and the removal of foreign troops from Britain. The German, Danish, Dutch, and Nor-wegian Social Democratic and Labor parties emphasize moving toward "transarmament," whereby the national militaries are made "struc-turally incapable" of committing aggression while retaining a defense capability.[15]

Third, the nuclear issue and the peace movement created a fissure in most northern Social Democratic parties between the Left Nationalist and Right "Atlanticist" factions found in most such parties.[16] Simply stated, some elements in the parties of the Left found it to be politically expedient to promote the peace movement so as to radicalize the parties' foreign policy orientation. In Germany this would be likely with the Erhard Eppler/Oskar LaFontaine faction, whereas in Britain party radi-cals such as Tony Benn stood to strengthen their hand by manipulating the nuclear and peace issues. Josef Joffe notes that in Germany, the nuclear issue pushed party power toward Willy Brandt.[17] This may well be so, but the image of Brandt promoting the peace movement to drive his party to the Left is greatly exaggerated, if not plain wrong. More accurately, Brandt saw the potential electoral influence of the peace movement and pushed his party to the Left in an attempt to co-opt it. The German Social Democratic party faces not only a severe internal schism between its Left (LaFontaine, Eppler) and Right (Rau, Schmidt, Vogel) but is under external pressure as the Green party continues to erode the SPD's electoral base. To fail to address the policy challenges posed by the Greens and the peace movement would guarantee the Social Democrats electoral failure at the national as well as the land level.

The relationship between the Protestant churches and the German Social Democratic party has developed since the late 1960s. While originally a nonclerical or to some, an anticlerical party, the SPD has come to embrace the Protestant churches as well as to appeal to some leftist Catholics. The 1959 Bad Godesberg program of the SPD jettisoned the Marxist baggage that the party had carried since its inception. By stating that "socialism is no substitute for religion," the new program opened the door to SPD-church cooperation. In 1973 the party established a standing liaison to the Protestant churches. Since that time SPD-EKD consultation has been systematic and cooperation has been frequent.[18] This relationship is made more concrete by the presence of leading Protestant lay activists such as Erhard Eppler and Henning Scherf among the ranks of SPD leadership. In sum, Joffe's observation that the peace movement became significant in those states where the leftist parties fostered it[19] appears to be accurate but must be balanced by a Dutch scholar's comment that without the support of the *church,* the antinuclear movement would not have gained the power that it did.[20] Again, no single church, party, or grass-roots organization held a commanding position within the peace movement. However, church support was certainly one critical element in fostering and maintaining the vitality of the peace movement. Without the existence of such a vital peace movement in northern Europe—particularly Germany and the Netherlands—it is doubtful that the Social Democratic parties would have moved as far to the Left as they have with regard to security issues.

The Church as an Actor in the Peace Movement

Numerous interesting observations can be made concerning the role of the church in the peace movement insofar as the difference between Protestants and Catholics, the difference between church hierarchy and lay organizations, the role played by the intensely religious as opposed to those with less religious fervor, and the difference between religious and nonreligious.

First, the differing role of Catholic and Protestant churches is significant. While there is usually very little difference in the attitudes of Catholics and Protestants regarding their support of NATO nuclear strategy, there is a dramatic difference in their willingness to become involved as active participants in the peace movement. Perhaps this trend is most obvious in Germany. For a number of reasons the Lutheran church has been more supportive of the peace movement. The 1945 Stuttgart Confession of Guilt for tolerating and not opposing the Hitler regime oriented the church toward talking a more constructive and actively political stance in the future.

Also, the fact that what was East Germany was overwhelmingly Lutheran, whereas in West Germany the Lutheran church had bare majority ranking, was not lost on church officials. *Ostpolitik* and the process of German reunification were particularly appealing for obvious reasons, and support for *Ostpolitik,* German, and indeed, European reunification runs deep in much of the peace movement.

In East Germany the Lutheran church was active in the peace movement as well. Since the church, before the revolutionary events of 1989–90, was one of the few remaining elements of civil society not overwhelmingly penetrated and manipulated by the Communist party (SED), it was able to provide facilities and a rather safe political haven for peace activists to meet and plan their activities.[21] The East German church responded to its Western counterpart's *Kirchentags* (national lay meetings to discuss religious and social issues) with its own similar conferences. However, because the East German church entered into an arrangement with the SED in 1978 promising to be the "church in socialism" in exchange for party support of the church, church leadership had to take some steps toward limiting its opposition to state policy. Therefore, as elements of the Western peace movement (Greens, Dutch Interchurch Peace Council, etc.) began to forge informal links with the East German peace movement,[22] and as the peace groups began to become more active while operating under the umbrella of church legitimacy, the church took steps to suppress the movement. For example, at the 1987 *Kirchentag* the youth peace workshop was canceled by church authorities. In response, peace movement leaders quickly devised a "churchday from below," holding their activities without the sanctity of the church.[23] This background will no doubt present problems for the Lutheran church in the future as reunified Germany completes the process of social integration. By associating too closely with the now thoroughly discredited Communist government, the church may well have tarnished its image and claim to moral leadership for the people of the eastern portion of Germany. The same might be said with regard to the too cozy relationship that existed between the West German Social Democrats and the East German SED. This no doubt tainted the image of the Social Democrats and helped boost the electoral fortunes of the Christian Democrats in the December 1990 election.

The situation of the Catholic church in Germany is quite different because the Catholic hierarchy did not accept guilt for tolerating nazism and, therefore, did not carry the burden of penance. Perhaps more important, Konrad Adenauer, the first chancellor of the Bonn republic, was intensely Catholic, and during his fourteen-year tenure in office he framed the policy of West German rearmament, NATO membership, and deterrence with American nuclear weapons—policies that were opposed by significant numbers of leading Protestants. Adenauer's Catholic credentials and profound influence upon the new government left a lasting legacy whereby the Catholic hierarchy would tend to support nuclear deterrence, the weapons systems, and the alliance upon which it was predicated. Perhaps Jean-Francois Bureau best sums up the difference in the orientation of the two religious perspectives: "The churches which, in northern Europe have played an important role in the growth of the movement, play in Catholic Europe a more prudential role."[24] That prudential role would include moral and ethical critique and guidance of government policy, but with regard to the leading issues of the peace movement of the 1950s (conscription, rearmament, nuclearization) and the 1980s (INF modernization), the Catholic church was far more supportive of government policy than were the Protestant churches.

Further, many observers have stressed that Catholics and Protestants are reacting to very different perceptions of the nuclear situation. Specifically, the Catholic church perceives the problem in terms of the possibility of nuclear war. Protestant churches on the other hand tend to perceive the problem as being the militarization of society.[25] If nuclear war is the focus, deterrence might well make sense and weapons systems designed to underwrite it—neutron bombs, cruise or Pershing II missiles—are not necessarily provocative or immoral. If, however, the militarization of society is the issue, additional weapons systems will likely be viewed as unacceptable because their very presence corrupts society and destroys that which they were designed to protect.

Second, there is a marked difference in attitude between church hierarchy and lay organizations associated with the church. Throughout Western Europe, lay organizations typically take a more strident stance in their demand for nuclear disarmament, are more hostile to deterrence, and are more critical of NATO policy—but not necessarily critical of NATO itself[26]—than are the church hierarchies. For example, in the early 1980s Britain's Anglican church appointed a committee to examine the changing nuclear environment in Europe and to propose an Anglican response to the situation. The committee proposed unilateral nuclear disarmament and the removal of all U.S. nuclear weapons from Britain.[27] The church hierarchy found the proposal far too controversial and instead issued a statement questioning the morality of nuclear deterrence.

Similarly, in Germany the 1981 and 1983 Evangelical Lutheran synods that had traditionally been "sedentary gatherings of church elders" became vast gatherings of over 150,000 participants who tried with considerable success to shift the focus of the congresses to anti-nuclear issues.[28] The same was true in East Germany, but there the participants numbered in the tens of thousands instead of hundreds of thousands.

Third, it has been observed that the intensity of religious commitment is negatively correlated with activism in the peace movement. Specifically, Josef Joffe notes that the most religious members of society tend to be "least infected by the spirit of protest."[29] Furthermore, in their survey-based study of European attitudes toward Western defense, Flynn and Rattinger note that the less religious Europeans are more critical of nuclear deterrence, whereas the more religious are also more supportive of nuclear deterrence.[30]

Finally, most peace activists are either nonreligious or are not closely associated with a particular church. Nonetheless, the churches have served as meeting places and sometimes sponsors of peace meetings, discussion groups, et cetera. Many researchers have noted that the flocking of European (East and West) youth to ecclesiastical synods should not be construed as a religious reawakening.[31] Rather, the churches' role in the movement is a way of reaching out to youth.[32] Josef Joffe, for example, states that "prominent Protestant theologians have been eager to lend the cachet of religious authority to the political cause."[33] In a more cynical mood, David Gress claims that the "political theologians of the 1980's are wholly secular in their thinking and use their moralism, which is all that is left of traditional religion, to achieve ends that are strictly political."[34] The movement tends to use religious symbols, slogans, and images but this should not necessarily be interpreted as a newfound commitment to the church.[35] In East Germany, for example, a "Swords into Plowshares" shoulder patch was more likely to be a symbolic antistate act than a display of Christian commitment. In Germany, the Netherlands, or Scandinavia, an Easter peace march is only remotely related to a day of religious observance. However, by staging such events on religious days or by lacing dialogue with religious vernacular, the sometimes precarious alliance between the peace movement and the church is more easily maintained.

Religious Challenge to State Authority

In no case did the peace movement or its church affiliates threaten the constitutional order of a Western European state. However, the legitimacy of particular administrations and especially of particular security policies was indeed challenged. Blechman and Fisher claim that West Germany went through a process of "securitization."[36] That is, the saliency of security issues became so great and so continuous that the public will now routinely pay attention to them and react when they see a policy they cannot support. Religious and other peace movement leaders can be expected to offer cues to the public. As a result, government will increasingly have to consider public reaction before it implements security policy. Foreign and security policy-making, which previously has been largely reserved for members of government, is increasingly being challenged by the counterelite.

The securitization of West German politics is mirrored in other northern European polities. The Netherlands, Britain, Denmark, and perhaps Belgium face this phenomenon as well. Security policy-making will no longer be reserved for a governmental elite. The Dutch Interchurch Peace Council, the (British) Campaign for Nuclear Disarmament, and similar actors work with enormous grass-roots organizations and are capable of exerting great pressure on government.

Today it appears that the peace movement has disappeared. The Easter marches of 1990 mobilized thousands of Protestants in East and West Germany, but the events were minuscule compared to the marches of the early 1980s. However, one cannot extrapolate from this that the peace movement is dead. Rather, one should realize that the issues critical to the movement have been addressed and therefore many participants are satisfied or at least satisfied enough to refrain from protest. To assume that the movement is dead because the protest activity has ceased is similar to assuming that a labor union is dead because it is not on strike.[37] Surely, the securitization of German politics is now so thorough that unpopular nuclear policies would quickly reawaken the movement.

Ironically, in East Germany dissident Protestant leaders took a critical position in facilitating the transfer of power from the Communist SED to the transitional government. Three members of the coalition government of Lothar De Maiziere are Protestant clergy: foreign minister Markus Meckel (SDP), defense and disarmament minister Rainer Eppelmann (Democratic Awakening), and development aid minister Hans-Wilhelm Ebeling (German Social Union). Additionally, the De Maiziere government selected the Reverend Friedrich Magirius, superintendent of the Leipzig Lutheran church, as East Germany's first president.[38]

The East German Lutheran church, which became the "church in socialism," systematically worked with the Communist government. As a result it lost significant following and prestige.[39] However, the church simultaneously challenged state power and developed the capability to question government nuclear policy and to serve as a "pace-setter in new thinking."[40] By doing so, church leaders such as Friedrich Magirius and Rainer Eppelmann developed a public status that caused them to be recruited to play an active role in establishing the new political order.

While the peace movement and the church have not succeeded in "changing the nature of state power" in the West, they have indeed succeeded in "unsettling parliament" and in dramatically influencing national policy.[41] The Euromissile crisis appears to have passed, and the securitization of northern European politics indicates that parliaments, governments, and parties could be "unsettled" again as the NATO states continue to pursue security in a rapidly changing political and strategic environment. The churches can also be expected to play a key role in shaping that environment, as well as in facilitating the social reintegration of the newly reunified Germany.

Notes

1. Nils Ørvik, ed., *Semialignment and Western Security* (New York: St. Martin's Press, 1986), 5.

2. Cited in H. Stuart Hughes, *Sophisticated Rebels: The Political Culture of European Dissent* (Cambridge, Mass.: Harvard University Press, 1988), 141.

3. Pierre Lellouche, "La contestation pacifiste et l'avenir de la sécurité de l'Europe," in *Pacifisme et dissuasion: La contestation pacifiste et l'avenir de la sécurité de l'Europe,* ed. Pierre Lellouche (Paris: Institute Francais des Relations Internationales, 1983), 19.

4. Thomas R. Rochon, *Mobilizing for Peace* (Princeton: Princeton University Press, 1988), 129.

5. Sergio Rossi and Verigilio Ilari, "Pacifisme à l'Italienne," in Lellouche, *Pacifisme et dissuasion,* 141.

6. Alice H. Cooper, "The West German Peace Movement and the Christian Churches," *Review of Politics* 50 (Winter 1988).

7. Jean Klein, "Les Chrétiens, les armes nucléaires, et la paix," in Lellouche, *Pacifisme et dissuasion,* 207.

8. Cooper, "The West German Peace Movement and the Christian Churches," 85.

9. Mark Cioc, *Pax Atomica: The Nuclear Defense Debate in West Germany during the Adenauer Era* (New York: Columbia University Press, 1988), 93–95.

10. Frederic Spotts, *The Church and Politics in Germany* (Middletown, Conn.: Wesleyan University Press, 1973), 130.

11. Ingemar Dorfer, "La Scandinavie ou la defense de la virginité nucléaire," in Lellouche, *Pacifisme et dissuasion,* 113.

12. Jeffrey Herf, "War, Peace, and the Intellectuals: The West German Peace Movement," *International Security* 10 (Spring 1986).

13. Independent Commission on Disarmament and Security Issues (Palme Commission), *Common Security* (New York: Simon & Schuster, 1982).

14. Alva Myrdal, *The Game of Disarmament* (New York: Pantheon, 1976).

15. See Gene Sharp, *Making Europe Unconquerable* (Cambridge, Mass.: Ballinger, 1985); and Dieter S. Lutz, "Towards a New European Peace Order," in *Consolidating Peace in Europe,* ed. Morton Kaplan (New York: Paragon House, 1987).

16. See, for example, Bruce George and Tim Lister, *European Democratic Socialist Parties and NATO* (Washington, D.C.: Atlantic Council of the United States, 1987).

17. Josef Joffe, *The Limited Partnership* (Cambridge, Mass.: Ballinger, 1987), 112.

18. Gerard Braunthal, *The West German Social Democrats, 1969–1982: Profile of a Party in Power* (Boulder, Colo.: Westview Press, 1983), 170–71.

19. Joffe, *Limited Partnership,* 112.

20. Alfred van Staden, "Pays-Bas et Belgique: La tentation neutraliste," in Lellouche, *Pacifisme et dissuasion,* 100.

21. "East Germany," in Helsinki Watch Report, *From Below: Independent Peace and Environmental Movements in Eastern Europe and the USSR* (New York: Helsinki Watch, 1987), 40.

22. J. A. Emerson Vermaat, "Neue Trends in Westeuropas Friedensbewegung," *Aussenpolitik* 37 (Spring 1985): 56.

23. Helsinki Watch Report, *Independent Peace and Environmental Movements,* 45–47.

24. Jean-Francois Bureau, "La contestation des armes nucléaires et les parties politiques en Europe de l'Ouest," in Lellouche, *Pacifisme et dissuasion,* 192.

25. Klein, *Chrétiens,* 200; and Pedro Ramet, "Disaffection and Dissent in East Germany," *World Politics* 37 (October 1984): 94.

26. William Domke, Richard Eichenberg, and Catherine Kelleher, "Consensus Lost? Domestic Politics and the 'Crisis' in NATO," *World Politics* 39 (April 1987): 384.

27. Rochon, *Mobilizing for Peace,* 129.

28. Joyce Mushaben, "Anti-Politics and Successor Generations: The Role of Youth in West and East German Peace Movements," *Journal of Political and Military Sociology* 12 (Spring 1984).

29. Joffe, *Limited Partnership,* 107.

30. Gregory Flynn and Hans Rattinger, eds., *The Public and Atlantic Defense* (Totowa, N.J.: Roman & Allanheld, 1985), 133.

31. Barry Blechman and Cathleen Fisher, *The Silent Partner: West Germany and Arms Control* (Cambridge, Mass.: Ballinger, 1988), 150.

32. Van Staden, "Pays-Bas et Belgique," 100.

33. Joffe, *Limited Partnership,* 107.

34. David Gress, *Peace and Survival: West Germany, The Peace Movement, and European Security* (Stanford, Calif.: Hoover Institution Press, 1985), 149–50.

35. Rochon, *Mobilizing for Peace,* 134–35.

36. Blechman, *Silent Partner,* 52–53.

37. Philip P. Everts, "Where the Peace Movement Goes When It Disappears," *Bulletin of the Atomic Scientists* 45 (November 1989).

38. Mark Fisher, "East Germans Set a 5-Party Government," *Boston Globe,* April 10, 1990, 2.

39. Mary Kaldor, "Transforming the State: An Alternative Security Concept for Europe," in Björn Hettne, ed., *Europe: Dimensions of Peace* (Atlantic Highlands, N.J.: Zed Books, 1988), 217.

40. "East German Churches Faces New Issues," *Christianity Today,* January 15, 1990, 48.

41. Helmut Fritzche, "The Security Debate in the Evangelical Church of the GDR," in Ole Waever, Pierre Lemaitre, and Elzbieta Tromer, eds., *European Polyphony* (New York: St. Martin's Press, 1989), 46–47.

PART V

The Middle East and Islamic Africa

8.

Challenge and Conciliation: Religion and State in Israel

ALLAN METZ

This chapter addresses the challenge/accommodation theme concerning the relationship between religion and state in Israel. Charles S. Liebman and Eliezer Don-Yehiya[1] and Ervin Birnbaum[2] emphasize the interrelationship, and thus accommodation, between religion and state in Israel. In comparison, Bruce M. Borthwick[3] and Ephraim Tabory,[4] while well aware of the conciliatory aspects of this relationship, focus more on the conflict between religion and state.[5] The case studies examined in this chapter reflect both the accommodative and the conflictive aspects of this sometimes paradoxical relationship. In the health policy process, for example, as demonstrated by the abortion and autopsy issues, the findings of a study by Yael Yishai[6] point to accommodation, despite the great divide between religious and secular forces on these sensitive issues. At the governmental level, the system has proved less successful in resolving the political stalemate, as we can see in the study of the 1988 election and the political turmoil generated first by the fall of Prime Minister Yitzhak Shamir and the National Unity Government in March 1990, and then by the failure of Labor's Shimon Peres to form a government the following month. The resulting political uncertainty will have an impact on the broader issues of the Middle East.

Theoretical Framework and Historical Background

According to Charles S. Liebman and Eliezer Don-Yehiya, two prevailing assumptions regarding religion and state in the West, and particularly in the United States, are (1) that democratic political states

159

are not successful in dealing with matters of religion, with the politiciz-
ing of religion posing a threat to the political system; and (2) that
political involvement undermines and corrupts religion. However, in
Israel religion and politics constitute a symbiotic relationship. In other
words, one cannot understand religion in Israel without seriously considering the political milieu, nor can one understand politics without
religion. Despite Western assumptions, Israel still maintains a democratic form of government, and the religious forces in Israel do not seem
to have been corrupted by involvement in politics. However, the blend-
ing of religion and politics undoubtedly can have serious implications
for both political stability and religious integrity. In the broader view,
this mix is unavoidable in certain societies. Moreover, both the religious
establishment and polity may benefit from this arrangement; thus, a
separation of religion and state would not only be impractical, but also
might not even be in Israel's best interests.

Liebman and Don-Yehiya make the point that a discussion of
religion and state involves more than political controversy regarding
religious matters, such as the operation of public transportation on the
Sabbath; control of marriage and divorce by the religious establishment;
the definition of a Jew based solely on *halakah* (Jewish law), or by other
standards as well; the amount of public expenditure for religious-related
causes or institutions; if the conservative and reform movements within
Judaism should be granted official state recognition; and the impact of
religious parties on the Israeli polity in representing their constituencies.[7]

Such issues or case studies are important in a consideration of
religion and politics in Israel but should be viewed within a broader
context. To consider specific issues in isolation would be misleading,
placing too much emphasis on "religion as a politically divisive issue" of
a particular interest group. Of course, deep cleavages and divisions exist
among Israelis on a variety of religious matters. Religion, however, also
unifies society and affords a means of socialization and political legitimacy that a focus on religious conflict might not consider. Furthermore, a consideration of religion and state as only a study of religious
issues in the public sphere overlooks interrelationships between religion
and state, such as the impact of politics on religion and vice versa, the
implications for the Israeli political scene of being a Jewish state, the
political ramifications of the religious parties, how such parties differ
from their more secular counterparts due to their religious faith, and
how political views are shaped by religious beliefs. Thus, Liebman and

Don-Yehiya believe that it is important to study the interrelationship of religion and state. The case studies presented herein regarding particular controversies on religious matters are considered within the framework of this religion-state interrelationship, resulting in a more accurate evaluation of the situation of religion and politics in Israel.[8]

Perhaps most indicative of the interrelationship between state and religion, a sense of compromise, and the mutual recognition for the need of a *modus operandi* is the "status quo" agreement. The basis for the resolution of conflicts over religion-polity issues depends on agreement between secular and religious forces on the need to preserve national unity and maintain the Jewish nature of the state. This ongoing consensus is termed the "status quo,"[9] an uneasy coexistence between secular and religious forces, as explained by Ervin Birnbaum, who describes state and religion in Israel as the "politics of compromise." If the militant religionists could impose their will, they would abolish the existing parliamentary democratic system[10] and replace it with a theocracy. If the secularists could have their way, they would discard what they view as the unnecessary hindrances of religion, which prevent the fulfillment of the "rule of law" and "freedom of conscience." The "rule of law" in secular parlance refers to laws passed in the Knesset, as distinct from the "rule of the Torah" (i.e., religious law or *halakah*), which is viewed as the ultimate law by religionists. However, from the secularist perspective the "rule of law" must predominate in a democracy, the belief being that secular legislation has a distinct right to make laws that will have priority over Torah law when there is a conflict between the two.

The phrase "freedom of conscience," as understood in Israel, may have the opposite meaning as it is perceived in the United States and Western Europe. From the secularist point of view, freedom of conscience means freedom from religious interference in the lives of secular Israelis who, for example, oppose the enforcement of kosher (i.e., religiously permissible) food in the military and in government facilities. They view this as an infringement of the freedom of conscience of most Israelis, who then are compelled to eat kosher food and not the food they would prefer. Under this rubric of freedom of conscience, secularists oppose, among other things, Sabbath travel restrictions and religious laws pertaining to marriage and divorce. Religionists take a diametrically opposing view, holding that a Jew can best maintain his freedom of conscience if he obeys *halakah,* which, for example, bans travel on the Sabbath and the eating of nonkosher food.

The rule of law and the rule of the Torah have occasionally come into conflict, coming close to, if not sometimes producing, explosive confrontations. And conflicting interpretations of freedom of conscience have resulted in equally difficult circumstances that have strained the political order in Israel. The political leadership has done its best to avoid open conflicts over these issues and when they have occurred, to minimize their impact. However, both religious and secular forces have recognized that an accommodation between the two is imperative. To this end, the status quo has been introduced. Religion is to remain as it was in May 1948, the date of Israel's independence. However, in spite of the status quo agreement, both sides have accused each other of taking advantage of the agreement by interfering in their respective spheres, by infringing on their freedom of conscience. Moreover, while this is confusing enough from a Western perspective, the situation becomes even more complex when one considers that the secularist parties command a great majority (around 85 percent) of the popular vote and representation in the Knesset, whereas the religious parties only account for approximately 15 percent. It is clear, then, that the religious camp, through the religious parties, has a disproportionate impact on the Israeli political system.

Birnbaum notes that the art of political compromise in Israel predates the formation of the Jewish state. It was already well established in the two organizations that led the way for the creation of the new nation: the Knesset Israel (Jewish Community) and the Zionist Organization. During the British Mandate in Palestine from 1920 to 1948, in the Knesset Israel, a number of parties formed a ruling coalition. Despite their at times considerable disagreements, they wielded their limited home rule power through "mutual concession and accommodation." In the Zionist Organization, which was essential in the eventual formation of a Jewish state, the "politics of compromise" was in effect since the organization's beginnings in 1897.

This status quo and emphasis on compromise continued following Israeli independence in May 1948. The nature of government, the political party and electoral systems, and party relationships were preindependence legacies. Therefore, Israel inherited a system that has had a profound impact on its constitutional and political development. Another legacy from the preindependence period was the religious establishment, which has engendered highly complex problems. Its origins can be traced to the ancient past. These political and religious inheritances are deeply ingrained in Israel, and attempts at political change have not been successful due largely to the interdependence of politics and religion that is so characteristic of the Israeli political system. This system of interdependence helps to perpetuate the politics of compromise, whereby the official governmental position does not represent just one party, but rather attempts to take into account the views of all the parties that form a coalition government. The degree to which a party can shape a government's program, if the other coalition parties do not share its view, depends on its importance, size, and influence.

In any political system, but especially in Israel, a premium is placed on compromise if the system is to be efficient and promote stability, since the Israeli political system depends on a general consensus of several parties with diverse views to form a government. This multiparty system tends to blur authority, leaving little room for clear-cut policy, and offers indirect ways to handle controversial issues. This could be the salient characteristic of the politics of compromise in Israel.[11]

In sum,

> the status quo agreement supplies a pragmatic resolution to religious-secular tensions and facilitates political leadership at the national level. The status quo is a dynamic solution: its provisions change delicately and subtly according to new balances of power and new circumstances. The principle, however, has remained constant since the establishment of the state.[12]

Distinct from Liebman and Don-Yehiya and Birnbaum, who place more emphasis on accommodation and the interrelationship between politics and religion in Israel, are Bruce M. Borthwick and Ephraim Tabory, who offer a more conflictive interpretation of religion and state in that the former has made gains at the latter's expense. Borthwick presents a dichotomy between secularization and religion. Secularization has been a popular topic since it generally is linked to modernization, during which process societies become increasingly secularized. According to Donald Eugene Smith, the "secularization of the polity has been the most fundamental structural and ideological change in the process of development."[13] Smith defines secularization as "the separation of the polity from religious ideologies and ecclesiastical structures, the expansion of the polity to perform regulatory functions in the socioeconomic sphere which were formerly performed by religious structures, and the transvaluation of the political culture to emphasize nontranscendent temporal goals and rational, pragmatic means, that is secular political values."[14] Smith goes on to delineate four secularization patterns: (1) polity-separation secularization, where religion and state are separate; (2) polity-expansion secularization, in which the polity increasingly exerts its control over social and economic areas previously regulated by religious authority; (3) polity-transvaluation secularization, referring to the secularization of the political arena; and (4) polity-dominance secularization, in which the state attacks the religious foundation of culture and forcibly imposes a secular ideology on political life.[15] The first pattern has not taken place in Israel because that country has never had a distinct independent religious establishment. Similarly, the fourth pattern is not represented because the state has no desire to eliminate or destroy religion. Even the most secular Israelis concede that religion enhances the Jewish character of the state.

Borthwick then proceeds to study Israel in terms of the patterns of polity-expansion secularization and polity-transvaluation secularization. For countries in the process of polity-expansion secularization, "the polity expands at the expense of religion. It is a zero-sum game, and what the polity wins, religion loses." The conflict generally occurs in legal, educational, social, and economic matters. Increasing restrictions are placed on a previously all-powerful religious law. Education becomes more and more secularized and is removed from religious control. As for societal structure, a struggle ensues between religious authorities who wish to maintain a hierarchical society while secularists call for an egalitarian society. In some societies religion wields significant economic power through, for example, large land holdings, while the state seeks to diminish this religious economic power.[16]

Israeli history in the postindependence period demonstrates, however, that polity-expansion secularization has not occurred. Jewish settlers who came to Palestine from 1905 to 1914 and who, following World War II, founded and led the government were "Labor-Zionists." Their ideology mixed socialism and Jewish nationalism, and their goal was to fashion "a democratic, egalitarian, secular, nationalist Jewish state" in Israel. However, in both the mandate and independence periods, Labor Zionism has not been able to govern exclusively. For example, the major Labor-Zionist party, Mapai, and then its successor, the Labor party, had to rule in coalitions with the National Religious party. In 1977, Likud predominated but had to form its own coalition with the National Religious party. And, in return for its support, the latter has exacted concessions in the form of specific laws benefiting religion,[17] such as state-enforced observance of the Sabbath, Jewish dietary laws, rabbinic authority over marriage and divorce, and the "Who is a Jew" Amendment.[18] Moreover, Israel does not have a written constitution since there is no consensus as to whether the state should be secular, theocratic, or something in between.

Borthwick points out that Israeli secular political parties have never been able to rule with a majority and have had to accede to the demands of the religious parties in return for the latter's support. Moreover, the secular parties are not wholly against what the religious parties demand. The former "have surrendered to some of the demands of the religious parties because they do not totally reject religious values, nor do they desire a totally secular state."[19] Advocates of secularism wish to maintain the society's Jewish character to which, they believe, religion makes a contribution. They want Israel to be a Jewish state, not merely a state with a majority of Jews.

Thus, Borthwick concludes that polity-expansion secularization is not occurring in Israel. On the contrary, since Israel's independence, secularists in the political system have been in "steady retreat," painfully accepting laws and policies that increase religion's authority and power. For a modern nation, this is rather unusual. While Israel is certainly not theocratic, neither is it secular.[20] Israeli society and politics constitute a mixture of the secular and the religious and most likely will remain as such.[21] Borthwick coins the term "polity-contraction sacralization" to more accurately describe what has taken place in Israel, as opposed to polity-expansion secularization, which certainly has not occurred.

Borthwick next considers the other pattern of secularization, polity-transvaluation secularization, which has three aspects: (1) secularization of the polity, with an accompanying decrease of religious values; (2) secularization of the foundation of legitimacy, whereby "religion ceases to be a potent source of legitimacy for governments, politicians, or political movements"; and (3) group identity secularization involving the "displacement of religious values and loyalties by those associated with the nation as the prime orientation to social and political life."[22]

The Labor-Zionists who founded the state of Israel endeavored to achieve all of these aims. They were thorough secularists and wished to create a new Jewish state that was not theocratic but rather was democratic, socialist, and egalitarian, deriving its legitimacy from the people. The Labor-Zionists were inspired by the humanitarianism of socialism and emphasized a Jewish group identity with a national consciousness, but one lacking a religious orientation. While in ancient

Jewish history religion was intimately tied to the nation, the founders of Israel wished to make a separation, viewing God euphemistically as the "Rock of Israel" or the "Eternal of Israel." Redemption was a religious term given "a new exclusively national meaning." For example, the establishment of Israel is viewed as the "redemption" of the Jewish people. The founders of Israel also secularized the religious ideal of Israel serving as a "light to the nations." The founders of Israel took religious concepts like the Bible, redemption, and Israel as a "light to the nations," made them devoid of theological significance, and applied them to the modern world in a secular-nationalistic manner; they were not completely successful. Thus, since independence the Labor-Zionist notion of "transvaluing or cleansing" Jewish history, symbols, and ceremonies of their religious significance has failed, since religion has grown in importance in national life. Labor-Zionist secularism has been unable to mobilize and gain the adherence of Israel's multifaceted society,[23] and a majority of Israelis agree that there is at least some linkage between "being Jewish . . . (and) the Jewish religion. . . . If being Jewish is what Israel is all about, then in some however vague and undefined way, there has to be some connection between Israel and religion."[24] Israelis are required to make tremendous sacrifices for the state, such as general conscription at age eighteen, long reserve duty, and high taxes. This dedication and commitment will only come from a populace willing to give their loyalties in an unconditional way to the state. Such sacrifices are more readily made when there is a connection between religion and the state, with religion being integrated into the national culture.

In sum, in the case of Israel, neither polity-expansion secularization nor polity-transvaluation secularization has occurred. Rather, the polity has declined relative to religion and has become more "sacralized." It has emerged as a secular and religious mixture. The state's legitimacy is based, partially, on its historical association with ancient Israel, which had a definite link to religion; Israeli national identity has clear religious and national origins.

Several immediate reasons may be offered to explain why secularization has not kept pace with the growing influence of religion, as reflected in religious party strength, rabbinic authority, and a conciliatory spirit that permeates most political factions. Although the secularists constitute most of the citizenry and are the major political force, they are not going to arbitrarily impose their will on the religionists. A longer-term answer is the eternal relationship between "the religion, the nation and the land" in all of Jewish history. In establishing a new Jewish state in the ancient Jewish homeland, it was not possible to exclude religion because the bond has been too powerful.

In addition, the Israeli leadership has been very concerned with threats posed by persecution and assimilation. These threats have reinforced the need for the return of Jews to their ancient homeland and the need to reestablish a Jewish state there. To be fully Jewish and to ensure the Jewish character of the state, as opposed to being just a nation in which a large number of Jews live, Israel must accept religion as an integral part of the nation's life.

While the link between the Jewish nation and religion has been very strong and continuous, the one between the Jewish state and religion has been tenuous. Throughout history, Jews in ancient Israel and in the Diaspora have had to live in servitude or under various degrees of domination by foreign powers. Depending on the time and circumstances, Jews have had varying amounts of autonomy or self-governance. This self-rule legacy from the Diaspora was reflected in Israel when, at its establishment, Jews were accustomed to self-government without a state and would not accept excesses once their own state came into being. "Thus, an unusual situation was created: a state precariously governed by the secular Labor-Zionist party balanced off by well organized and strong religious organizations. The result has been an equilibrium in which neither the secularists nor the religionists ever completely get their way."[25]

Like Borthwick, and in contrast to Liebman and Don-Yehiya and Birnbaum, Ephraim Tabory focuses more on religious-political contention in Israel resulting from the intertwining of state and religion. The place of religion in Western industrialized nations, in which there is a structural separation of state and religion, has engendered religious tolerance and lessened inter- and intrareligious conflict. According to Peter Berger, this is so because religion is not of vital importance to Western society as a whole, but remains so on an individual level.[26] In contrast, in societies where religion plays a significant role, as in Iran, for example, there is the potential for much conflict and turmoil. The ideological basis of religious conflict mitigates against compromise, since the latter can undermine doctrinaire religious beliefs. The potential for tension between religious forces is heightened when religion and state are intermingled, as is the case for Israel. To some extent, Tabory argues, there is "no freedom from religion" in Israel, since theologically based law is pervasive and in some cases binding on both religious and secular Israelis, which causes animosity on the part of the latter, who feel coerced. Moreover, potential conflict between religious and secular Jews is seen as representing "one of Israel's greatest social problems." Thus, the purpose of Tabory's article is to study the impact that the mixing of state and religion in Israel has had on the conflict between religious and secular Israelis.

The pervasiveness of Judaism in Israel can be studied from two levels. First there is the ideological issue of state legitimation and the definition of societal character and traditions. This essentially is a question of how to determine "who is a Jew." Religionists maintain that *halakah* (i.e., the doctrine and precepts of Judaism) must be the ultimate authority in establishing standards for such matters as marriage, divorce, and conversion. Secularists are amenable to more flexible standards for defining who is a Jew. This issue is significant due to the *raison d'être* of the Jewish state: Jews throughout the world are eligible for citizenship there, and whether the civil or religious courts have the final authority in passing judgments on this sensitive issue is a thorny question.

The second level affected by religion concerns the general nature of the Jewish state and the daily impact of religious laws on its citizens, as typified on a national scale by the requirement that all public institutions, such as airlines and ships, must follow *Kashruth* (i.e., the Jewish dietary laws). Also, travel restrictions on the Sabbath, when mass transit does not operate, make it difficult for those Israelis who cannot afford more expensive modes of transportation and for whom this is the only day of leisure since Israel has a six-day workweek.

The public has occasionally protested such laws, but not at length, despite the fact that the majority of Israelis are not religious, the Orthodox only constitute a minority (from 20 to 30 percent)[27] and, according to Tabory, secularization has made great advances in Israeli society.[28] (This observation by Tabory is in contrast to Borthwick's belief that secularism has retreated in Israel.) The secular-religious conflict has not been more contentious for two reasons: the political system and the Jewish culture in Israel.

Israel's parliamentary system is based on coalition governments. The participation of religious parties in the political system has channeled the demands of the religious and secular parties into political outlets, resulting in moderation and compromise. In a way, the religious and secular parties have co-opted each other, with the religious groups benefiting the most,[29] because they have had a considerable impact on the political system, disproportionate to their approximate 15 percent of the seats in the Knesset.

Furthermore, on the political level, the working relationship between religious and secular groups in preindependence Israel has been retained in the postindependence period. As discussed previously, this status quo agreement stipulates that certain religious provisions already in place must be retained and that any effort to change the existing religious arrangement will be viewed as a violation of the status quo and will not be tolerated. While there have been conflicting interpretations of the status quo, this agreement has done more overall to prevent contention regarding religious issues than it has caused.

In addition to the political factors that have reconciled the religious and secular forces, another factor is Jewish culture in Israel. In its history, Judaism has imbued religious significance into secular and daily life. This has resulted in a continual process of searching for one's Jewish roots, particularly since a special meaning is given to Israel as a Jewish state and extraordinary demands are made on its citizens. This search includes nonreligious Israelis.

This search for answers to Israel's significance as a Jewish state is related to its civil religion.[30] The combination of nationalistic symbols and religious practice is common in Jewish culture in Israel,[31] including such symbols as the national flag—which is fashioned after the tallis or Jewish prayer shawl—or more emotion-invoking experiences, like the religious ceremonies that form an essential role in civil ceremonies, such as those held on Memorial Day. This mixture of religious and nationalistic symbolism results in a general acceptance of the part religion plays as a unifying force in society.

What bodes well for religious tolerance[32] in Israel is that Judaism is a ritualistic religion, based on repeated cycles. Even secular Israelis perform to a large extent a number of such rituals, similar to Reform Jews in the United States. A case can be made that even a basic level of religious observance by a majority of Israelis contributes to the acceptance of religious practice on a state level.

Finally, the segments of the population that are most affected by religious-based laws constitute another factor enhancing political/religious accommodation. The religious legislation that probably has had the most impact on Israelis in general is the lack of bus service on the Sabbath. However, this does not affect members of the relatively well-off middle class, who have private transportation or can afford taxi service, which does operate on the Sabbath. Sabbath restrictions thus impinge most on the lower classes, but the latter tend to be the most traditionally religious groups and so would not mind such restrictions as much.[33]

Another religious issue poses a threat to the fundamental relationship between secular and religious Israelis. The religious political parties have traditionally been concerned with internal religious matters as opposed to external issues.[34] However, the possible trade-off of land for peace with Israel's Arab neighbors has politicized this issue. The *Gush Emunim* (Block of the Faithful) has been formed by some Orthodox youth who believe that Israel has a duty, based on a religious rationale, to annex the territory west of the Jordan River. The strident position of *Gush Emunim* has been to polarize traditionally temperate religious parties, compelling them to take a similar stance. According to Tabory, matters of secular law and human rights are of secondary importance to *Gush Emunim*. To a large degree, this movement views itself as a new form of messianism.[35] The impact of this movement in the field of foreign policy could extend to growing opposition on religious issues at the local level. If the religious parties no longer can moderate religious demands, as has been the case, the larger ruling parties may feel compelled to join with other parties that are less sympathetic to traditional Judaism. If this, hypothetically, were to lead to increased secularization, with a relaxation of religion-based laws on the national level, then the religious groups would become alienated and could even withdraw and form their own subcommunity within Israeli society.

This does not mean, however, that the answer to preservation of Israeli unity would be a total concession to religious demands, because the situation is not that simple. Although generally there has not been overt conflict concerning religion-based laws, the issue is potentially divisive. Secularists may be willing to accept the growing demands of religionists only to a certain extent. The status quo agreement has been used more frequently by religious groups to prevent any weakening of religious practice, but they have also endeavored to add to religious legislation. If efforts to make religious law into national law increase, powerful secular groups will be affected and will not necessarily tolerate a steady erosion of their sphere. For example, a law based on Jewish religious law placing severe restrictions on autopsies went into effect in December 1980 and incurred the wrath of the medical establishment. Some physicians openly declared that they would not abide by it. (This issue will be discussed in more detail later in the chapter.)

The attempt to achieve a balance between tradition and change in order to preserve political and social stability in Israel has been termed the country's "perpetual dilemma."[36] Israel is still a relatively new society made up of immigrants from a wide variety of nations. Both ethnic and religious cleavages have the potential to threaten general national unity. While religious legislation is directed through the political system, the views of religious and secular groups vis-à-vis state and religious law have a direct bearing on the relationship between religious and secular individuals. Though religious strife does not prevail in Israel, societal unity does not exist either, whereby religious differences would be relatively unimportant. Moreover, studies have indicated relatively little social interaction between religious and secular Israelis and little bonding between them.[37] Tabory thus concludes that "a resolution of the religious question is necessary to ensure the unity and social identity of Israel."[38] The theoretical framework of the relationship between religion and politics that has been established, together with some historical background, provides the context for case studies epitomizing the challenge/accommodation theme as it relates to health policy issues and electoral politics. The health policy study reflects accommodation while the electoral study is more indicative of a conflict that could not be resolved by the system and of the challenges posed by the Israeli political system.

Health Policy and Religion: Abortion and Autopsies

The complex relationship between state and religion has been one of the unique features of the Israeli political system. Issues on religion have been channeled politically through various parties and groupings that attempt to consolidate the position of religion in the political culture.[39] This case study examines the impact religious values have on two important health policy issues, abortion and autopsy, and provides a comparison of the processes involved in determining health policy.[40] These issues reflect great disagreement between religious and secular groups and demonstrate how public policy is formulated. While the details of these issues are beyond the scope and general nature of this paper, the findings resulting from a comparison of the abortion and autopsy issues are relevant to the topic of religion and state, as they relate to the nature of the problem, the problem-solving process, and decision making.

There are two factors to consider regarding problem formation: (1) abortion was just beneath the surface of the public debate, and (2) autopsy was expressed by interested advocates. Political parties were more successful in promoting the abortion issue, whereas pressure groups had more of an impact politically with the autopsy issue as it grew and remained in the public debate. This difference is linked to the nature of the problem. Giving the abortion issue universal applications was much more successful than similar attempts in the case of autopsy. A connection was made between the abortion issue and national priorities like demographic growth[41] and social equality. The autopsy issue was essentially a conflict between zealous religious groups and the medical establishment, each accusing the other of promoting personal interests, thereby ignoring the universality of the problem.

As for problem solving, the major players in the abortion issue were political parties, or groups acting on their behalf. In the autopsy case, these groups were the main source of problem resolution. Although they interacted with political parties, these groups were not viewed as "mediators but as decision makers."[42] The abortion and autopsy issues indicate that the making of health policy in Israel does not have a rigid structure. Instead, there are numerous ways to exert influence by various types of political groups.

In both instances, decision making reflected compromise and accommodation. The decisions on changes in abortion policy differed slightly from previous practice. As for autopsy, calls for radical change were not accepted and the political establishment agreed to the initial solution, which itself was a compromise. The sense of accommodation in formulating health policy pertaining to these issues had three underlying principles. First was the right to follow one's own beliefs. The need for compromise, more prevalent among secularists, was based on the idea that there should be a minimum of coercion, particularly in issues of conscience. The second principle was political, based on the necessity of compromise involved in coalition bargaining. Negotiations with religious parties have always involved issues in which the nonreligious majority had to concede to the religious minority. The third principle resulted from the unique relationship between religion and polity in Israel. Despite differing views on the nature of this relationship, or what it should be, there is acceptance that the state is Jewish, with traditional faith and practice reinforcing nationalism. Given the political milieu in Israel, one cannot disregard or overrule the demands of religionists.[43]

For the abortion and autopsy issues, the decision-making process was both dynamic and painstaking. Since no easy solution could be formulated to satisfy both secular and religious demands, the process is a continual one. These cases offer clear examples of how the power of an "intensive minority"[44] results from the influence of religion on the Israeli political system. While the religious parties only attract approximately 15 percent of the national vote, they exert disproportionate strength on issues of concern to them. The very intense emotions generated by these controversial issues together with considerable pressure wielded by religious or secular groups have preserved a sense of accommodation in which only partial answers have been found among the parties involved. According to one scholar,

> the Israeli system maintains an open political market in which health policy is a target of influence for political parties and pressure groups. The competition between the actors has resulted, at least in the cases of abortion and autopsy, in policies which are perhaps not fully compatible with medical needs, but do reflect, to a large extent, the intricacies of the social system and its political imperatives.[45]

In sum, the influence of religious values and groups on two health policy issues, abortion and autopsy, caused much contention between religious and secular groups. The comparison of these issues was based on three policy-making stages: problem formation, problem solving, and decision making. Two patterns of influence on public policy emerged: one in which political parties tried to suppress issues and another pertaining to a well-defined issue resolved by groups who went directly to decision makers. The party pattern pertains to the abortion issue, which was suppressed in the public debate because of an adherence to national and religious values. The group pattern pertains to the autopsy issue, which essentially was and continues to be a source of controversy between the medical establishment and religious groups. The decision-making process reflected "a pattern of compromise and accommodation" that resulted in little difference from previous practice. The decisions arrived at were indicative of the complexities of the political system in Israel and the transcendence of religious values in the formulation of health policy.[46]

Electoral and Coalition Politics

The national election of 1988 and the coalition negotiations that characterized the Israeli political landscape in the spring of 1990 reflect the relationship between religion and state in Israel. The November 1988 election serves as a necessary background to more recent attempts at forming new governments. This election has been characterized as an "all-loser election" where "no political party, faction, or group won."[47] Despite its strong electoral showing in gaining 18 of the 120 Knesset seats, the Orthodox bloc of four religious parties[48]—National Religious party (NRP) or MAFDAL, Agudat Yisrael, Shas (Sephardi Torah Guardians), and Degel HaTorah (Flag of the Torah)[49]—made so many demands (such as stricter enforcement of *Kashruth* and Sabbath restrictions)[50] in their negotiations with Likud and Labor as preconditions for their participation in a possible coalition, that the two major parties once again formed a government, as had been the case in 1984. But the National Unity Government (NUG), which emerged from the 1988 election, left Likud in a stronger position, with Labor more as a junior partner. The painstaking political negotiation[51] between Likud, Labor, and the Orthodox bloc following the election once again thrust the issue of state and religion into the limelight (an issue that prior to the election was not viewed as a major concern). A majority of the Israeli public protested against Orthodox demands and renewed calls for electoral reform were voiced across the political spectrum from the Knesset[52] to break the Israeli political deadlock.[53]

This discussion of the 1988 election serves as a prelude to a consideration of coalition negotiations in the spring of 1990[54] that demonstrates the political paralysis that can result from the interaction of politics and religion on the governmental level. The demise of the uneasy alliance between Likud and Labor, belying the name of National Unity, began on March 3, 1990, when American president George Bush stated that he opposed Jewish settlement in East Jerusalem. His statement touched off a crisis within the coalition, with Labor supporting and Likud opposing a U.S. proposal for Israeli-Palestinian peace talks.[55] On March 13, Prime Minister Yitzhak Shamir of Likud fired Deputy Prime Minister Shimon Peres, causing the other Labor party members of the coalition to resign.[56] On March 15, Shamir lost a confidence vote in the Knesset and his fifteen-month-old government fell.[57] Peres accused Shamir of "murdering the peace process" and Shamir, in turn, called Peres a "shameful" appeaser of the Arabs.[58] Israeli president Chaim Herzog gave Peres on March 20 a mandate to form a new government, and Peres convened the Knesset on April 11 for that purpose.[59] However, sudden defections by two Agudat Israel supporters on the orders of Rabbi Menachem Mendel Schneerson, an eighty-eight-year-old right-wing Lubavitcher rebbe of Brooklyn, New York, thwarted such efforts. Finally, on April 26, Peres had to admit his failure to form a government; Herzog then requested that Shamir form a government and thereby break the deadlock in the 120-member Knesset.[60] Thus, religion again played a decisive role politically by helping to bring down the National Unity Government (when Shas was absent from a no-confidence vote) and then when two Agudat Yisrael members, Avracham Verdiger and Eliezer Mizrachi, suddenly withdrew their pledge of support to Shimon Peres, reflecting the disproportionate influence of religious parties on electoral politics.[61] This opened the way for Shamir to try to form a narrow right-wing coalition government[62] that would accelerate the settlement process in the West Bank and reject the Baker peace initiative.[63]

While it is difficult to speculate on Israel's political future, the "present political reality is that the Likud is likely to play the dominant role in the next government, whether it is broadly-based or narrow."[64] This process could lead to more deadlock, meaning new elections, likely to result in "yet another standoff. Only ending the proportional-representation system that awards Knesset seats to the tiniest minority will produce majority rule. And when will that come? Israeli cynics say the Messiah will arrive first."[65] In view of Israel's electoral systems, it is practically impossible to foresee how much time Shamir will require to form a new coalition government, who Likud's partners will be, or if Shamir will be successful.[66] However, should Shamir succeed, Peres has predicted that the outcome will be "an extremist right-wing government the like(s) of which Israel never had."[67] The muddled political situation was reflected in an observation made by President Chaim Herzog on April 28, 1990, that Israel was "in a state of political and public confusion such as it has never known since its founding"[68] and that "among the public there is a feeling of heavy depression."[69] Moreover, the spectacle of the major parties (i.e., first Labor, then Likud) engaged in a bidding war for the support of the minority religious parties has brought the "legitimacy of the whole political system . . . into question."[70] Thus, the political outlook is quite uncertain for Israel, which will probably continue in its "political stalemate, one that will also be imposed on the larger issues of Middle East peace."[71]

Conclusion

This chapter has demonstrated the theme of challenge and accommodation in regard to the relationship between religion and state in

Israel. A theoretical framework, including some historical background, of this relationship was provided by several commentators. Charles S. Liebman and Eliezer Don-Yehiya and Ervin Birnbaum emphasized the spirit of compromise in this relationship while Borthwick and Tabory, though also acknowledging this aspect, placed more emphasis on the challenges posed by religion to the state. Borthwick and Tabory hold that in the give-and-take between religion and the state, the former has benefited more—despite the relatively small percentage (15 percent) it commands among the electorate—due to the nature of Israel's parliamentary system. The two case studies point to both the success and failure of the political system in reconciling religious and secular differences. Regarding health issues such as abortion and autopsy, pragmatic solutions not differing very much from past precedent have prevailed, reflecting accommodation and compromise between religion and state. On the other hand, the example of the 1988 election and, particularly, the political events of the spring of 1990 that resulted in political stalemate, point to both the religious and political challenges posed to the state. The excessive demands of the religious parties in the negotiations following the 1988 election dissipated what electoral strength they did gain, prompting Likud and Labor to form another National Unity Government; in 1990, the religious bloc proved that it could make or break a government in the current political situation characterized by a rift between the principle parties, Likud and Labor.

In sum, Israel is a nation in which "even simple matters become complicated." Therefore, it is no surprise that the relationship between state and religion is highly complex. This complexity, as studied in this chapter, is due largely to "the nature of Judaism, the Jewish religion and, consequently, of Israel as a Jewish state" and the prevailing parliamentary political system, which gave disproportionate influence to the religious parties.[72]

Thus, the state of Israel is engaged in a delicate balancing act regarding concessions made to secularists and the religious. Such concessions (i.e., state enforcement of the Sabbath and *Kashruth* in government facilities), however, amount to accommodations, not solutions, and are ultimately unsatisfactory to both secularists and religionists. These conflicting groups do not share a common vision for Israel and, as a result, "Israel as a state has not been able to precisely define its relationship to Judaic norms."[73] "In the absence of a final religion-state definition, religious issues assume political overtones and character." Israelis have yet to work out a definitive relationship between secular authority (i.e., the Israeli body politic) and religion, reflecting the paradox of reconciling the historical desire of Jews in the Diaspora to practice their private faith without public policy restrictions with "the problem of how Judaism can flourish within the framework of a sovereign democratic Jewish state."[74] This "situation ensures the continuation of a struggle between a determined [religious] minority and a patient, hesitant, and disunited [secular] majority."[75]

Notes

1. Charles S. Liebman and Eliezer Don-Yehiya, *Religion and Politics in Israel* (Bloomington: Indiana University Press, 1984). Unless otherwise noted, all further references to Liebman and Don-Yehiya pertain to this book.

2. Ervin Birnbaum, *The Politics of Compromise: State and Religion in Israel* (Rutherford, N.J.: Fairleigh Dickinson University Press, 1970). Unless otherwise noted, all further references to Birnbaum pertain to this book.

3. Bruce M. Borthwick, "Religion and Politics in Israel and Egypt," *Middle East Journal* 33, no. 2 (Spring 1979): 145–63.

4. Ephraim Tabory, "State and Religion: Religious Conflict Among Jews in Israel," *Journal of Church and State* 23, no. 2 (Spring 1981): 275–83. Unless otherwise noted, all further references to Tabory pertain to this article.

5. For more on religion and state in Israel, see also Amnon Rubinstein, "State and Religion in Israel," *Journal of Contemporary History* 2, no. 4 (October 1967): 107–21; Daniel J. Elazar and Janet Aviad, "Religion and Politics in Israel," in *Religion and Politics in the Middle East,* ed. Michael Curtis (Boulder, Colo.: Westview Press, 1981); Izhak England, "Law and Religion in Israel," *American Journal of Comparative Law* 35, no. 1 (Winter 1987): 185–208; Shlomo Deshen, "Israel: Searching for Identity," in *Religions and Societies: Asia and the Middle East,* ed. Carlo Caldarola, Religion and Society, no. 22 (Berlin: Mouton Publishers, 1982), 85–118; S. Clement Leslie, *The Rift in Israel: Religious Authority and Secular Democracy* (New York: Schocken Books, 1971).

6. Yael Yishai, "Health Policy and Religion: Conflict and Accommodation in Israeli Politics," *Journal of Health Politics, Policy and Law* 5, no. 3 (Fall 1980): 431–46.

7. There have been numerous articles written about the religious parties and their political influence. Among them are Atef A. Gawad, "The Growing Role of the Religious Parties in Israel," *Middle East Insight* 2 (March/April 1982): 35–41; David Nachmias, "The Right-Wing Opposition in Israel," *Political Studies* 24, no. 3 (September 1976): 268–80; Yehuda Litari, "The Fanatic Right in Israel: Linking Nationalism and Fundamentalist Religion," *Dissent* 32, no. 3 (Summer 1985): 315–19; Shimshon Zelniker and Michael Kahan, "Religion and Nascent Cleavages: The Case of Israel's National Re-

ligious Party," *Comparative Politics* 9 (October 1976): 21–48; Avishai Margalit, "Israel: The Rise of the Ultra-Orthodox," *New York Review of Books* 3 (November 9, 1989): 38–44; Jonathan Marcus, "Israel: The Politics of Piety," *World Today* 42, no. 11 (November 1986): 188–92; Matthew Nesvisky, "The Orthodox Establishment and Everyone Else," *Present Tense,* Autumn 1984: 15–19; David Biale, "Zionism, Politics, and Settlement in Israel: The Messianic Connection," *Center Magazine* 18, no. 5 (September/October 1985): 35–45; Eliezer Don-Yehiya, "Religious Leaders in the Political Arena: The Case of Israel," *Middle East Studies* 20 (April 1984): 154–71; Ian S. Lustick, *Study on Jewish Fundamentalism in Israel* (Washington, D.C.: Defense Academic Research Program, 1986); Ilan Greilsammer, "Fonctions interpretatives et representatives des partis religieux en Israel," *Revue française de science politique* 36, no. 3 (June 1986): 349–73; Rosemary Radford Ruether and Herman J. Ruether, *The Wrath of Jonah: The Crisis of Religious Nationalism in the Israeli-Palestine Conflict* (San Francisco: Harper & Row, 1989); Dan Gordon, "Limits on Extremist Political Parties: A Comparison of Israeli Jurisprudence with that of the United States and West Germany," *Hastings International and Comparative Law Review* 10, no. 2 (Winter 1987): 347–400; Alan Dowty, "Religion and Politics in Israel: No Theocracy but Growing Religious Influence," *Commonweal* 110, no. 13 (July 15, 1983): 393–96; Gary S. Schiff, *Tradition and Politics: The Religious Parties of Israel,* Modern Middle East Series, Middle East Institute, Columbia University, New York, vol. 9 (Detroit: Wayne State University Press, 1977).

8. Liebman and Don-Yehiya, *Religion and Politics,* vii–viii.

9. Ibid., 27.

10. For more on Israel's parliamentary system, see Samuel Sager, *The Parliamentary System of Israel* (Syracuse, N.Y.: Syracuse University Press, 1985).

11. Birnbaum, *Politics of Compromise,* 27–32.

12. Liebman and Don-Yehiya, *Religion and Politics,* 40.

13. Donald Eugene Smith, *Religion and Political Development* (Boston: Little, Brown, 1970), 2.

14. Ibid., 85.

15. Ibid., 91–123.

16. Ibid., 96–113.

17. Borthwick, "Religion and Politics," 147–48.

18. Ibid., 145.

19. Norman L. Zucker, *The Coming Crisis in Israel: Private Faith and Public Policy* (Cambridge, Mass.: MIT Press, 1973), 13.

20. Borthwick, "Religion and Politics," 148.

21. Ibid., 146.

22. Smith, *Religion and Political Development,* 114–17.

23. Borthwick, "Religion and Politics," 148–52.

24. Charles S. Liebman, "Religion and Political Integration in Israel," *Jewish Journal of Sociology* 17 (June 1975): 19.

25. Borthwick, "Religion and Politics," 52–53.

26. Peter L. Berger, *The Sacred Canopy: Elements of a Sociological Theory of Religion* (Garden City, N.Y.: Anchor Books, 1967, 128–35.

27. Sammy Smoocha, *Israel: Pluralism and Conflict* (London: Routledge & Kegan Paul, 1978), 73–75.

28. Elihu Katz and Michael Gurevitch, *The Secularization of Leisure: Culture and Communication in Israel* (Cambridge, Mass.: Harvard University, 1976).

29. Borthwick makes the same point.

30. More on Israel's "civil religion" may be found in Charles S. Liebman and Eliezer Don-Yehiya, "Israel's Civil Religion," *Jerusalem Quarterly*, no. 23 (Spring 1982): 57–69; and S. Daniel Breslauer, "Zionism, Judaism, and Civil Religion: Two Paradigms," *Journal of Church and State* 31, no. 2 (Spring 1989): 287–301.

31. Liebman, "Religion and Political Integration," 17–27.

32. For more detail, see *The Status of Religious Pluralism in Israel* (Jerusalem: American Jewish Committee, 1982).

33. Alan Arian, *The Choosing People: Voting Behavior in Israel* (Cleveland: Case Western Reserve University Press, 1973), 67.

34. Michael Brecher, *The Foreign Policy System of Israel: Settings, Images, Process* (Oxford: Oxford University Press, 1972), 179.

35. More on *Gush Emunim* can be found in Janet O'Dea, "Gush Emunim: Roots and Ambiguities," *Forum on the Jewish People* 25 (1976): 39–50; Kevin A. Avruch, "Traditionalizing Israeli Nationalism: The Development of Gush Emunim," *Political Psychology* 1, no. 1 (Spring 1979): 47–57; Kevin A. Avruch, "Gush Emunim: The 'Iceberg Model' of Extremism Reconsidered," *Middle East Review* 21 (Fall 1988): 27–33; Kevin A. Avruch, "Gush Emunim: Politics, Religion and Ideology in Israel," *Middle East Review* 11, no. 2 (1978): 26–31; Ehud Sprinzak, "Gush Emunim: The Iceberg Model of Political Extremism," in *The Impact of Gush Emunim: Politics and Settlement in the West Bank*, ed. David Newman (New York: St. Martin's Press, 1985); Ehud Sprinzak, *Fundamentalism, Terrorism, and Democracy: The Case of the Gush Emunim Underground*, Occasional Paper, no. 4 (Washington, D.C.: Wilson Center, 1986).

36. S. Zalman Abramov, *Perpetual Dilemma: Jewish Religion in the Jewish State* (Jerusalem: World Union for Progressive Judaism, 1976), 400–402.

37. Simon N. Herman, *Israelis and Jews: The Continuity of an Identity* (Philadelphia: Jewish Publication Society of America, 1971), 106.

38. Tabory, "State and Religion," 283.

39. Martin Seliger, "Positions and Dispositions in Israeli Politics," *Government and Opposition* 3 (Autumn 1968): 465–84.

40. Yishai, "Health Policy and Religion," 431–46.

For more on the abortion issue in Israel, see, for instance, Zeev W. Falk, "The New Abortion Law of Israel," *Israel Law Review* 13 (1978): 103–10; Roberto Bachi, "Abortion in Israel," in *Abortion in a Changing World*, vol. 1, ed. Robert E. Hall (New York: Columbia University Press, 1970): 274–83; Fred Rosner, "The Jewish Attitude toward Abortion," *Tradition* 10 (Winter 1968): 48–71. On the autopsy issue, see, for example, Yael Yishai, "Autopsy in Israel: Political Pressures and Medical Policy," *Ethics in Science and Medicine* 6 (1979): 11–20.

41. Concerning the demographic issue in Israel, see Dov Friedlander, "Israel," in *Population Policy in Developed Countries,* ed. Bernard Berelson (New York: McGraw-Hill, 1974), 42–97.

42. Yishai, "Health Policy and Religion," 442.

43. Regarding this facet of Israeli politics, see Emanual Gutmann, "Religion in Israeli Politics," in *Man, State and Society in the Contemporary Middle East,* ed. Jacob M. Landau (London: Pall Mall, 1972), 122–34.

44. For more on the concept of intensive minority, see Robert A. Dahl, *A Preface to Democratic Theory* (Chicago: University of Chicago Press, 1956).

45. Yishai, "Health Policy and Religion," 443–45.

46. Ibid., 431.

47. Don Peretz and Sammy Smoocha, "Israel's Twelfth Knesset Election: An All-Loser Game," *Middle East Journal* 43, no. 3 (Summer 1989): 401, 389.

48. For more about the four religious parties, see Peretz Kidron, "A Guide to Israel's Religious Parties," *Middle East International,* no. 372 (March 30, 1990): 4. "The so-called 'bloc' of religious parties is in fact divided into four parliamentary factions, each representing a coalition of conflicting sub-factions and groups loyal to different rabbis."

49. For more information on the impact of religion on politics during the 1988 election campaign, see Robert O. Freedman, "Religion, Politics, and the Israeli Elections of 1988," *Middle East Journal* 43, no. 3 (Summer 1989): 406–22, particularly 421–22.

50. Rosalie Beck and David W. Hendon, "Notes on Church-State Affairs: Israel," *Journal of Church and State* 31, no. 2 (Spring 1989): 338.

51. Regarding the complex parliamentary negotiating process, see, for example, Birnbaum, *Politics of Compromise,* 31–32.

52. Peretz and Smoocha, "Israel's Twelfth Knesset Election," 404–5. An excellent historical overview of proposed electoral reform is provided by Avraham Brichta, "Forty Years of Struggle for Electoral Reform in Israel, 1948–1988," *Middle East Review* 21, no. 1 (Fall 1988): 18–25.

53. Peretz and Smoocha, "Israel's Twelfth Knesset Election," 399–401.

54. For more on Peres's attempts to form a government, see *New York Times,* March 21, 1990, A5; *New York Times,* March 22, 1990, A16; *Wall Street Journal,* March 22, 1990, A11.

55. Regarding Bush's remarks, see also *U.S. News & World Report,* March 26, 1990, 32–33; and *Wall Street Journal,* March 14, 1990, A16.

56. *New York Times,* March 14, 1990, A1; and *New York Times,* March 16, 1990, A1.

57. For more on the no-confidence vote and the demise of the unity government, see *New York Times,* March 14, 1990, A1; and *New York Times,* March 16, 1990, A1; "Israel: The Government Takes a Fall," *Time,* March 26, 1990, 28; "Israel's 'Week of Hell': For the First Time in 42 Years, a Government Falls," *Newsweek,* March 26, 1990, 28; "Shamir Loses Confidence Vote, Israeli Government Falls," *Facts on File* 50, no. 2573 (March 16, 1990), 171–72.

58. *Time,* March 26, 1990, 28.

59. *New York Times,* April 12, 1990, A3; *Washington Post,* April 12, 1990, 1, 40; *Washington Times,* April 12, 1990, 1, 6.

60. *Washington Times,* April 26, 1990, 1, 6. All these events received front-page coverage in the *Jerusalem Post,* International ed., for the following dates: March 3, 10, 17, 24, 31, and April 7, 14, 21, 28, 1990.

61. *Washington Post,* April 12, 1990, A1, A40.

62. *Jerusalem Post,* May 5, 1990, 1, International ed.; *Jerusalem Post,* May 12, 1990, 1, International ed.

63. *Washington Times,* April 27, 1990, 1, 10.

64. *Jerusalem Post,* April 2, 1990, 24.

65. David Makovsky, "Israel's Soap-Opera Politics," *U.S. News & World Report,* April 2, 1990, 38. Peretz and Smoocha argue, however, that even reform of the electoral system still would not resolve the political stalemate, since the deep divisions among the Right, the Left, and religious factions within the Israeli body politic would still remain, as reflected, for example, in the returns of the 1988 national election (p. 405).

66. *Los Angeles Times,* April 26, 1990, A7.

67. *Wall Street Journal,* April 27, 1990, A6.

68. *Los Angeles Times,* April 29, 1990, A16.

69. *New York Times,* April 28, 1990, A3.

70. *New York Times,* April 27, 1990, A15.

71. Peretz and Smoocha, "Israel's Twelfth Knesset Election," 405.

72. Rubinstein, "State and Religion in Israel," 107.

73. Carlo Caldarola, "Introduction," in *Religion and Societies: Asia and the Middle East,* ed. Carlo Caldarola, Religion and Society, no. 22 (Berlin: Mouton Publishers, 1982), 33.

74. Zucker, *Crisis in Israel,* 2–4.

75. Rubinstein, "State and Religion in Israel," 120–21.

9.

The Muslim Brotherhood in Egypt: Reform or Revolution?

ANN M. LESCH

The elections to the Egyptian Peoples Assembly on April 6, 1987, marked a critical breakthrough for the Muslim Brotherhood. Thirty-six Islamists won seats. Although the ruling National Democratic party retained a commanding majority with 78 percent of the contested seats, that represented a distinct drop from the 87 percent gained in the parliamentary election of 1984. Moreover, the secular-liberal New Wafd party's representation shrank from 13 percent in 1984 to 8 percent in 1987, in part because the Muslim Brotherhood defected from its 1984 electoral alliance with the Wafd. Instead, the brotherhood became the dominant partner in an alliance with the Labor and Liberal parties. Islamist candidates were positioned at the top of the electoral lists and Islamic slogans and banners festooned the rallies and posters. On their own, Labor and Liberal would not have won any seats in the assembly, as they had failed to do in 1984. Teamed with the brotherhood, they gained 14 percent. That was a striking achievement for the brotherhood, an organization that lacked official registration as either a social institution or a political party.

The Brotherhood under the Monarchy

The emergence of the Muslim Brotherhood as a significant force in the parliamentary arena occurred on the sixtieth anniversary of the founding of the society in Ismailiyya. That town was a foreign enclave, administered by French interests and guarded by the British army, since it served as the headquarters for the lucrative Suez Canal Company. The twenty-two-year-old teacher Hasan al-Banna, who was already active in efforts to promote Islamic values and to counter Christian missionaries' influence, was shocked at the European domination in Ismailiyya and receptive to the idea proposed by a handful of associates to form a society that would seek a "practical path which will lead to the glory of Islam and the welfare of the Muslim people."[1]

Banna linked his concern for moral rejuvenation with his determination to end foreign domination. The Muslim Brotherhood could lead the way to a rejuvenated and righteous society by providing tangible "good works" for the Egyptian people and working toward an Islamic polity. The Muslim Brotherhood established social and educational programs that met a serious need at a time when the government did not provide welfare benefits, and public education was woefully inadequate.[2] Banna constructed a mosque, girls' school, boys' technical institute, and medical clinic in Ismailiyya, supplemented by a soup kitchen and the provision of money and clothing for the poor. By 1949, the division of charity and social services in the brotherhood had five hundred branches with a wide array of activities. One clinic in Cairo, for example, assisted 51,300 patients in 1947. The affiliated Muslim Sisters had a parallel set of activities, and the Workers Section provided health and disability benefits as well as aid to widows and the aged for Brothers who were employed in industry.[3] The brotherhood pressed the government to provide minimum wages and guarantees of employment and promotion, to hasten the Egyptianization of the economy, and to undertake large-scale development projects such as a high dam at Aswan.

The socioeconomic programs were not ends in themselves. They ideally would lead to the creation of a harmonious Islamic society in which the upper class would not exploit the poor, the manager would not oppress the worker, and the profit would be tempered by piety and good works. The Islamic state that would emerge from that society would combine social solidarity with a genuine democracy. Banna likened such a polity to the mosque: the mosque belongs to God, and all believers are equal before God and form an equal and compact mass behind the *imam* (prayer leader). The mosque embodies unity and order. However, if the *imam* stumbles or makes a mistake, all those rowed behind him "have the imperative duty to tell him of his error in order to put him back on the right road."[4] The *imam* must accept their advice. Translated into political terms, the ruler is responsible before God and his people. He has a contract to protect their interests and is accountable to them. The form of rule is not so important as long as the ruler is incorruptible and accountable, and the nation is united in its basic purposes.[5] In the long run, an Islamic League of Nations would be formed, encompassing all rightly guided countries, and the league would choose a caliph by consensus. Reviving the caliphate would restore the symbol of Islamic unity.[6]

In the late 1930s, as Banna gradually built the movement, he argued for patience and the careful preparation of the steps toward creating an Islamic system. However, his construction of a strict hierarchical order, with small cohesive cells (known as families) at the base and affiliated groups of paramilitary scouts, caused concern among the other political groups. Youth affiliated with the brotherhood clashed with rival groups linked to the Wafd and Young Egypt. Moreover, Banna's attack on the terms of the Anglo-Egyptian Treaty of 1936 and his outspoken criticism of the continuing British presence caused the British to intern him from May 1941 to February 1942, as a threat to the Allied war effort.

The arrest apparently marked a turning point in Banna's approach. He was released by the Wafd government, which acceded to his demands to prohibit alcoholic beverages, ban prostitution, and close down gambling houses, in return for which Banna agreed not to run for Parliament from Ismailiyya.[7] Nonetheless, he founded the underground "secret apparatus" to prepare for a violent showdown with the British forces and the Egyptian regime. The secret apparatus orchestrated bombings of British clubs during World War II and assassinated Egyptian officials—including a judge and a police chief—in 1948. Although the brotherhood had gained esteem from its participation in the fighting in Palestine in 1947–48, its resort to internal violence and its attacks on corruption in the palace led to a showdown with the regime. The government banned the brotherhood in December 1948, closed its headquarters and branches, confiscated its accounts, and froze its funds. The secret apparatus retaliated immediately by assassinating the prime minister, Fahmy al-Nuqrashy Pasha. Hasan al-Banna, in turn, was assassinated on government orders on February 12, 1949. The brotherhood, based on concepts of social justice and solidarity, was decimated in a paroxysm of violence.

One careful observer of the brotherhood speculated as to the route that Banna might have taken if he had not had the premature confrontation with the British in 1941 and had been elected to Parliament in 1942:[8]

He could have followed a conventional path to power within the framework of government institutions; his "religious association" would have become a formal political party; and he might, just possibly, have gained control of the government by constitutional means. . . . He could then have tried to establish the Islamic state which he had long advocated. But as it was, he remained outside the government . . . and his Brotherhood gradually turned into a subversive organization.

Those observations point to a basic dilemma in assessing the brotherhood and an inherent tension within the movement. The brotherhood sought a long-term sociopolitical transformation, but faced short-term realities that contradicted those aims. When blocked by the external and internal power structure in Egypt, its members became impatient with the gradualist approach. The idea of an immediate violent transformation became credible and attractive to the most ideologically committed members. Instead of letting the situation ripen, the Brothers forced the issue. Their tactics discredited them in the public eye and weakened their ability to turn to their advantage the political situation that emerged following the Free Officers coup d'état on July 23, 1952.

The Nasser Era

The Muslim Brotherhood registered as an association for the first time in 1951, a move that enabled the Wafd government to release its members from jail. They resumed many social programs and played a leading role in the guerrilla operations against the British in the Suez Canal Zone. They were, however, seriously weakened by the death of Banna and the contest of leadership, particularly between a founder of the secret apparatus, Salih Mustafa al-Ashmawi, and the former legal advisor to Banna, Judge Hasan Ismail al-Hudaybi. The selection of Hudaybi as general guide in October 1951 was viewed by the Ashmawi faction as a capitulation to the Wafd government. Moreover, the brotherhood was no longer influential in the student and worker movements[9] and remained peripheral to the secret plans of the Free Officers.

Nonetheless, the Brothers quickly sought to assume ideological leadership over the Free Officers. Hudaybi and the Guidance Council not only pressed for representation in the government but also issued a list of requested reforms.[10] They ranged from a purge of the political system and promulgation of a new constitution to land reform, revised labor legislation, and Egyptianization of the National Bank. The capstone was the demand to implement *Shari'a* (Islamic law), which would be accompanied by banning alcohol, gambling, nightclubs, immoral films, and antireligious books. Colonel Gamal Abdul Nasser apparently told Hudaybi that those reforms were far too comprehensive to be implemented at once. He singled out *Shari'a* as particularly difficult to institute immediately.[11] But the Free Officers did not want to antagonize the brotherhood and so they released some members from prison, reopened the investigation into Banna's assassination, and invited the Brothers to provide three ministers for the first cabinet. The relationship cooled when they could not agree on the names of ministers and when the Free Officers pointedly rejected guardianship by the Muslim Brotherhood, in the form of consultation prior to issuing laws. One senior Brother asserted that he would base his support for the regime on the implementation of *Shari'a,* an indication that confrontation was possible and that the Brothers thought they had the popular support to win a showdown.[12]

The Free Officers wanted to avoid a direct clash, since they were preoccupied with taking steps to abolish the monarchy, annul the Parliament, close political parties, and arrest politicians from the Wafd. The brotherhood could object neither to those actions nor to the government's sweeping social reforms. Labor laws, social insurance, agricultural reform, and the expansion of health and educational services to the poor were measures that they had espoused for many years. However, those reforms began to undercut the brotherhood's base of support. The urban lower and lower-middle classes, which had welcomed the brotherhood's social aid programs in the past, now had an alternative support system to which they could turn. Moreover, Nasser's establishment of the Liberation Rally, with its branches throughout the country and its effort to mobilize youth in social action projects, threatened to compete with the brotherhood.[13] The first clash between the two groups took place in January 1954 on the Cairo University campus. Nasser promptly clamped Hudaybi, Ashmawi, and 450 other Brothers in jail.

Having lost the first round, the brotherhood tried to recoup by supporting General Muhammad Naguib in his power struggle with Nasser during February and March 1954. But Nasser released the January detainees, thereby inducing Hudaybi to withdraw his support from Naguib.[14] The accord was short-lived. Nasser signed a new treaty with Britain on October 19 that provided for their troops' withdrawal from the Suez Canal within two years but included a clause permitting them to return under certain conditions. The brotherhood denounced Nasser as an agent of British imperialism, no better than the dethroned king. That criticism hit a sensitive spot and appeared to turn public opinion away from the young officers. When a gunman attempted to assassinate Nasser on October 26, blame was quickly placed on the secret apparatus of the brotherhood. Thousands were arrested, Naguib was confined to his home, and the brotherhood was dissolved. Six senior members were executed for treason, and more than eight hundred were sentenced to long terms in jail. They included Hudaybi and Ashmawi.

Nasser's move undermined the principal mass organization that challenged his rule. Once again, the Brothers miscalculated their power. They had demanded a controlling voice in the new government and then had pressed toward confrontation. If they had followed through more systematically in supporting Naguib, they might have tipped the balance in his favor. The assassination attempt, however, shifted the moral force to Nasser's side and gave him the excuse to decapitate the movement.

The second crackdown in less than a decade led to a profound crisis within the brotherhood. Members sought to examine the causes of their failure and reached sharply diverging conclusions. A relatively small number decided that they should accommodate to Nasserism.[15] Although they objected to the secular bases of his rule and to his imposition of state control over the religious institutions, including al-Azhar and the courts, they found promise in his social reform program. Moreover, they supported his plan to construct the Aswan High Dam, his nationalization of the Suez Canal in July 1956, and his showdown with the Israeli, British, and French forces that autumn. They backed the strengthening of the armed forces and the promotion of Arab nationalism. This group established itself as the New Muslim Brotherhood in December 1958. In return, the government improved their conditions in jail and released some of them early.

The central trend, supported by the underground Guidance Council, the Muslim Sisters, and the sympathetic Muslim Women's Society led by Zeinab al-Ghazali, maintained that the brotherhood should concentrate on developing a truly comprehensive program concerning Islamic education, social structure, and legislation. They argued that their lack of preparation in specific alternatives had harmed them when the Revolution took place in 1952. With a ready-made plan for an Islamic curriculum or well-formulated measures related to *Shari'a*, they could have had a substantive impact on the actions of the Free Officers.[16] In the late 1950s, Ghazali and the Guidance Council initiated research and study groups to develop a program of Islamic education that they would implement over a thirteen-year period, corresponding to the thirteen years that Muhammad spent in spreading the faith in Mecca. At the end, they would survey the Egyptian public: if 75 percent wanted Islamic rule, they would demand the immediate establishment of an Islamic state. If only 25 percent favored that, they would work another thirteen years to convince people. That cautious, low-keyed approach was appropriate to the straitened circumstances in which the Brothers found themselves. The approach also reflected Banna's view that Egyptian society was receptive to Islamic concepts, despite the secularism of the government.

A third approach was conceptualized by Sayyid Qutb, a leading Islamist thinker who was jailed from 1954 to 1964. His essays charted a course for the Islamic movement in an era of persecution.[17] Although Qutb supported the education program outlined by the Guidance Council, he was fundamentally pessimistic about the prospects for gradual, peaceful change. Qutb maintained that Egyptian society had fallen into a *jahili* (ignorant) condition, resembling the period prior to Islam. However, this era was worse than the pre-Islamic era in that the people had knowingly deviated from the path prescribed in the Qur'an and the *Hadith* (sayings of the Prophet). Some had even fallen into *takfir* (unbelief) by following "human gods,"[18] an implied reference to the adulation accorded Nasser. Some thought that the people could be provided with their material needs without meeting their spiritual needs. Given the depth of this decline, mere reforms would not suffice:[19]

> The old system which was built in the Jahiliyya . . . cannot remain . . . nor can it be patched up by the Islamic vision. Rather, a total shaking and destruction of the old system is necessary that it may be rebuilt according to the new plan and the new design. . . . There is a difference between having a certain design for a building you want to erect little by little and the repair of an existent building which is built according to a different plan. Repairs will not in the end give you a new building.

The only way to transform the social and political system, Qutb believed, was to establish *jama'at* (societies) of believers, who would live according to the precepts of the faith and confront the pressures of the *jahili* society surrounding them:[20]

When the number of Believers reaches three, then this faith tells them: "Now you are a community, a distinct Islamic community, distinct from the jahili society which does not live according to this belief or accept its basic premise." Now the Islamic society has come into existence. These three individuals increase to ten, the ten to a hundred, the hundred to a thousand, and the thousand increase to 12,000—and the Islamic society grows and becomes established. . . . [Meanwhile] a struggle would already have started within the jahili society.

Qutb believed that the Islamic vanguard would suffer torture and death in its struggle with the *jahili* society. In the long run, it would be victorious and would totally transform the system. He argued that efforts should focus on purifying the individual and restoring the Islamic beliefs rather than detailing the nature of that future Islamic system. He criticized movements that placed so much stress on social programs that they lost sight of spiritual needs and the duty to institute *Shari'a*.[21]

Finally, some members of the brotherhood believed that sabotage, assassination, and coups d'état were the only way to alter the political reality and install an Islamic government. Elements of the secret apparatus were involved in this group, which planned to overthrow the government, drew maps, and smuggled in arms. Their plans were apparently known to Qutb and the Guidance Council, although their approach deviated from the long-term educational program that the council had articulated. Moreover, Qutb sent a message from prison urging them to cancel the plots, both on the grounds that the violence would be futile and that a coup d'état was not the appropriate means.[22]

Nevertheless, those strands converged in mid-1964 when Qutb and a substantial number of Brothers were released from prison in a general amnesty that also encompassed political activists on the Left. Qutb quickly assumed the intellectual leadership of the movement and sought to concentrate on the long-term educational plan in order to build the nuclei of an Islamic community.[23] But the government uncovered the sabotage network in August 1965 and rearrested thousands of Brothers, accusing them of plotting a coup. Qutb, charged with masterminding the plot, was hanged in September 1966.

Once again the contradictory tendencies within the brotherhood had caused its demise. The trend that sought a long-term transformation was contradicted by the desire for immediate revenge against the government. Impatience and failure to adhere to a comprehensive strategy damaged the brotherhood in the late 1940s, just as the monarchical system disintegrated. In 1965–66 the crackdown came shortly before Egypt experienced a profound national trauma that inadvertently helped to make the climate more receptive to Islamist thought.

The Sadat Era

The Israeli defeat of Egypt's army in June 1967 caused a profound shock. The illusions of military strength, economic transformation, and Arab unity crumbled overnight. Some Egyptians argued that they had been defeated because they had not completed the socialist transformation or because they had not closed the technological gap with Israel.[24] Others attributed the defeat to a lack of piety: Qutb's warning about worshiping false gods resonated in the public mind. Members of the brotherhood charged that the defeat was God's revenge for Nasser's oppression of the Egyptian people and for aligning the country to the atheist Soviet Union to advance his secular, materialist interests. Even those who questioned such sweeping charges turned to religion: faith can help to sustain people in times of crisis.

With Nasser's death in September 1970, the political climate changed markedly. Anwar Sadat sought to build new bases of power, in part to undermine the power of rivals who saw themselves as the true heirs of Nasser. He cultivated support from the rural notables who predominated in the Peoples Assembly and had suffered from the Nasserist land reform; encouraged the private entrepreneurs who had been battered by the socialization measures and the postwar austerity; and built up the professionalism of the armed forces, whose officers chafed under the humiliation of the 1967 defeat and the embarrassment of the war in Yemen. Sadat also released members of the Muslim Brotherhood from jail and invited them to help draft a new constitution, promulgated in May 1971. One clause referred to *Shari'a* as "a source" of legislation.[25] As the de-Nasserization campaign swelled, Sadat increasingly invoked religious symbols. He called himself the "believing" president, code-named the October War of 1973 "Badr" in symbolic reference to the Prophet's victorious battle in 624 A.D., and did not scoff at the idea that the improved military performance in that war was due to renewed faith, rather than improved thinking.[26]

In that relatively receptive atmosphere, the Muslim Brotherhood found three routes to influence: through the parliamentary process, through the press and publishing houses, and through the Islamic student movement in the universities.

Sadat undermined the control of the single party, the Arab Socialist Union, by first allowing independents to run for Parliament and then by permitting political parties to compete for seats. Some prominent associates of the Muslim Brotherhood were elected as individuals, including such MPs who won in 1987 as Shaykh Salah Abu Ismail and Hasan al-Gamal. They pressed for Islamic regulations: the prohibition of alcoholic beverages; the establishment of dress codes for women in universities and workplaces; the separation of men and women in public transportation and schools; the prohibition of usury; a ban on female private secretaries and stewardesses; and a ban on male hairdressers working in salons for women.[27]

Although the government bottled up those proposals in committees, Sadat charged the legislative committee with examining all the existing laws to ascertain whether they conformed to *Shari'a*. That move pleased the brotherhood but agitated the Coptic community.[28] When the Justice Ministry began to draft laws in 1977 to institute *hudud* (prescribed forms of punishment), ban usury, and execute any person who renounced Islam, the Coptic pope Shenouda III led his community in a five-day protest fast. Sadat hastily withdrew the bill on apostasy, and discussion of implementing *hudud* was silenced. The brotherhood thus found Parliament a partially satisfactory forum in which to air its views. But the Brothers could not have a decisive impact. The size of their representation was also limited by the parties law, which banned the establishment of parties based on religion. That measure had been instituted to prevent a potentially divisive clash between Islamic and Christian parties.

The second route proved highly successful.[29] A long-established theological journal, *al-I'tisam* (Perseverance), issued by the *Shari'a* Society, began to espouse brotherhood views. Moreover, Sadat allowed *al-Da'wa* (The call) to resume publication in June 1976, after a twelve-year absence, under Salih al-Ashmawi, the previous editor. Publishing houses attached to those newspapers issued editions of Banna's writings, Qutb's essays, and current analyses. Cassette tapes of popular preachers were sold inexpensively at kiosks on street corners. Even though the Brothers remained illegal, their publications spread their message widely in a society that was receptive to religious perspectives.

Third, the Islamic societies (*al-jama'at al-islamiyya*) among students at the universities indirectly helped the brotherhood to influence the thinking of the youth.[30] Sadat allowed those societies to flourish in the early 1970s as a counter to the left-wing and Nasserist youth movements. By 1976–77 they controlled most student unions and dominated the National Student Union. The Islamic societies tried to alter some of the practices on campus: they insisted on setting aside rooms for prayer, sometimes stopped classes at prayer time, and pressured female and male students to sit on different sides of the lecture halls. They also provided Islamic dresses at low prices for female students, chartered special buses to transport female students, organized Islamic literary exhibits, and subsidized textbooks, lecture notes, and Islamic books. Through their control of the student unions they organized summer camps that combined sports activities with religious indoctrination. The brotherhood, however, could not control the Islamic societies directly. They had their own leaders and own agenda. Nonetheless, the Brothers sought to provide guidance and support for the societies' activities. Some activists—such as the medical student Essam al-Iryan and the geologist Muhammad Habib—came under the brotherhood umbrella after graduation and were elected to Parliament under its aegis in 1987.

In pursuing the triple routes of Parliament, the press, and mobilization of the youth, the brotherhood sought legitimacy and respectability. The leaders emphasized that they renounced violence and sabotage. They indicated that they had returned to the populist approach of Banna in the 1930s and canceled the charge of *takfir* that Qutb had leveled against the society in the 1960s. Consequently, the brotherhood denounced the coup d'état attempted by a group linked to the Liberation party (*Hizb al-Tahrir*) in 1974 and decried the actions of *al-Takfir wal-Hijra* (generally, but inaccurately, translated as Repentance and Holy Flight) in 1977.[31] The first group had declared that it must remove the ungodly government that was turning to the West and seeking peace with Israel. The second group revived Qutb's call for the establishment of *jama'at* that would serve as the vanguard in the struggle against the *jahili* society. Its founder, Ahmad Shukri Mustafa, was a former Muslim Brother who had been jailed from 1965 to 1971. He organized *al-Takfir wal-Hijra* as a tightly knit group, containing nearly five thousand persons by 1977. Following a violent showdown with the government that July, more than four hundred were arrested and Mustafa was executed after a military court trial.

The Muslim Brothers explicitly criticized the ideological framework of *al-Takfir wal-Hijra*. They argued that no one has the right to judge others as unbelievers (i.e., *takfir*), but only to counsel and advise. Moreover, believers should not separate themselves from the society (i.e., *hijra*) but must work from within to reform the society. They thereby divorced themselves decisively from the logic of Qutb's thinking. Nonetheless, the Brothers also criticized the government for overreacting to Mustafa's group. They feared that Sadat would tar all the Islamists with the same brush.

In fact, tension grew between Sadat and the Islamist trend after 1977. Sadat tightened political life in general after the food riots of January 1977 and in the face of mounting criticism of his peace initiatives with Israel. The New Wafd party shut down after only three months and left-wing Tagammu's newspaper was closed after six months. A hastily called parliamentary election in 1979 excluded Tagammu and the most outspoken independent MPs. Even the Labor party, created as a loyal opposition in 1978, decried Sadat's foreign policy and criticized his economic measures, embodied in the Open Door (*infitah*) policy.

The Muslim Brotherhood's tacit coexistence with Sadat frayed. The leadership had supported Sadat's curtailing of the Left and the Nasserists, his break with Moscow, his ties with conservative Arab monarchies, and his privatization of the economy. Many Brothers had become prosperous businessmen, with ties to Saudi Arabia. However, they strongly opposed other policies: the opening of Egypt to Western economic and cultural influence, the close ties with the United States, and especially the peace treaty with Israel. The brotherhood viewed Israel as an illegitimate state, established on land usurped from the Muslims; only war would return Palestine to the Muslim world.[32] The Brothers' criticism of the treaty was intensified by the break that it caused in Egypt's relations with the Arab world, including Saudi Arabia. The brotherhood's dream of a Muslim alliance to counter the triple enemies—capitalism, communism, and Zionism—was demonstrably thwarted by Sadat's actions. A final blow occurred in March 1980 when Sadat allowed the deposed Shah of Iran to settle in Cairo, despite public enthusiasm for the Islamic Revolution in Tehran.

Sadat's curtailment of the Islamic student movement irritated the brotherhood. Sadat placed security guards on the campuses and dissolved the National Student Union in 1979. By then its leaders had called on him to end the "state of jahili injustice, corruption and nepotism . . . and [to implement] Islamic Sharia in all the economic, political, and social legislative aspects of life."[33] The brotherhood also found their influence limited in the Peoples Assembly. Although Article 2 of the Constitution was amended in May 1980 to make *Shari'a* the only source of legislation, specific measures to implement that were blocked. Moreover, such antithetical laws as revision of the personal status code were implemented over the Brothers' objections. Islamist intellectuals even asserted that Sadat was preventing democratization: under Islamic *shura* (consensus), the ruler is held accountable, whereas Sadat was above criticism.[34]

The brotherhood, however, did not court a showdown with Sadat. They had business interests to protect and remembered vividly the years of repression under Nasser. Despite their frank criticism in *al-Da'wa,* they did not deliberately foment violence. General Guide Umar al-Tilmissani tried to calm the atmosphere when Muslim-Coptic tension flared into violent attacks on Christian property. But the brotherhood was caught up in Sadat's sweeping arrests in September 1981. Sadat jailed some fifteen hundred of his political opponents, who ranged from secular leaders of Tagammu, Wafd, and the bar association to the heads of the brotherhood (including Tilmissani) and a large number of Islamic militants. Coptic activists were also detained and Pope Shenouda III was exiled to a monastery in the desert.

Sadat signed his death sentence with those sweeping arrests. *Al-Jihad,* an underground Islamist organization, began to plot his assassination. *Al-Jihad* had been established by young university graduates, influenced by the campus *jama'at* and espousing Qutb's beliefs. A key leader, Abd al-Salam Farag, wrote in *al-Farida al-Gha'iba* (The absent obligation) that the current Muslim rulers were *takfir* and the minority of believers had the right to impose their will by force (*jihad*) on the majority.[35] Farag disagreed with Shukri Mustafa's belief in *hijra* (flight) from the *jahili* society, but rather sought to confront the unbelievers head on. The *Jihad* group also attacked Coptic property and plotted to kill Pope Shenouda. They argued that the Copts sought a separate Christian state, along the lines of the Maronite forces in Lebanon. Although *al-Jihad* was small, two leaders served in the armed forces. They had access to the parade grounds on October 6, 1981, and carried out their bold plot to kill the president.

Political Participation under Mubarak

The Muslim Brotherhood emerged relatively unscathed from the assassination of Sadat and Husni Mubarak's succession. Mubarak sought to control the militant Islamist groups through the security forces and the emergency laws. But he differentiated between the underground groups and nonviolent critics. He avoided Sadat's excesses and reasserted the rule of law and parliamentary processes. He released the political prisoners, including Tilmissani, and allowed Islamist journals to resume publication. Shenouda returned from internal exile and regained his position as the Coptic pope. Moreover, Mubarak did not challenge the court decision that allowed the New Wafd to return to the political arena. When elections were held for the Peoples Assembly in May 1984, the Wafd was the only opposition party to win seats. Even though it had but four months to prepare for the campaign, the cachet of its prerevolutionary name attracted support from a wide range of voters.

The Muslim Brotherhood lent its support to the Wafd in the campaign, and eight Islamists won seats through the joint list. Since the new electoral law banned nonparty candidates, the brotherhood was compelled to link itself to a registered party if it wanted to contest the elections. The Wafd was the only opposition party apt to win seats, and therefore joining forces was a plus tactically. Moreover, the brotherhood's grass-roots supporters could assist the Wafd in the campaign and bolster its votes. The alliance, however, seemed ideologically incongruent: in the past the Wafd had upheld national unity and liberal democracy, whereas the brotherhood sought Islamic rule and had questioned the tenets of both liberalism and democracy.

In practice, there was a logic to the electoral alliance. The Wafd viewed itself as an umbrella organization under which a wide range of ideological trends could be encompassed. When revived briefly in 1978, Wafdist MPs ranged from the Marxist lawyer Ahmad Taha to the Islamist Shaykh Salah Abu Ismail. Abu Ismail served informally as the Wafd spokesman in the Peoples Assembly and he pressed for the electoral alliance in 1984. Moreover, the two groups pointed to periods of cooperation in 1942–44 and 1950–51, and they shared a common hostility to the July Revolution. They agreed on the importance of bolstering the private sector and economic ties with the Arab world, and they both criticized the peace treaty with Israel. Nonetheless, the alliance was fundamentally opportunistic: it provided a means for both to ensure representation in Parliament.

The Wafd maintained the upper hand in the alliance.[36] Brothers were not admitted into the Wafd's decision-making bodies and only eighteen of the seventy candidates that they sought were accepted onto the Wafd list. Although the electoral program asserted support for the constitutional stipulations that Islam is the religion of the state and that the principles of Islamic law are the main source of legislation, the program also emphasized the importance of providing justice for both Muslims and non-Muslims. And Wafd leaders insisted that the implementation of *Shari'a* could only take place with the concurrence of the Copts.

The alliance began to fray within weeks of the election. Some Brothers had criticized the relationship from the start, as had many Wafdists. Coptic supporters were particularly dismayed at the ties to an Islamist movement. In mid-June, Tilmissani stated bluntly that the brotherhood had entered Parliament to put into effect Article 2 of the Constitution, which referred to *Shari'a.* The Brothers were not interested in other issues, he stated.[37] By September, he was fulminating against the hypocrisy of party leaders: in their campaigns they promised to implement *Shari'a* and when they took the oath as MPs they swore to uphold the Constitution, but now they refused to implement the law of God. Applying *Shari'a* would eliminate social differences and decrease crime, extremism, and bureaucratic problems since the people would unhesitatingly follow God's commands rather than laws issued by humans. The devil caused the delay in applying *Shari'a,* Tilmissani concluded.[38]

Shaykh Abu Ismail was also irritated by the Wafd, especially when the party leaders bypassed him in selecting their spokesman in the assembly. The secular lawyer Mumtaz Nassar became Wafd spokesman and head of the opposition. Within a year, Abu Ismail stormed out of the Wafd, charging that its leaders were treasonous liars who pretended to be religious but really mocked the word of God.[39] He claimed that the Wafd had stabbed him in the back: when he collected signatures from MPs to support *Shari'a* and when he spoke up in the assembly for *Shari'a,* Nassar and the other Wafdists refused to back him. They asserted that he was speaking merely as an individual.

Abu Ismail tried unsuccessfully to form his own party and then joined the virtually moribund Liberal Socialist party, which had received less than 1 percent of the votes in 1984. Abu Ismail became the second-in-command and radically reoriented the party's newspaper. He later stated bluntly that he had replaced the Nasserist editor of *al-Ahrar* with an Islamist, convinced the party to drop "socialist" from its name, and persuaded the leaders to denounce the peace treaty with Israel. Thus, he had "purified it of its negative aspects."[40] Cynical observers termed it a takeover deal: Abu Ismail bought out the newspaper, the party's only tangible asset, to ensure a public platform for his views.[41]

Meanwhile, Ibrahim Shukri, the secretary general of the Labor party, wooed the Muslim Brotherhood. He felt humiliated at accepting three parliamentary seats on the basis of appointment by Mubarak, since the party failed to attain enough votes on its own. Shukri allegedly approached Tilmissani immediately after the 1984 election to win him away from the Wafd. Moreover, he appointed Adel Hussein editor of the party newspaper, *al-Sha'ab,* in late 1984, in part to build bridges to the brotherhood.[42]

When Tilmissani died in 1986, the brotherhood's general guide, Hamid Abul Nasr, brought new people into the Guidance Council. They were impatient with the Wafd alliance. The Labor and Liberal parties were attractive targets because they were weaker and potentially more malleable than the Wafd. The triple alliance formed in February 1987 had its roots in those prior contacts.

The brotherhood outmaneuvered Shukri in setting the terms of the alliance, thereby becoming the dominant partner. Shukri had sought a comprehensive alliance that would include the Wafd and Tagammu as well as Labor, Liberal, and the brotherhood.[43] Shukri felt that a broad electoral bloc was the only means to confront the governing National Democratic party. When the Wafd decided to run alone, Shukri offered to host an alliance of the remaining parties. But ideological tension between Tagammu and the brotherhood prevented their running under the same umbrella. That left three groups in the potential alliance. The brotherhood and the Abu Ismail–dominated Liberal party insisted that the formula for composing the joint list be based on forty percent brotherhood, forty percent Labor, and twenty percent Liberal, a formula that wildly overrepresented the Liberals and tipped the balance to the Islamist side.

When Ma'mun al-Hudaybi and other Brothers threatened to bolt the alliance and return to the Wafd, Shukri capitulated to their terms. He even agreed that half of the number one slots on the election lists should be granted to the brotherhood.[44] (The threat to return to the Wafd appears to have been pure bluff, since the Wafd's Fuad Serageddin had no intention of realigning with the brotherhood.)[45] Some of the Labor alliance election lists were composed entirely of Islamist candidates and the election platform overwhelmingly reflected the brotherhood's concerns. Shukri and many of the Labor party activists upheld the alliance—which outpolled the Wafd on election day, thereby gaining Shukri the role as opposition spokesman in Parliament—but some long-term party members refused to campaign for it. Three members of the Labor party executive were removed from their posts for their critical stances.[46] The question remained as to the extent to which the three groups would function as a bloc within the Peoples Assembly. In their leaders' statements there were hints that they would pursue their separate agendas in that forum.[47]

The Brotherhood in the Elections

The election campaign demonstrated the durability and deep roots of the Islamist movement. Numerous veteran members, such as Hasan al-Gamal and Mustafa al-Wardani, who had been active since the early 1940s and jailed in the 1950s, were elected to Parliament. Ahmad Saif al-Islam Hasan al-Banna, who was fifteen years old when his father died, was imprisoned in the early 1970s, and serves on the Guidance Council of the brotherhood, was also elected, as was Ma'mun Hasan al-Hudaybi, son of the general guide in the 1950s, former counselor in the Cairo appeals court, and member of the Guidance Council.

Room was made for new blood and for idiosyncratic personalities. Former student leaders from the 1970s were incorporated into the parliamentary team. The most notable were Dr. Essam al-Iryan, professor in the Faculty of Medicine at Cairo University and a member of the Doctors Syndicate,[48] and Dr. Muhammad Habib, professor of geology at Assiut University and head of its teachers club. Their political bases lay in the Islamic *jama'at* of the academic and professional communities, which the brotherhood had reached out to in the 1970s.

The Islamist movement also included the maverick Shaykh Salah Abu Ismail, who entered Parliament as an independent in the 1970s, engineered the brotherhood's alliance first with the Wafd, and then shifted to the Liberal party. The outspoken representative of a crowded, lower-class district in Giza, Abu Ismail won 42,700 votes in 1987, leaving all three opponents trailing in his wake with a combined total of 25,000. Similarly, the Populist preacher Yusif al-Badri trounced the minister of state for military production, even though the district included the main military factories, whose workers had been expected to vote en masse for the minister. The parliamentarians connected with the brotherhood provided evidence of the movement's range of activists and broad appeal. But they did not indicate that it was a tightly knit group, since each representative had his own base of power and his own focus of interest. Tension was evident during and after the campaign, for example, between Abu Ismail and Badri, and between both of them and the leaders of the brotherhood. They united under the banner "Islam is the Solution," but the problems addressed and the solutions proposed were not necessarily identical.

The Muslim Brotherhood's participation in the election was highly controversial in Egyptian political circles. Zaki Badr, the tough minister of interior, stated bluntly that the brotherhood's presence in the campaign was unconstitutional and illegal: since the brotherhood was not registered as either a society or a political party, it had no right to sponsor candidates.[49] The government viewed the thirty-six Islamist MPs as members of the Labor party. Badr considered the brotherhood subversive and disruptive. He stoutly defended the detention of poll watchers connected with the brotherhood, which had kept them away from the polling booths the entire election day. Badr argued that they were plotting to disrupt the voting and impose their views on the voters, rather than to observe quietly the election process. Badr also defended the police forces for blocking brotherhood leaders who were not themselves candidates from participating in election rallies. In at least one instance, Hamid Abul Nasr, the general guide, was detained on the road from Cairo to Suez to prevent him from traveling to a rally.

Mainstream journalists echoed the minister in decrying the de facto participation of the brotherhood and in blaming the brotherhood for its anomalous legal status. An editor with close ties to Mubarak asserted that the brotherhood was a political party that denied it was a political party because it did not want to be accountable for its actions.[50] Brotherhood spokesmen responded that the assertion was invalid: the brotherhood had not applied for party status, knowing that the application would be rejected. Their members could have run for the forty-eight independent seats in the Peoples Assembly, but that would not have provided them with an adequate base.[51] By coordinating in the alliance they could both acquire a legitimate structure and press more effectively for official recognition of their movement.[52] That pressure was precisely what officials and commentators feared.

Behind the discussion of legality lay the concern as to the Muslim Brotherhood's aims. Was it prepared to accept a multiparty democracy? Would it only accord legitimacy to groups that supported Islamic law? What did the slogan "Islam is the Solution" mean? If the brotherhood articulated the word of God, were critics nonbelievers or even performing the work of the devil? What would be the structure of an Islamic state? What would be its social and economic policies? What impact would implementing Islamic law have on the Coptic community? Such questions were asked repeatedly and anxiously by commentators in the press.

Spokesmen for the Wafd resented the Islamists' implication that other parties were atheist. The Wafd underlined the paramount importance of national unity, which it had upheld since the Revolution of 1919.[53] Representatives of the Progressive Grouping (Tagammu party) asserted their counterslogan: "Religion is for God and the Nation for All."[54] They derided the brotherhood's premise that Egypt's crisis was moral and that turning to religion would solve the social and economic problems facing the people. They argued that the brotherhood's proclamation that private investment was a religious duty indicated the opportunistic nature of the movement and its willingness to manipulate religion to suit the ends of its wealthy supporters.[55]

The most pointed criticism came from Adel Eid, a former MP from Alexandria who ran for Parliament as an independent. He had long been active in the Islamist movement but remained outside the brotherhood. In the 1987 elections, the alliance ran a candidate against Eid who accused him of being a Communist hiding under an Islamic cloak, apparently because Eid asserted the importance of promoting social reform to assist the poor and of maintaining the public sector as a fundamental element of the economy. Eid responded bitterly to those attacks; he accused the brotherhood of being shallow, narrow-minded, and intolerant, of asserting slogans without content, and of stressing the surface rituals of the religion without deeply comprehending its meaning.[56] He articulated his own view of the Islamic path: the creation of a just society that would guarantee the rights of the poor, respect the rights of the minority, and honor a multiplicity of views. There is no one Islamic way, Eid maintained. The Prophet did not impose his views but rather benefited from discussing alternatives. Imposition of the *hudud* prior to establishing a just society and without taking into account religious differences would damage Egypt's social fabric and stability rather than serve the cause of the Islamists.

The Muslim Brothers responded sharply to those who accused them of presenting a "magic formula"[57] that would appeal to the "simple people."[58] They argued that the alliance had formulated a detailed program, based on the fundamental belief that the misery, poverty, and lack of identity experienced in Egypt were caused by disbelief and mocking of the Qur'an: God promised that if the people followed the correct path, he would open the doors of prosperity.[59]

The alliance program called first for democratic reform—institution of a genuine multiparty system with complete freedom to form parties. That call related to the brotherhood's demand to operate independently in the political arena.[60] Second, the program insisted that Islamic law be applied, on the grounds of religious duty and national necessity. A decision in principle to apply Islamic law would have to be made quickly, followed by the amendment of any current legislation that violated *Shari'a* and then the promulgation of new laws explicitly based on *Shari'a*. Such laws would encompass not only *hudud* but also the media, education, and the economy. The media and cultural activities would have to strengthen religious values; decadent shows and immoral attitudes would be eliminated. *Haram* (religiously forbidden) places for tourists, such as nightclubs, would be closed. No betting or gambling would be allowed, and factories that manufactured alcoholic beverages would be closed. Education would inculcate noble values and government officials would be expected to set an example to the people in virtue and incorruptibility.

According to the program, the Islamic renaissance would require not only moral and political regeneration but also sound economic development. The size of the government bureaucracy and public sector would have to shrink, and officials would be held accountable and compelled to adhere to high standards of productivity. The private sector would provide the backbone of the economy, since productive investment is a religious duty. A non-interest-bearing banking system would replace the existing system derived from Western, usurious models. *Zakat* (alms) would be incorporated into the reformed tax system to assist the poor. Foreigners from the West would not be allowed to interfere in the Egyptian economy, but integration with Muslim economies, such as Saudi Arabia, would be promoted. Military integration would also be sought with Islamic states in the context of a foreign policy strategy that would eliminate Western influence and promote the self-reliance of the Islamic *ummah* (community). Superpower hegemony would be opposed: the program condemned both Soviet aggression in Afghanistan and American penetration in the region. The Camp David accords would be frozen, Israelis would be boycotted in Egypt, and the Palestinian *jihad* would be supported.

The lengthy program bore the imprint of the Muslim Brotherhood in all its sections and spelled out in detail the meaning behind the slogan "Islam is the Solution." Nonetheless, questions remained. The program specified that Coptic Egyptians were citizens, with the same rights and duties as Muslims, and that the alliance sought to promote brotherhood and unity. But it did not state how equality would be guaranteed. The sympathetic editor of *al-Sha'ab* even criticized that lacuna: we need to reassure our Coptic brothers, he argued, by specifying the voting, legislative, and administrative systems under an Islamic constitution, not merely by asserting that their interests will be protected.[61]

Moreover, the Brothers seemed ambiguous about engaging in debate and self-criticism, and accepting the legitimacy of other perspectives. Critics feared that they were using the democratic route to destroy democracy. One journalist accused them of believing that they were the shadow of God on Earth and that any disagreements with them were differences with God.[62] A leading Brother responded: we are advocates, not judges, but those who accuse us of such beliefs must feel guilty for straying from the faith.[63] Another Islamist insisted that the brotherhood does not charge others with atheism since it is *a* group of Muslims, not *the* Muslims.[64] Nonetheless, their tone implied that the program was sanctified and unchallengeable. After the election, Hudaybi commented: we cannot merely purify the existing laws, since they were based on European legal systems; God has ordered us to implement *Shari'a* in obedience to our faith, and we must carry out the will of God.[65] More pointedly, an Islamist editor, in denouncing the rigging and harassment on election day, exclaimed: it is God's law that the devil never withdraws from battle in peace and quiet.[66]

Clearly, the vigorous campaigning by the Islamists and the election of thirty-six Islamic advocates to the Peoples Assembly caused profound concern among Egyptian politicians and intellectuals. That concern exceeded the actual weight of the brotherhood in the assembly, since Islamists controlled only 8 percent of the seats. Islamists could express their views in committees and plenary debates but could not block measures proposed by the government. Moreover, they were not a cohesive bloc: the independently based Islamists had their own agendas, which might differ from the brotherhood.

Nonetheless, attaining a publicly acknowledged presence in the Peoples Assembly was a significant achievement for the Muslim Brotherhood. It testified to the staying power of a sociopolitical movement that had been declared dead three times in the past—after crackdowns in 1948–49, 1954, and 1965–66. Moreover, the movement had maintained a striking continuity in its goal of implementing *Shari'a* as a step toward the establishment of an Islamic state.

The participation in the assembly signaled, however, a consolidation of the shift in the brotherhood's mode of operation. Whereas the brotherhood had resisted entering the official political arena under the monarchy and had been driven underground by the Free Officers, some of its leaders cautiously participated in the constitutional system established by Sadat. The effort to participate in and manipulate the system became more explicit and systematic in the 1980s.

The social bases and attitudes of the brotherhood also altered over time. Banna envisaged a corporatist society in which differences between the rich and the poor would be unimportant and class struggle would yield to the common interest. That vision faced difficulties and contradictions when put to the test. The Brothers' violence in the 1940s expressed frustration at the government's hostility to their views, even though the brotherhood's socioeconomic and educational programs attracted broad support. Qutb later undertook a deeper critique of the sociopolitical environment. He concluded that the society itself was *jahili*—not only the rulers—and needed to be fundamentally transformed. His approach formed the basis for the radical groups of the 1970s, in particular *al-Takfir wal-Hijra* and *Jihad*. The brotherhood, however, generally did not endorse Qutb's views but adhered to the more optimistic tenets of Banna. Long-term education, renewed social programs, and a growing political presence were viewed as the route to an Islamic polity.

In the late 1980s, contradictions persisted both within the brotherhood and between it and the political environment. Within the movement, differences were discernible between the leadership and the base. The leaders were increasingly conservative on socioeconomic issues. They became wealthy through Saudi connections and established profitable private businesses in Egypt. They were oriented toward the private sector and sought to consolidate the benefits that have accrued to the rich under the Open Door policy. In contrast, the lower and lower-middle class supporters of the movement had suffered reduced living standards, decreased social services and constricted career prospects. The attraction of the militant Islamic groups has been linked in part to those social strains. The brotherhood and related Islamist societies have tried to provide educational and health services for the urban poor. Their effort to fill the vacuum in government services was an important factor in their success in the elections. Moreover, their appeal to moral and religious causes for Egypt's economic woes provided an understandable explanation to many Egyptians, bewildered by the changes occurring in their lives. However, the stress placed by some Islamist MPs on enhancing the free operation of private enterprises, reducing the government's role in the economy, and ending rent control and price subsidies contradicted the interests of the urban lower-middle class. If the MPs were to push for such changes in Parliament, their popular support could erode.

Moreover, Islamist MPs differed on the specific policies that should be introduced. Some supported the private sector, while others backed strong social welfare programs. Some viewed the current legal system as basically sound while others demanded a comprehensive overhaul of the laws. Some criticized the Coptic community while others called for reconciliation. Some supported the Islamic Republic of Iran while others decried its excesses. Such disagreements were partly based on philosophical differences and partly rooted in personal rivalries. In either case, the divergencies called into question the existence of *the* Islamic solution and thereby made Islamists vulnerable to criticism by other political groups.

Moreover, contradictions persisted between the brotherhood and the overall political system. Mubarak opened up political life significantly, but the bureaucracy and the military establishment remained the backbone of the regime.[67] Emergency regulations limited freedom of assembly and action by political parties, the governing party continued to monopolize the local councils and dominate the Parliament, and Mubarak won a second term as president in October 1987 unopposed. The room for maneuver by nongovernmental political forces remained constricted. That was especially the case for the Muslim Brotherhood and other Islamist groups. The government was determined to prevent the brotherhood from forming a separate political party, in part because that could exacerbate communal tension and open the door to Lebanon-type religious strife. In addition, the government feared that the brotherhood had the greatest potential of any current political movement for becoming a real challenge to its authority and legitimacy. The achieving of power by the brotherhood also could result in the curtailment of political freedom, since the Brothers' commitment to democracy remained suspect. Officials wanted to keep the brotherhood within manageable limits.

The government faced perplexing dilemmas after the 1987 election. Allowing the Islamist movement to function freely in the political arena could result in co-opting it into the constitutional political structure and compromising the absolutism of its goals. Alternatively, that freedom could encourage the Islamists to escalate their demands and enhance their strength. Similarly, establishing an Islamic party could reduce the anomalies in the parliamentary arena or could cause the democratic process to fracture along sectarian lines. The perceived risks in opening up the system contributed to the government's policy of putting brakes on the democratization process. And yet, those limits themselves could exacerbate public alienation and accelerate the growth in pent-up demand and tension. That tension, in turn, could help to spawn extralegal movements that resort to violence to express their frustration and attain their ends. That vicious circle deepened the dilemma facing the regime.

Mubarak's effort to contain the Islamists is likely to continue. He is apt to accord them minimal access to the political arena and to clamp down on those who use violence. However, he will not agree to the Islamists' core demands to implement Islamic law and establish autonomous political parties. The ability of the government to maintain that balancing act remains problematic, just as the willingness of the Islamic movement to live with the contradictions remains unknown. In the past, the inherent tension has erupted in violent showdowns in which the Islamists have been severely defeated. A replay of the confrontation need not, however, lead to the same result.

Notes

1. Christina Phelps Harris, *Nationalism and Revolution in Egypt: The Role of the Muslim Brotherhood* (Stanford, Calif.: Hoover Institution, 1964), 149.

2. Karen Aboul Kheir, "The Moslem Brothers: Quest for an Islamic Alternative" (Master's thesis, American University in Cairo, 1983), 55–58.

3. Ellis Goldberg, "Moslem Union Politics in Egypt: Two Cases," in *Islam, Politics, and Social Movements,* ed. Edmund Burke III and Ira M. Lapidus (Berkeley, Calif.: University of California Press, 1988), 233; on the Brothers' concept of society, see also 232, 240–41.

4. Hasan al-Banna, "New Renaissance," in *Political and Social Thought in the Contemporary Middle East,* ed. Kemal H. Karpat (New York: Praeger, 1968), 121.

5. Aboul Kheir, "Moslem Brothers," 44–45.

6. Ibid., 42.

7. Harris, *Nationalism and Revolution,* 182–83. Aboul Kheir, "Moslem Brothers," 59, says that Prime Minister Mustafa Nahhas threatened to exile Banna and dissolve the brotherhood if he ran for election.

8. Harris, *Nationalism and Revolution,* 183.

9. Joel Beinin, "Islam, Marxism and the Shubra al-Khayma Textile Workers: Moslem Brothers and Communists in the Egyptian Trade Union Movement," in Burke and Lapidus, eds., *Islam, Politics,* 225.

10. Harris, *Nationalism and Revolution,* 193; Aboul Kheir, "Moslem Brothers," 79.

11. Aboul Kheir, "Moslem Brothers," 80.

12. Statement by Secretary Abdel Hakim Abdein, paraphrased in ibid., 80–81.

13. Harris, *Nationalism and Revolution,* 214.

14. Aboul Kheir, "Moslem Brothers," 83–84.

15. Ibid., 101–4.

16. Ibid., 99–100, 123.

17. Ibid., 90–96, 105–14.

18. Ibid., 94.

19. Quoted in Yvonne Yazbeck Haddad, *Contemporary Islam* (Albany: State University of New York Press, 1983), 164. See also Haddad's excellent chapter, "Sayyid Qutb: Ideologue of Islamic Revival," in *Voice of Resurgent Islam,* ed. John L. Esposito (New York: Oxford University Press, 1983), 67–98.

20. Sayyid Qutb, *Milestones* (Cedar Rapids, Iowa: Unity Publishing, n.d.), 102.

21. Abol Kheir, "Moslem Brothers," 108–11. That might be seen as implicit criticism of Banna's approach, which brought thousands of supporters to the movement on the basis of its social aid programs and schools but failed to deepen their ideological commitment to the extent that they were willing to defy and overcome the *jahili* attacks.

22. Ibid., 124–25; Hamied N. Ansari, "The Islamic Militants in Egyptian Politics," *International Journal of Middle East Studies (IJMES)* 16, no. 1 (March 1984): 140.

23. Aboul Kheir, "Moslem Brothers," 124–25.

24. Nazih N. M. Ayubi, "The Political Revival of Islam: The Case of Egypt," *IJMES* 12, no. 4 (December 1980): 489. Eric Davis argues against overemphasizing the importance of the defeat in 1967 to the growth in Islamic movements in the 1970s, in "Ideology, Social Class and Islamic Radicalism in Modern Egypt," in *From Nationalism to Revolutionary Islam,* ed. Said Arjomand (Oxford: Macmillan, 1984), 153.

25. Abd al-Monein Said Aly and Manfred W. Wenner, "Modern Islamic Movements: The Moslem Brotherhood in Contemporary Egypt," *Middle East Journal (MEJ)* 36, no. 3 (Summer 1982): 348–49. They note that the Moslem Brotherhood wanted the clause to refer to *Shari'a* as *the* source of legislation, not only *a* source.

26. Ayubi, "Political Revival in Islam," 490.

27. Israel Altman, "Islamic Movements in Egypt," *The Jerusalem Quarterly* 10 (Winter 1979): 92–94; see also Saad Eddin Ibrahim, "An Islamic Alternative in Egypt: The Moslem Brotherhood and Sadat," *Arab Studies Quarterly* 4, nos. 1–2 (Spring 1982): 81; and Aly and Wenner, "Modern Islamic Movements," 349–50.

28. Hamied Ansari, "Sectarian Conflict in Egypt and the Political Expediency of Religion," *MEJ* 38, no. 3 (Summer 1984): 400–402; Louis J. Cantori, "Religion and Politics in Egypt," in *Religion and Politics in the Middle East,* ed. Michael Curtis (Boulder, Colo.: Westview Press, 1981), 83–85; and John Waterbury, "Egypt: Islam and Social Change," in *Change and the Moslem*

World, ed. Philip Stoddard (Syracuse, N.Y.: Syracuse University Press, 1981), 56–57.

29. Altman, "Islamic Movements," 90, 95–96; Ibrahim, "Islamic Alternative," 81–82.

30. Altman, "Islamic Movements," 96–97; Aboul Kheir, "Moslem Brothers," 145–46, 189, 191–92.

31. For analyses of those groups see, in particular, Altman's "Islamic Movements," Ansari's "Islamic Militants," Davis's "Ideology," and Saad Eddin Ibrahim, "Anatomy of Egypt's Militant Islamic Groups," *IJMES* 12 (1980): 423–53. Criticism of the groups by the Moslem Brotherhood is also noted by Aboul Kheir, "Moslem Brothers," 175–76, and Aly and Wenner, "Modern Islamic Movements," 358.

32. Ayubi, "Political Revival," 493; Ibrahim, "Islamic Alternative," 85–89.

33. Aboul Kheir, "Moslem Brothers," 188, quoting *al-Da'wa,* June 1976; also Aly and Wenner, "Modern Islamic Movements," 356–58.

34. Aly and Wenner, "Modern Islamic Movements," 352; Ibrahim, "Islamic Alternative," 83–85.

35. Ansari, "Islamic Militants," 135–40; Ansari, "Sectarian Conflict," 307–15. Some scholars argue that the blind shaykh Omar Abd al-Rayman wrote *al-Farida al-Gha'iba.*

36. Bertus Hendricks, "Egypt's Election, Mubarak's Bind," *MERIP Reports,* no. 129 (January 1985): 18.

37. Tilmissani column in *al-Wafd,* June 14, 1984.

38. Tilmissani column in *al-Wafd,* September 6, 1984.

39. *Al-Ahrar,* January 12, 1987.

40. Ibid.

41. For example, Makram Mohammad Ahmad editorial, *al-Musawwar,* March 20, 1987.

42. Mamduh Qinawi, secretary of central committee in Labor, ibid. Qinawi opposed the alliance with the brotherhood and broke with the party during the election campaign.

43. See, for example, Shukri's statement to *al-Musawwar,* ibid.

44. Qinawi, ibid.

45. *Al-Musawwar,* February 27, 1987.

46. *Al-Sha'ab,* April 14, 1987.

47. Mustafa Kamil Murad, Liberal party head, *al-Sha'ab,* February 17, 1987; Ahmad Harak, MP and member of Labor's executive committee, *al-Wafd,* April 17, 1987.

48. According to Ansari, "Sectarian Conflict," 412, Iryan came from the same village in Giza as Abbud al-Zomor, a key figure in the *Jihad* group. Iryan married the sister of one of the participants in the attack on the Military Technical College in 1974 and he preached *Shari'a* but rejected the idea of

takfir. In a speech at a conference following the Zawiya al-Hamra violence in 1981, Iryan decried the destruction of homes and shops but criticized the Copts, arguing that they sought a separate state with its capital in Assiut and that Pope Shenouda resembled Sa'd Haddad, the Israeli-supported commander in south Lebanon. Iryan was arrested in the September 1981 roundup.

49. *Al-Musawwar,* April 24, 1987.

50. Editorial, Makram Muhammad Ahmad, *al-Musawwar,* March 20, 1987.

51. Mustafa Mashhour, *al-Ahrar,* April 13, 1987.

52. Ma'mun al-Hudaybi, *al-Wafd,* April 17, 1987.

53. Dr. Wahid Rifaat, *al-Musawwar,* March 27, 1987.

54. Rifat al-Said, secretary general, ibid.

55. *Al-Ahali,* February 25, 1987.

56. *Al-Musawwar,* March 27, 1987.

57. Ahmad Bahaeddin, *al-Ahram,* April 9, 1987.

58. Makram Muhammad Ahmad, *al-Musawwar,* April 10, 1987.

59. Salah Shadi, *al-Sha'ab,* April 14, 1987.

60. Complete text of alliance program in *al-Sha'ab,* March 17, 1987.

61. Adel Hussein, *al-Sha'ab,* January 27, 1987, criticizing an editorial by the brotherhood's Hamza Di'bes in *al-Nur.*

62. M. M. Ahmad, *al-Musawwar,* April 10, 1987.

63. Salah Shadi, *al-Sha'ab,* April 14, 1987.

64. Mustafa Mashhour, *al-Ahrar,* April 13, 1987.

65. Ma'Mun al-Hudaybi, *al-Sha-ab,* April 21, 1987.

66. Adel Hussein, *al-Sha-ab,* April 14, 1987.

67. See A. M. Lesch, "Egyptian Politics in the 1990s," in *Workshop Report: US-Egyptian Security Relations in an Era of Economic Constraints* (Fort McNair: National Defense University, 1988); and "Democracy in Doses: Egypt under Hosni Mubarak," *Arab Studies Quarterly* 11, no. 3 (Fall 1989): 87–107.

IO.

Religion and Politics in Islamic Africa

JOHN O. VOLL

Islamic fundamentalism is an important force in Islamic Africa. In numerous countries, it is reshaping the role of Muslims in the relationship between religion and politics. In clearly Muslim countries like Egypt, this development is now well known and possibly expected. However, it is also significant in countries where Muslims are not the dominant majority. The ways that Muslims view and work with the state and identify with the nation reflect this trend.

"State" and "nation" are key concepts in examining religion and politics in Islamic Africa. The concepts are subjects of increasing interest and scholarly attention. As one scholar has noted, "After decades of neglect, the concept of the state is once again a central object of theory and empirical research."[1] However, much of this new interest is expressed in terms that are difficult to apply within the Islamic context. As a result, scholars examining the Islamic resurgence of the 1970s and 1980s often express conceptual reservations when discussing the state. In a study of state and religion in Afghanistan, Iran, and Pakistan, for example, Ali Banuazizi and Myron Weiner note that the "term 'state' itself is an elusive one, for it is so associated with modern European conceptions that in some respects it is not appropriate to apply the term to the institutions of these countries [Iran, Afghanistan, and Pakistan]."[2]

Similarly, the perception of "nation" and "nationalism" that is embedded in much of the terminology is not always the most effective perception for analysis of Islamic experience. A relatively common usage identifies "state" and "nation-state" as being the same thing, although the territorial nation-state is a relatively new phenomenon in world history.[3] This "modern state" is a "particular form which originated in

Europe in the fifteenth century, evolved into a nation-state by the end of
the eighteenth century, and became diffused throughout the globe by
imperial conquest and anticolonial revolt or defensive adaptation."[4]

When the state is assumed to be a nation-state, it possesses
"nationality," which means that the state represents "a transcendent
embodiment of its civil society . . . [and] an expression of citizenry as a
collective self."[5] For a considerable time, the process of creating such
nation-states has been seen as the major political problem for societies in
Africa and Asia as they worked to adapt to the conditions of the
contemporary world. This is the heart of the classic analyses by scholars
like Rupert Emerson and Dankwart Rustow.[6]

This assumption that a modern state is necessarily a nation-state
poses problems for the analysis of Muslim politics. It is useful and, in
fact, necessary to distinguish between state and nation. Muslims in the
context of African societies, at least, sometimes make a distinction
between the state and the nation. Some of the strictest Islamic fundamentalists will cooperate with state institutions, even when they are not
Islamic, but have grave reservations about accepting a part in a national
identity unless that identity is clearly associated with Islam. In making
this distinction, it is also important to recognize that the Islamic
conceptualizations of state and nation may vary from those used by non-
Muslim political analysts.

In this framework, what is often called Islamic fundamentalism is
the call for a rigorous affirmation, in belief and practice, of the Islamic
vision as presented in the Qur'an and Traditions of the Prophet. This
perspective interprets these sources relatively literally and strives to
eliminate what it feels are the unjustified additions to faith and practice
that have come about as an adaptation to local conditions or as compromises in the modern context, with Western ideas and practices. In the
fundamentalist view, their vision is comprehensive and universal. However, the implications of their vision vary depending upon the local
environments in which they find themselves.

The subject of the rise of Islamic fundamentalism in the context of
religion and politics in Muslim Africa thus requires combining several
considerations. The conceptual heritage of Islam with regard to the
concepts of state and nation needs to be noted. This provides the
foundation for the ideology and discourse of African Muslims. Then,
specific examples of Islamic resurgence in Africa need to be examined. It
is important to look at the leading case, which is the experience of
Egypt. However, it is also important to recognize the diversity of
Islamic Africa and to look at the rise of fundamentalists in other African

contexts. An examination of fundamentalism in Sudan, Nigeria, and South Africa provides a broad spectrum of experience.

Islamic Political Perspectives

Religion and politics are strongly linked in Islamic perspectives. Many people note Bernard Lewis's belief that there is in Islam "an intimate and essential relationship between religion and politics, creed and power."[7] At the same time, certain institutions within Muslim societies perform functions that can be called religious, and other structures can be called states. The distinction between a shah and an ayatollah in Iran, for example, is part of the basic shape of Iranian society even before modern concepts of secularism were incorporated into Iranian political life. "Most Muslim societies were and are built around separate state and religious institutions."[8]

Although it is possible to say that for believing Muslims, there is no separation of religion and politics, it is also necessary to recognize that religious and political institutions do, in fact, exist in Muslim societies. These two points are not contradictory unless the analyst makes the further assumption that such a distinction means that the political institution is therefore secular, and by that definition, is not Islamic. What distinguishes the Islamic perspective is not that it lacks a sense of different dimensions of life (e.g., devotional, political, economic), but rather that it believes that none of those dimensions is independent. Instead, all are seen as part of and subject to the Islamic vision. It is in this sense that one can say that Islam is not a *religion* in the modern Western meaning of that term. It is, rather, a total way of life and worldview.

In the framework of Islam as a worldview or as a vision of a world order, there are institutional distinctions between religious and political dimensions of life. However, both are part of the Islamic vision, so there is no secular arena within which the values and symbols of Islam are not believed to be the ultimate authority. This is the ideal, but especially in the modern era, Muslims are exposed to significant secular and non-Islamic influences. To the extent that a Muslim accepts the secular assumptions of Western civilization, he or she will not be disturbed by this. However, one of the major dimensions of the Islamic resurgence is that a growing number of Muslims perceive the existence of a secular, non-Islamic arena as being undesirable.

The modern issues raised for Muslims by the nation-state have foundations in the broader stretches of Islamic history. The subject of religion and politics any place within the Islamic world reflects old images and debates as well as the new conditions created by the interaction of Islamic societies with the West. Some of these issues take special form in Africa but they are not without precedents elsewhere.

Although the nation-state is a modern phenomenon, dealing with national identity and state structures is an old issue in Islamic society. With regard to state structures, Muslims have the ideal of a unified polity that includes all Muslims, as was actually the case during the lifetime of the Prophet and his immediate successors. However, Muslims came to accept a plurality of territorial polities in the medieval era.[9] In the long run, Muslims were able to cope with the problems of the political disunity of the world of Islam and the creation of many different forms of states. Classical medieval Islamic political thought, at least in the Sunni world, came to terms with the state. Perhaps the most extreme case of adjustment was the acceptance by many medieval Muslim political philosophers that authority is preferable to anarchy, and the view of the fourteenth-century scholar Badr al-Din Ibn Jama's that forty years of tyranny from the ruler were better than the abandonment of his subjects for one hour.[10]

Military rule was accepted, even if it meant some tyranny, in this medieval framework. Even the loss of political unity was finally recognized. However, there was a limit. None of the commanders was recognized as having formal sovereignty. They were accepted, rather, as instruments of God's will. It is this way that Muslims accepted the state: as a subordinate instrument of God, not as a sovereign, independent institution. In Islamic thought there was and continues to be a rich symbolism associated with the issue of the ruler who tries to be sovereign. The Qur'anic prototype of such a ruler is Pharaoh, who became the symbol of the attempt to disobey God and claim sovereign power for himself. In contemporary Islamic writings this can be seen in the works of people like Ali Shariati, thought by many to be the intellectual parent of the Iranian Revolution.[11] Killing Pharaoh was the symbolism used by those who killed Anwar Sadat of Egypt. In the sweeping terms of Gilles Kepel, "In the Middle East of the 1980s, largely alien to Western political categories, the message of Muhammad the Prophet threatens to become ever more insistent the greater is the execration of Pharaoh."[12] Islam does not prohibit or oppose the state but it insists that the state is not sovereign—it opposes Pharaoh.

The issue is similar with regard to nations and nationalism. The Qur'an speaks of different communities, and Muslims frequently have seen these as nations with special linguistic or ethnic identities. However, these identities, in the Islamic ideal, are not to create sovereign groups that might dominate other groups. A leading intellectual in the Muslim Brotherhood in Egypt, Sayyid Qutb, presented the standard fundamentalist view of nationalism when he said that Muhammad the Prophet had not adopted an Arab nationalist program because it "would not have been appropriate that Allah's creatures were subjected to Arab tyranny after being freed from the clutches of Roman or Persian imperialism. . . . All nations belonging to any colour or race, whether Arabic, Roman, or Persian, in the eyes of this faith enjoy equal status under Allah's banner."[13]

The issue, again, in Islamic terms is not whether to accept the legitimacy of an ethnic or communal or national identity. It is to be able to put such an identity within a proper set of priorities, keeping the universal community of God as the primary identity. In this worldview, nationalism can become a form of idolatry but it does not have to.

Islam thus does not prescribe a specific state structure or a particular ethnic or cultural identity. Instead, it defines a set of priorities. This does not create a monolithic unity since Muslims have created a wide variety of state structures and community identities. It does, however, mean that Islamic perspectives and worldviews, based on Qur'anic images and symbols, provide the basis for what can be called Islamic positions with regard to the relationship between religion and politics. In the modern context, Muslims have difficulty in accepting the legitimacy of the modern nation-state concept, not because it involves a state or a sense of national identity, but because it presumes that the nation-state is its own ultimate, sovereign authority.

In the great diversity of African societies, Muslims have worked out many different ways of adjusting to the local realities while maintaining a sense of their adherence to Islam. In these adjustments, the problems of defining their relationship to the state and to national identities are very important. The conceptual place of state and nation within the Islamic worldview provides a possible vehicle for developing a broader picture of the patterns of interactions of religion and politics in Islamic Africa.

African Societies and Islamic Fundamentalists

Muslims in the continent of Africa live in a wide variety of contexts. "Islamic Africa" includes all Muslims in that continent. This broad perspective makes it possible to create a more inclusive interpretation of the interactions of religion and politics.

In Africa, Muslim communities range from constituting virtually 100 percent of the population to representing less than 1 percent of the population. There is no single, typical Muslim African national community. Relatively large communities exist in both large and small states. Muslim national communities can be grouped into four different types. About half of the Muslims in Africa live in countries where they comprise 90 percent or more of the population. Most of these countries are strongly influenced by Arab tradition and culture and have long been a part of the Islamic world. The largest are those countries on the Mediterranean coast of Africa.

The second grouping of Muslim national communities includes those where Muslims are the majority, but they coexist with non-Muslim communities of significant size. Although these countries only account for about 10 percent of the total Muslim population of Africa, two of them—Sudan and Chad—are well known because of their internal conflicts, which have often involved fighting between Muslims and non-Muslims.

The third and fourth groupings are the Muslim minority communities. Almost 40 percent of African Muslims live as minorities within their societies. The largest Muslim national community in Africa is such a minority, in Nigeria. Most of these communities are expanding and their importance is increasing. The third group of Muslim communities includes those that are minorities but represent a significant, possibly near-majority, proportion of their country's population. These large-but-minority communities tend to be in West Africa, and all of them are in a belt of societies stretching across the middle of the continent just south of the Sahara. The fourth group of Muslim communities includes those where Muslims comprise less than one-fifth of the population. These are often small communities in terms of number of people, as well. However, even these small communities seem to have some developing significance.

Clearly the size of the community and its strength within society will be an important influence on how religion and politics interact within any of the African states. However, this variable is not a sufficient condition for explaining the emergence of a fundamentalist type of religion-politics interaction. One of the remarkable features of Islamic Africa is that size and strength, at least in terms of numbers and proportions, do not seem to correlate directly with the development of

Islamic fundamentalism. In each group, some countries contain a viable and influential Muslim fundamentalist presence, and some do not. In every African Muslim community, there are probably a few people who could be considered to be fundamentalist. However, these people, even at the beginning of the 1990s, do not always play a significant or visible role in the Islamic life of the country.

Among those countries where virtually the entire population is Muslim, there are significant and globally visible Islamic fundamentalist groups. Egypt can be regarded as the homeland of Sunni Muslim fundamentalism of the modern style. Its experience is examined in more detail later in this analysis. In Tunisia the development of the Islamic Tendency movement in the 1970s and 1980s showed the strength of the Islamic resurgence in one of the most secular countries in the Arab world. At the same time, such activism has relatively little significance in other large majority communities, such as Mali or the Gambia.

In the second group, where Muslims are only a bare majority, this same diversity is present. An influential Muslim Brotherhood movement is active in the Sudan, but in Chad, with roughly the same proportion of its population being Muslim, there is little significant fundamentalist activity.

Where Muslims comprise between 20 percent and 50 percent of the population, there are both communities with active fundamentalists and without them. The huge Muslim population of Nigeria contains a wide range of Muslim activist organizations and is worth further examination. However, in this same category, other states have Muslims who are politically active but not especially fundamentalist or revivalist in orientation. The various Muslim-supported liberation groups in Ethiopia, for example, do not have a fundamentalist reputation and places like Ivory Coast have little fundamentalist activism.

In the fourth category, where Muslims form less than one-fifth of the population, one would expect fundamentalist activism, where it exists at all, to be concentrated primarily in missionary work. To a large extent this is true. Muslim communities are not strong enough to represent a significant political force within the country. Also, existing, well-established small communities tend to have a survivalist mentality that is not suited to a fundamentalist orientation. This is the case in Malawi. However, in some of these relatively small communities, highly visible fundamentalist groups have emerged and are playing increasingly significant roles, both in their own communities and in the large Islamic world. One such community is in South Africa.

In view of this diversity, a study of Islamic fundamentalism in Africa that attempts to provide insight into the interaction of religion and politics could profitably examine more closely four cases, one drawn from each group of states, where fundamentalism is an important or visible feature. Useful examples are Egypt, Sudan, Nigeria, and South Africa. A detailed analysis of each of these situations is not possible in this chapter. However, some of the significant features can be identified for purposes of developing generalizations about this subject.

It is useful to ask: (1) What are the conditions involved in the development of fundamentalism in the country? (2) What are the attitudes of the fundamentalists toward the state in their country? (3) What are the attitudes of fundamentalists toward their nation or national community or society? On the basis of the answers to these questions, generalizations can be formulated about religion and politics in African Islam, particularly with regard to the global issue of the rise of religious fundamentalism as a transnational movement in the final quarter of the twentieth century.

Islamic Fundamentalism in Egypt

The Islamic experience of Egypt is complex. Fundamentalism has deep roots in the modern history of Egypt and much has been written about that experience. [14] For many people, both Muslim and non-Muslim, the development of Islamic fundamentalism in Egypt is almost the paradigmatic experience of Islamic fundamentalism in the Sunni world. In general, Egypt has been a pioneer in all of the major developments of the modern Middle East. Egypt was one of the first Muslim societies to be involved in a major effort at Westernizing reform, beginning with the efforts of its ruler, Muhammad Ali, in the first half of the nineteenth century. Late in that century Egypt experienced both the Pan-Islamic efforts of Jamal al-Din al-Afghani and the pioneering efforts in Islamic modernism of Muhammad Abduh. In the twentieth century, Egyptian nationalism was one of the early mass movements of modern-style opposition to Western imperial control, and in the 1950s and 1960s, Jamal Abd al-Nasir (Nasser) was one of the leading formulators and advocates of Arab socialism.

It is not surprising that pioneering efforts in creating a modern style of Islamic fundamentalism also appeared in Egypt. Although individual intellectuals and activists might have been considered fundamentalists earlier, the organizational beginnings of Egypt's contemporary fundamentalism occurred in 1928 with the establishment of the Muslim Brotherhood by Hasan al-Banna. In the "sweep of developments in the Arab world beginning with the movement of the Wahhabiyya [in Arabia] in the late eighteenth century, the Society of the Brothers emerges as the first mass-supported and organized, essentially urban-oriented effort to cope with the plight of Islam in the modern world."[15]

When the brotherhood was founded, this "plight" primarily involved the loss of control by Muslims over their own lands and destinies. This critical sense of unease has been described in an often-quoted passage by Wilfred Cantwell Smith: "The fundamental *malaise* of modern Islam is a sense that something has gone wrong with Islamic history. The fundamental problem of modern Muslims is how to rehabilitate that history: to set it going again in full vigour, so that Islamic society may once again flourish as a divinely guided society should and must."[16] The brotherhood worked to bring about this rehabilitation through a rigorous affirmation of Islam in what can be thought of as a fundamentalist response.

In its early years, the brotherhood was a response to the victories of the West. It appeared that Islamic values were being lost in the processes of reform and Westernization. Al-Banna saw the corruption that this involved in Egyptian society. In this sense, the brotherhood's mission had two major dimensions. One was the reaffirmation of the truth of Islam in the face of the Westernizers, and the other was the effort to help the common Egyptian survive in the face of the corruptions and inefficiencies of modernizing Egyptian society.

Although the brotherhood gained some mass support or sympathy, it was not as successful as the movements of Egyptian nationalism, the largest of which was the Wafd party, or the later combination of Arab nationalism and socialism of Nasser. In the 1950s and 1960s the brotherhood was suppressed and the dominant perspective of the time was Nasser's Arab socialism. However, by the 1970s the situation had changed. Nasser died in 1970, and there was a high level of disillusionment with his style of radicalism. In the context of the more pragmatic rule of Anwar Sadat, the brotherhood and other fundamentalist groups began to emerge as important political forces in Egypt.

In the final quarter of the twentieth century there has been a resurgence of Islam in Egypt that is broader than simply the revival of the fortunes of the Muslim Brotherhood.[17] Many specific explanations have been given for this resurgence. However, at the risk of oversimplifying complex phenomena, most of these explanations involve three basic dimensions. The first, a perceived threat to the Islamic identity of Egyptians and their society, is that which inspired Hasan al-Banna. The brotherhood was an important part of the response to that threat and attempted to reaffirm the fundamental Islamic identity that seemed about to be lost. In other words, there was, and is, a strongly defensive dimension.

The second explanation rests on the experience of the Islamic world, including Egypt, in the 1960s. By the end of that decade it was clear that the great nationalist efforts and radical socialist programs had failed to bring significant success or power to Egypt (and other Islamic countries). Nasser's great promises all appeared to have crashed with the stunning defeat of the Arabs by Israel in the Six-Day War of 1967. The borrowed ideologies, whether Marxist, liberal, or capitalist, were all viewed as having failed. In this situation, "Islam constitutes a 'fall back' ideology to capture the alienated, the disoriented and the angry."[18] In even broader terms, by the early 1970s the social and ideological confusions visible in the West itself made it possible for Muslims to start from an assumption that the West had itself basically failed.[19]

The third explanation takes a more positive view and argues that, for Egyptians in the 1980s, Islam represented an effective source of strength for coping with contemporary problems. In fact, in many ways, Islamic institutions and approaches were relatively successful in the 1980s. The Islamic Revolution in Iran, although its problems are recognized, is seen as proof that an Islamic movement can succeed in transforming the state. Islamic banks and investment companies have good records. In general, the Islamic world is playing a more important role in world affairs than it has for centuries. This provides positive incentives for the affirmation of the Islamic message and vision.

In summary, Islamic fundamentalism has emerged as an important force in Egypt in the last decades of the twentieth century as a response to challenges to the survival of an authentic Islamic identity, as a result of the vacuum created by the failure of borrowed ideologies, and as a consequence of the growing conviction of the value and strength of the Islamic alternative.

There are a number of different attitudes toward the state among Egyptian fundamentalists. However, all of these views start from the position that the state cannot be "Pharaoh's state." It must, in some way, recognize that ultimate sovereignty rests not with the state but with God. Disagreements do not arise over whether or not the Pharaohs of the world should be opposed, but rather, over the evaluation of the regime in control of the existing state.

The Muslim Brotherhood tradition has been quite flexible. "The ultimate goal of the Muslim Brothers was the creation of an 'Islamic order' (*al-nizam al-islami*). In practice, this phrase was sometimes loosely used to mean a 'Muslim state'; mostly, however, it referred to a set of legal (not political) principles which were regarded as fundamental to Muslim society whatever the particular form of political order."[20] The recognition and implementation of Islamic law (the *Shari'a*) and not the particular form of government has been the primary concern of the mainline Muslim Brotherhood. As a result, brotherhood leaders were willing to work for the reform of the old parliamentary system and in the 1980s, to participate in the political system of Mubarak's Egypt. The Muslim Brotherhood is, at the beginning of the 1990s, the leading force in the legal parliamentary opposition in Egypt. It accepts the state as reformable and therefore works within the existing political system to create the desired Islamic order.

A small but highly visible minority of the Egyptian fundamentalists does not accept the existing regime as legitimate or reformable. One such group, *al-Jihad,* was responsible for killing Sadat, which they saw as "killing Pharaoh." Another group sees the whole of society, not just the state, as decadent and sinful. They believe that the solution is to withdraw from society and to build a new order on the basis of a core community of true believers.[21] These extreme fringes are only a very small portion of the total community but their existence and potential appeal sets limits to the moderation of mainline moderate fundamentalists.

For most fundamentalists in Egypt, the state is seen as an appropriate arena for action. There is a sense that an authentic Islamic order can be created by modification and reform of the present system. The state is accepted but seen as being in need of significant reform—which is believed to be possible.

State structures are ancient in Egypt, and the relative homogeneity of Egyptian society has helped to create an identity between the state and the national community. Even though the fundamentalists are affirming a worldview that is not solely Egyptian, they tend to be Egypt-oriented in their perspectives. Although the Muslim Brotherhood had a significant impact on Muslims in other countries, Egyptian Brothers have not been significantly active in large numbers outside of their own country. (Members who were in exile during the Nasser years often prospered, but returned to Egypt in the 1970s where they resumed their active Muslim work.) The extremist groups of the 1980s were aware of the broader Islamic community and their part in it. However, the mainline brotherhood is very aware of the need for Egyptian national unity. In the 1987 elections they even gave a prominent place in their party organization to a Copt, who represented the largest non-Muslim community in Egypt.

The Egyptian national identity involves a recognition of Islam as an important component. Since the overwhelming majority of Egyptians are Muslim, it is difficult for fundamentalists to reject the nation as it developed. Egypt fits the traditionally acceptable pattern of being a distinctive nation but also recognizing that it is part of the Islamic world. Only when a leader attempts to withdraw Egypt from that world do fundamentalists become aroused. This occurred when Sadat signed the peace treaty with Israel and emphasized the slogan, "Egypt First."

For Egyptian fundamentalists, their attitude toward the state and the nation is shaped by the fact that Egypt is overwhelmingly Muslim. This allows the possibility of reforming the state, rather than rejecting it, to create an authentically Islamic order. The Egyptian national identity similarly can be accepted because it does not involve a departure from a type of Muslim identity.

Islamic Fundamentalism in Sudan

The assumption that state and society are both identifiably Muslim is an important part of the Muslim fundamentalist viewpoint in the Sudan. However, in contrast to Egypt, the demographic reality is different. While Muslims are a majority, more than a quarter of the Sudanese population is clearly non-Muslim. Islamic fundamentalism arises in the Sudan within the context of actual pluralism but of social and political dominance by Muslims.

The modern Sudan is a creation of the history of the past two centuries. Before the nineteenth century, the area included a number of small states and ethnic group domains, and the region had no formal unity. Much of the contemporary Sudan was brought under the control of Ottoman-Egyptian forces in the 1820s, and this "Turko-Egyptian" regime provided the first Sudanwide structures of communications and control. This rule by outsiders and the development of Islamic sentiments provided the context for a major revolt, led by a local Muslim teacher, Muhammad Ahmad al-Mahdi. The Sudanese Mahdi was fundamentalist in style,[22] and he formally proclaimed an Islamic state in much of the area of the modern Sudan in the 1880s.

This first fundamentalism arose out of resentment toward outside rule and toward widespread practices that were believed to be corruptions of true Islam. A new political order was established that laid the foundations for a tradition of direct political involvement by Islamic leaders of the Mahdist style. For the past century, this tradition has been identified with the continuing Mahdist movement (the adherents are called the Ansar) and the descendants of the Mahdi. The largest civilian party in the days of parliamentary politics has been the Ummah party, based on the Ansar, and the prime minister in the parliamentary era of 1986–89 was a great grandson of the Mahdi, Sadiq al-Mahdi.

The Mahdist movement survived the conquest by the British in 1898 and became one of the major political forces in the modern Sudan. In the first half of the twentieth century, the Ansar formed the core of the nationalist movement advocating the separate independence of the Sudan (as opposed to the other nationalist movement calling for unity with Egypt). The Ansar have provided a political power base for important Sudanese leaders throughout the twentieth century. However, the Mahdist leadership divorced itself from the chiliastic elements of the original Mahdist vision and represents a powerful sociopolitical establishment. The Mahdist tradition represents an already established Muslim identity, and Mahdist leaders have acted to preserve that position rather than become active advocates of fundamentalist reform in the Sudan.

When fundamentalism emerged in the twentieth century, it took a form similar to and was influenced by the Muslim Brotherhood in Egypt.[23] It was primarily a movement among the modern educated Muslim Sudanese that began in the years following World War II as a reaction to the secularism of popular leftist movements and the domination of local politics by Muslim sectarian power struggles. Smaller groups came together by the 1950s to form the Muslim Brotherhood in the Sudan. This brotherhood participated in the politics of nationalism and then worked to support parties involved in parliamentary politics.

During this era the best-known leader of the brotherhood, Hasan Turabi, set the pattern that has been followed. The brotherhood itself does not act as a political party. Instead, it defines its mission as working within society. It provided support for parties like the Charter Front in the 1960s and the National Islamic Front in the 1980s. The brotherhood advocates the implementation of Islamic law in the Sudan and the gradual Islamization of all of Sudanese society. Although initially only a small group of intellectuals, it has now become much larger and more influential. It continues to draw its major support from the modern educated rather than the more traditional elements in society. In this sense, at least, the growing significance of fundamentalism in Sudan is tied to the modernization of society.

In summary, the explicitly fundamentalist movement in the contemporary Sudan did not arise directly out of the tradition of nineteenth-century Sudanese fundamentalism. It did, however, emerge for some of the same reasons: a concern over the loss of an authentic Islamic identity in the face of both secularist and sectarian influences and over the failure of nationalism and sectarian-based politics to provide solutions for the problems of the Sudan. As in Egypt, fundamentalism in the Sudan can be seen as a response to a perceived challenge to the Islamic character of society, to the vacuum created by the weakness of competing world-views, and also as a positive affirmation by modern people of the viability of the Islamic alternative in the contemporary world.

There are three different approaches to the state among Sudanese fundamentalist traditions. The first is the Mahdist, which was originally revolutionary in character. The Mahdi did not attempt to take control of the Turko-Egyptian state. Instead, he defeated it and replaced it with a different political system based on explicitly Islamic grounds. The successors to the Mahdi in the twentieth century have not had this same revolutionary approach. Instead, Mahdist leaders have worked within the framework of the existing political system to gain influence and control. The major exception to this was when the Mahdists actively worked to overthrow the regime of Jafar Numayri in the 1970s and 1980s. In these cases, however, the Mahdists advocated a return to a parliamentary system rather than the creation of a fundamentalist state. Sadiq al-Mahdi was jailed for his open opposition to Numayri's Islam-ization program in 1983. The political organizations of the Ansar therefore have become identified with parliamentary state traditions rather than fundamentalist ones.

The Muslim Brotherhood, in contrast, has maintained a position similar to the Egyptian brotherhood. Although it has been actively involved in the political arena, the brotherhood has not seen its primary goal as gaining control of the state. A statement by Hasan Turabi in 1980 reflects the long-term view of the Sudanese brotherhood: "our objective was not to gain political power but to consolidate Islamic principles in public and private life."[24] This stance has made it possible for the brotherhood to work actively with the state both in eras of military regimes and in times of parliamentary politics. The Brothers have had opportunities to participate directly in cabinets and they have chosen to accept those opportunities rather than to create a movement of Islamic political revolution. At the beginning of the 1990s the revolutionary style of Islamic fundamentalism is not an overt force in the Sudan.

A third fundamentalist approach to the state in the Sudan is the military-authoritarian one. In 1983, Jafar Numayri, after trying a variety of other ideological foundations for his regime, instituted an idiosyncratic fundamentalist program in the Sudan. Numayri's Islamization program originally received the support of the Muslim Brotherhood, but brotherhood leaders had reservations about its content and mode of implementation. For all practical purposes, Numayri was the state, and his program represented the state adopting fundamentalism as a policy of survival.

The military regime established in the summer of 1989 under the leadership of Umar Hasan Ahmad Bashir is identified by many observers with the Muslim Brotherhood. The new regime came into power with an apparent ideological commitment to a fundamentalist approach and represents a further development in "military fundamentalism" in the Sudan. The long-term impact of the militarization of ideological fundamentalism was not clear at the beginning of the 1990s but it certainly changes the basic position of the brotherhood.

There has been little fundamentalist opposition to the state as state in the Sudan. The state as Pharaoh has not been a very strong image. The one leader who might have been attacked as being a Pharaoh, Numayri, was an implementer of Islamization. Instead, Sudanese political tradition seems to be more shaped by the Mahdist image of the state as a tool of the faith. It has always been possible to imagine the formal identification of the state as Islamic. There are thus struggles to control the state, but fundamentalism has not appeared as an alternative system. The extremes of the spectrum found in Egypt are less significant in the Sudan.

This situation is related to the Sudanese national identity. Despite the significant numbers of Sudanese who are non-Muslim, the national identity as it emerged was predominantly viewed as being Muslim. In the first half of the twentieth century, politics and nationalist feelings developed primarily in the northern, predominantly Muslim part of the Sudan. Integrating non-Muslims into the national political community has been one of the major challenges facing Sudanese leaders since independence in 1956.

Sudanese Muslims in general have resisted moves that would

secularize the Sudanese national identity. Older Muslim groups like the Mahdists maintain special traditions. The role of the fundamentalists in this process has been to move the issue into the arena of modern identities. Relatively secularist Sudanese have been the primary opponents of sectarian Muslim politics, but the Muslim Brotherhood has been increasingly successful in advocating a nonsectarian but still Islamic national identity. In this position, the fundamentalists are emerging as the most articulate opponents of developments that would de-Islamize the Sudanese national identity.

For Sudanese fundamentalists, their attitudes toward the state and nation are shaped by the fact that these have been historically accepted as significantly Muslim. The mission of fundamentalism is, then, to preserve and purify rather than to create. Because of the close association of traditional Muslim forces with state institutions, the state is seen as requiring further Islamization but it has not been seen as the state of Pharaoh. Similarly, the Sudanese nation has been defined by Muslims in Islamic terms. The national mission, in this framework, is defined as keeping the national identity from becoming godless. In the contemporary era of civil conflict, this has direct political implications because it puts the Muslim Brotherhood in direct opposition to the secularization of state and national identity demanded by increasingly active non-Muslim elements of Sudanese society.

Islamic Fundamentalism in Nigeria

Muslim fundamentalists in Nigeria are part of a long tradition of Islamic activism. Islam came to West Africa gradually through many channels. By the end of the eighteenth century, many states and societies just south of the Sahara had become significantly Islamized. However, this process of conversion involved compromises that combined Islamic and local African practices and perspectives. Beginning in the late seventeenth century, Muslim activists in several areas of West Africa began to work to "purify" local Islamic life.[25] One of the most important of these revivalists was Uthman dan Fodio, who began his fundamentalist mission in the area of present-day northern Nigeria in the late eighteenth century.

Dan Fodio's activities resulted in a successful preaching mission and holy war, and the establishment of an explicitly Islamic sultanate in the region of modern northern Nigeria. The descendants of these Islamic rulers dominated the area during the nineteenth century and their influence continued into the twentieth as a result of their recognition as "Native Authorities" by the British. Since independence in 1960, these northern leaders have been important political forces, in fact dominating much of the politics of the first parliamentary era (1960–66).

The colony that the British created and called Nigeria was not, however, exclusively or even primarily Islamic. Major non-Muslim peoples were included in the colony. These groups, concentrated in the southern regions of the country, were the most active in the modern sectors of society and were the most visible in the developing nationalist movements. The territory of Nigeria was very different from the land and state of Uthman dan Fodio. The independent state of Nigeria is an ethnically and religiously pluralist one. The political system is actively federalist in tone, in an effort to recognize the fact that no single group or region represents a majority in the country.

Although the Nigerian federal experiment began with great hopes, it failed to provide effective or stable government for the country. Since independence, military rule has alternated with periods of parliamentary politics. Amidst this unstable, pluralist environment contemporary Islamic fundamentalism has developed in Nigeria.

In the years immediately following independence, the most visible forms of Islamic activism and involvement in politics were the conservative party politics of the northern Muslim establishment and the relatively nonpolitical missionary activities in southern regions. Northern politicians were generally not reformist in perspective but they helped protect Islamic communal interests in the broader Nigerian political arena. The mission activities were remarkably successful, and a growing proportion of southern Nigerians had some Islamic identification. Much of this expansion involved an adaptation to local conditions instead of a fundamentalist approach. For example, the largest number of Muslims in the southern regions is among the Yoruba (about half of whom are Muslim), and it is said that "one of the most striking characteristics of present Yoruba religious practice is its open tolerance of divergence."[26]

There was little visible fundamentalism in the early years of independence. However, in the 1970s and 1980s, explicitly fundamentalist groups and individuals gained growing significance. Even the old establishments have become more open advocates of fundamentalist-style ideas and policies. This is in part a result of the weakening power of the old establishments and the growth of a modern educated Muslim constituency that is very concerned about maintaining a clear Islamic identity in the context of pluralism and unstable (and often corrupt) politics. This emerging Islamic advocacy is increasingly national rather than being tied to specific regional groups or interests. It has not taken the form of a single, national Islamic organization. Instead, "Islamic discourse, at the national level, has tended to become embedded in diverse institutions, above all in the media, the educational system, and the courts."[27] Although the older styles of Islamic life have not, of course, disappeared, these new, more countrywide and fundamentalist forms have gained increasing significance.

One reflection of this change has been the debate over the role of Islamic law in Nigeria. This became a major issue during the deliberations in 1977–79 creating the Constitution for the second civilian republic. When Muslims advocated the establishment of a *Shari'a* court system at the federal level rather than just in Muslim regions, the debate became so bitter that the military head of state had to intervene and stop the discussion. Rather than continuing the old style of Muslim politics where leaders of establishments worked within the balance of federal politics to ensure their own positions, this debate reflected the growing activist Muslim desire to reshape the political community of Nigeria as a whole.

Islamic activism has taken various forms in Nigeria in recent years. The most militant is the Maitatsine movement in the northern regions. This movement originated with the teachings of Mallam Muhammad Marwa, who preached against the modernization and corruption of Nigerian society. His messianic visions resulted in open conflict in some northern cities, which continued even after his death. Marwa's teachings are judged to have gone beyond the limits of Islam by most Nigerian Muslims, and his impact has been more messianic than fundamentalist. However, the widespread impact of the Maitatsine movement reflects the growing, active Islamic consciousness in Nigeria.

Two of the most prominent fundamentalists in contemporary Nigeria are Abu Bakr Gumi and Ibraheem Sulaiman. Gumi is an older figure with strong ties to the northern Muslim establishment. He has been a reformist in some traditional ways, opposing localist popular Islamic groups whom he accuses of diluting the faith with local customs. In recent years he became a popular radio preacher and is said to be "the foremost spokesman of what might be termed conservative Islamic reformism in northern Nigeria."[28] He has a large following but tends to give his support to established Islamically identified parties working within the existing political framework.

Ibraheem Sulaiman is more radical in his positions, being closer to people like Ali Shariati in Iran. He is a university lecturer who speaks primarily to students and the modern educated Nigerians, often writing in English. He identifies his position as being within the authentic West African Islamic revivalist tradition, having written significant studies of the holy war of dan Fodio and the Islamic state that he created.[29] His vision is of an Islamic society not bound by the traditional attitudes and structures of the old establishments that has liberated itself from the domination of the colonial heritage and Western ideas of secularism. He is active in opposition to both Marxism and secular African nationalism.

These two leading fundamentalists have contrasting views of the state, although both have as a long-term goal the Islamic transformation of the Nigerian political system. In the days of civilian party politics, Gumi worked closely with the party of the northern Muslim establishment. He accepted the constitutional framework and worked within it to reduce the influence of secularism and religiocultural pluralism. For him, the state, though corrupt and in need of significant transformation, was not Pharaoh. At the same time, he did not accept the fundamental principle underlying the Constitution, which was the recognition and acceptance of the pluralism of Nigerian society.

Sulaiman's position is more radical. "The country called Nigeria" is seen as a British creation, while the primary community is that of the caliphate created by dan Fodio and, more broadly, the Muslim world community.[30] In this context, while Sulaiman does not advocate open revolution against the state, he does not recognize its validity. For Sulaiman, "mankind is divided, in its beliefs and ideologies, into two distinct categories—the unbelievers and the believers. . . . This divide . . . transcends race and social and economic differences. . . . The difference that exists between a believer and an unbeliever is not merely one of opinion; it is a profound difference, embracing at once ideals, morality, politics, culture and attitudes."[31] In this context Sulaiman cannot accept the legitimacy of the Nigerian state and works to replace it by an Islamic one. Although his opposition is not violent, it is revolutionary in that it advocates the total replacement of the existing system by another.

For most fundamentalists in Nigeria, the state is not a legitimate entity. The differences among them relate to whether or not the state is reformable and the degree to which one accepts the existing pluralism. The existing state system accepts the reality of religiocultural pluralism in Nigeria and attempts to provide a balance among conflicting interests. Fundamentalists like Gumi seem to believe that this system can be transformed into an authentically Islamic one by working from within, while more radical fundamentalists do not accept that evaluation.

There is little relationship between the state and any specific national identity. Most Nigerians' primary identity is with their ethnic, linguistic, or religious community. In this context, most fundamentalists agree that the Muslim in Nigeria is primarily Muslim rather than Nigerian. "The greatest political problem for Nigerian Muslims, especially the northern majority, is the maintenance of their religion and ethnic distinctiveness."[32] The differences between Gumi and Sulaiman again emphasize the more radical stance of the latter. "Whereas Abubakar Gumi understands Islam as the value system and basis of identity of one of Nigeria's competing communities, Sulaiman tries to detach it from any particular communal basis, to present it as a universal as opposed to a particularist solidarity, as an ideology relevant to all Nigerians."[33] The Muslim community, however, for both is not the same as the Nigerian nation.

The attitude of Nigerian fundamentalists toward the state and nation is clearly shaped by the position of Islam as only one of a number of competing identities in the country. There is thus an implicit, and often explicit, vision of the end of the political order as it currently exists and the creation of a new state and political identity. Even though tactics may, as in the case of Gumi, involve participation, the fundamentalist position in Nigeria is inherently revolutionary.

Islamic Fundamentalism in South Africa

South African Muslim communities are relatively small but are well established. One major group is Southeast Asian in origin, descended from political exiles and slaves brought by the Dutch as early as the seventeenth century. This community is of Malay origin and is legally identified with the "Coloured" population of South Africa. Almost all of them live in the Cape Province and represent the Cape Muslim Community. At present they number more than 150,000 people and comprise slightly more than half of the total South African Muslim population.[34] The other half consists primarily of Muslims of South Asian origin, whose community began with immigration of workers and traders in the mid-nineteenth century. Most of the South Asian Muslims live in Natal and the Transvaal areas.

The general political evolution of South Africa affected the lives of these Muslim communities but both Cape and South Asian Muslims have maintained a significant degree of social isolation. As a small minority, their major effort, historically, has been to accommodate themselves to South Africa conditions while keeping their own Islamic identity. The result has been communities guided by religious leadership that has been eager to avoid upset or turmoil. In political terms, the Muslim establishment has been conservative. While some Muslims became politically prominent, they did so as individuals and Islam was not an important part of their public image.

This situation began to change significantly by the 1970s. The legal tightening of apartheid in the 1960s placed growing restrictions on Muslim communal life. The community in Cape Town began to organize protest meetings under the leadership of the local *imam*, Abdallah Haroon, but this type of action was opposed by the South African ulama establishment. Imam Abdallah Haroon was arrested in 1969 and died while in prison. He has become a symbol of Muslim activism for the younger generation of Muslims.

In the early 1970s, several new organizations emerged, the largest of which is the Muslim Youth Movement (MYM), established in 1970. The MYM was strongly influenced by the emerging global Islamic resurgence and was visited by prominent figures from the Egyptian Muslim Brotherhood and the Jamaat-i-Islami of Pakistan. The MYM concentrated on the comprehensive vision of Islamization presented by these thinkers and tended to hold itself aloof from the arena of activist politics in South Africa. Only in the mid-1980s, under pressure from other newer activist Muslim groups, did the MYM become more directly involved in South African developments.

A more militant group called Qiblah was established in 1980. Inspired by the success of the Islamic Revolution in Iran, Qiblah believed in the possibility of organizing an Islamic revolution in South Africa. The group was small but its militance appealed to Muslim youth in South Africa, which had an impact on the thinking of the larger Muslim organizations. When asked how an Islamic revolution could succeed in a country where Muslims comprise such a small proportion of the population, Ahmed Cassim, the leader of Qiblah, responded that "Islam does not look at the sociological reality of minorities versus majorities but at the divine reality of truth and falsehood."[35]

The Call of Islam, formed in the mid-1980s, is the Muslim group most directly involved in the South African nationalist effort. It is associated with the United Democratic Front and, more indirectly, with

the African National Congress. It was formed by MYM leaders who were
forced to choose between the isolation of the MYM and involvement in
the African national struggle in South Africa. Its leaders speak more of
universal values than of explicitly Islamic values. This has made the Call
of Islam seem "lukewarm to the most emphatic supporters of the
concept of Muslim solidarity and to those who advocate the ideal of an
Islamic state."[36] Call of Islam has thus emerged more as an explicitly
South African force than as an Islamic fundamentalist movement. Similar to the conservative ulama, Call of Islam integrates itself into the
South African scene, but in contrast to the ulama, it opposes the existing
system. Its aim is to have Muslims be "an integral part of that non-
racial, non-sexist, and democratic South Africa which will arise out of
the ashes of apartheid."[37]

The issue of relations with the state is of critical importance to
Islamic fundamentalists in South Africa. They represent part of a spectrum of approaches that range from the conservative survivalism of the
old establishments to the revolutionary antiapartheid position of the
Call of Islam. Neither of these nonfundamentalist parts of the spectrum
calls explicitly for the creation of an Islamic state. It is the fundamentalists, in groups like the old MYM or Qiblah, who are unwilling to accept
either a black or a white regime as being legitimate in Islamic terms.
The fundamentalists affirm the validity of an Islamic alternative, despite
their position as a very small minority within society.

The fundamentalists do not identify with the black nationalist
sentiments. Neither white nor black in the South African context,
Muslim fundamentalists find little that attracts them in any form of
South African nationalism. Islamic teachings that stress the universal
nature of the Islamic community have appeal. The development of
fundamentalism among the Muslim communities in South Africa has
opened the way to a greater sense of membership in the global Muslim
community and a willingness to hold back from too direct an involvement in the struggles of South African society. "In spite of its internal
differences often added to by contact with different Muslim countries,
the South African Muslim community is more and more becoming an
inseparable and integral part of the international Muslim ummah [com-
munity]."[38] It is the fundamentalists who are leading the way in this
development.

For South African Muslim fundamentalists, their attitudes toward
the state and nation are shaped by the fact that Muslims are a very small
part of their society and marginal to the great developments in politics

and culture. As a result, affirmation of Islam means a relative withdrawal from the state and units of national identity in favor of a purist isolation from the unbelievers. Parallel to this is an increasing effort to integrate the South African Muslim community into the larger world of Islam.

Conclusion

State and nation are significant focal points for Islamic action in Africa. The Islamic political experience in Africa, however, tends to keep these concepts separated. Analysis assuming that African political systems are emerging (or collapsing) nation-states will miss critical dimensions of the relations between religion and politics in Islamic Africa.

As fundamentalist groups have emerged, there has been a much greater tendency to accept or work with the state rather than to accept any type of non-Islamic national identity. Fundamentalists in Egypt have been willing to work with the state and also assume at least some stance of Egyptian nationalism, since both the Egyptian state and national identity have a visible Islamic component. However, even in this case, the challenge to that Islamic dimension raised by the secularism of modernizing development has caused more radical fundamentalists to reject both state and society as having departed from legitimate Islam. Similarly, to the extent that both state and national identity are tied to Islam in the Sudan, the fundamentalists there are willing to work within the system.

In Nigeria, the separation becomes more apparent. The state and the Nigerian identity are clearly not based on Islam. As a result, cooperating with the state is more a matter of political power balancing and is done more by the older establishments that by the fundamentalists. There is clear fundamentalist opposition to a non-Islamic national identity and this becomes an important factor in the potential instability of Nigeria. Finally, in South Africa, even when there is an appealing Third World cause, fundamentalists have been unwilling to act within a framework that is not clearly Islamic. The Call of Islam leaders have moved away from the more strictly fundamentalist conceptualization of their situation as they have become actively involved in the struggle against apartheid.

The state in contemporary Africa is not necessarily a nation-state. An analysis of the relationship between religion and politics in Islamic Africa helps to emphasize this point.

A second conclusion is also suggested by the Islamic fundamentalist experiences in Egypt, Sudan, Nigeria, and South Africa. Although some groups started much earlier, the beginnings of the current prominence of these fundamentalists are in the 1970s. The simultaneous nature of this rise to prominence might suggest a coordinated movement of transnational character. However, despite some mutual contacts, the rise of fundamentalism cannot be seen as simply a grand conspiracy on a global scale. In each of the four cases, special local conditions shaped the development of Islamic fundamentalism.

The common features in these otherwise very different societies are noteworthy. By the 1970s significant modernization and social transformation had occurred in each of these societies. Old patterns of social action and old socioreligious establishments were increasingly marginalized or co-opted by the emerging sociopolitical order. These changes presented a real challenge to the continuing Islamic identification of the communities of Muslims, and the old establishments were unable to cope with the changes. In that situation, a new generation, educated in the modern systems and not drawn from the old establishments (at least directly), stepped forward to champion Islam and reaffirm its validity. One common feature is, then, fundamentalism as a defensive action, undertaken by a new generation of Muslims who had despaired of the old establishments being able to act effectively.

A second common feature is that this defensive affirmation came in the 1970s, after a variety of other worldviews had been tried and found wanting. The rise of fundamentalism in Egypt, for example, did not come until after the corruption and failure of liberal nationalism, parliamentary democracy, and radical Arab socialism. In speaking of the brotherhood in Egypt, Ibrahim notes that the brotherhood's "religious populism is proving to be the functional equivalent to Nasser's national socialism."[39] By the mid-1970s there was an intellectual and ideological vacuum for many in the younger generation of African Muslims. Islamic fundamentalism seems for many to have filled that void.

Islamic fundamentalism is able to fill the vacuum in a way that reflects the third common feature—it is an appealing worldview in the contemporary world. It is not simply a nostalgic longing for medieval glories nor is it a Luddite reaction to the complexities of industrial and postindustrial society. As a result of the developing conceptual sophistication of writers in the 1950s and 1960s, Islamic fundamentalism emerged in the 1970s as a well-articulated and appealing contemporary ideology. This is true in all four of the cases examined in this chapter.

Islamic fundamentalism is not the worldview of the "traditional" rural person nor of the old-fashioned Muslim establishment figures. It is the worldview of the graduates of the schools of science, engineering, and medicine, and for many other modern educated people. For them, it provides a positive, viable alternative to the now confused and often discredited ideologies of the West, both capitalist and Marxist.

Islamic fundamentalism, as reflected in the experience of Islamic Africa, is emerging as an important element in the political scene of that continent. It is not a single monolithic force, but it is an important tendency that is shaping the relations between religion and politics in Africa. Its influence calls into question theoretical and practical assumptions about the viability of the nation-state model for African societies.

Notes

1. James A. Caporaso, "Introduction to a Special Issue on the State in Comparative and International Perspective," *Comparative Political Studies* 21, no. 1 (April 1988): 3.

2. Ali Banuazizi and Myron Weiner, "Introduction," in *The State, Religion, and Ethnic Politics: Afghanistan, Iran, and Pakistan,* ed. Ali Banuazizi and Myron Weiner (Syracuse, N.Y.: Syracuse University Press, 1986), 7.

3. For an interesting discussion of the emergence of the territorial nation-state, see Richard Rosecrance, *The Rise of the Trading State* (New York: Basic Books, 1986), 73–79, passim.

4. Crawford Young, "The African Colonial State and Its Political Legacy," in *The Precarious Balance: State and Society in Africa,* ed. Donald Rothchild and Naomi Chazan (Boulder, Colo.: Westview Press, 1988), 29.

5. Ibid., 30.

6. See, for example, Rupert Emerson, *From Empire to Nation* (Cambridge: Harvard University Press, 1960); and Dankwart A. Rustow, *A World of Nations: Problems of Political Modernization* (Washington: Brookings Institution, 1967).

7. Bernard Lewis, "Preface," in Gilles Kepel, *Muslim Extremism in Egypt: The Prophet and Pharaoh,* trans. Jon Rothschild (Berkeley: University of California Press, 1985), 10. See also Bernard Lewis, *The Political Language of Islam* (Chicago: University of Chicago Press, 1988), 2–3.

8. Ira Lapidus, "Islam and Modernity," in *Patterns of Modernity,* vol. 2, *Beyond the West,* ed. S. N. Eisenstadt (New York: New York University Press, 1987), 90.

9. See the discussion in James P. Piscatori, *Islam in a World of Nation-States* (Cambridge: Cambridge University Press, 1986), chapter 3.

10. E.I.J. Rosenthal, *Political Thought in Medieval Islam* (Cambridge: Cambridge University Press, 1962), 44.

11. See, for example, Mansour Farhang, "Resisting the Pharaohs: Ali Shariati on Oppression," *Race and Class* 21, no. 1 (Summer 1979).

12. Kepel, *Muslim Extremism,* 240.

13. Syed Qutb, *Milestones,* trans. S. Badrul Hasan (Karachi: International Islamic Publishers, 1981), 68–69.

14. See, for example, the discussions in Kepel, *Muslim Extremism,* and in John Obert Voll, *Islam: Continuity and Change in the Modern World* (Boulder, Colo.: Westview Press, 1982).

15. Richard P. Mitchell, *The Society of the Muslim Brothers* (London: Oxford University Press, 1969), 321.

16. Wilfred Cantwell Smith, *Islam in Modern History* (Princeton, N.J.: Princeton University Press, 1957), 41.

17. Saad Eddin Ibrahim, "Egypt's Islamic Activism in the 1980s," *Third World Quarterly* 10, no. 2 (April 1988).

18. R. Hrair Dekmejian, "The Anatomy of Islamic Revival: Legitimacy Crisis, Ethnic Conflict and the Search for Islamic Alternatives," *Middle East Journal* 34, no. 1 (Winter 1980): 11.

19. John O. Voll, "Islamic Renewal and the 'Failure of the West,'" in *Religious Resurgence,* ed. Richard T. Antoun and Mary Elaine Hegland (Syracuse, N.Y.: Syracuse University Press, 1987).

20. Mitchell, *Society of the Muslim Brothers,* 234–35.

21. See the discussion in Ibrahim, "Egypt's Islamic Activism," and Saad Eddin Ibrahim, "Anatomy of Egypt's Militant Islamic Groups: Methodological Note and Preliminary Findings," *International Journal of Middle East Studies* 12, no. 4 (December 1980).

22. John O. Voll, "The Sudanese Mahdi: Frontier Fundamentalist," *International Journal of Middle East Studies* 10, no. 2 (May 1979).

23. John O. Voll, "The Evolution of Islamic Fundamentalism in Twentieth-Century Sudan," in *Islam, Nationalism, and Radicalism in Egypt and the Sudan,* ed. Gabriel Warburg and Uri Kupferschmidt (New York: Praeger, 1983).

24. Voll, "Evolution of Islamic Fundamentalism," 135.

25. For a survey of this process see Sulayman Nyang, "West Africa," in *The Politics of Islamic Revivalism,* ed. Shireen T. Hunter (Bloomington: Indiana University Press, 1988).

26. Robert M. Wren, "Yoruba," in *Muslim Peoples: A World Ethnographic Survey,* ed. Richard V. Weekes, 2d ed. (Westport, Conn.: Greenwood, 1984), 874.

27. Allan Christelow, "Three Islamic Voices in Contemporary Nigeria," in *Islam and the Political Economy of Meaning,* ed. William Roff (Berkeley: University of California Press, 1987), 229.

28. Ibid., 231.

29. Ibraheem Sulaiman, *A Revolution in History: The Jihad of Usman dan*

Fodio (London: Mansell, 1986); and Ibraheem Sulaiman, *The Islamic State and the Challenge of History* (London: Mansell, 1987).

30. Sulaiman, *Islamic State,* 149.

31. Ibid., 1–2.

32. Akbar Muhammad, "Islam and National Integration through Education in Nigeria," in *Islam and Development,* ed. John L. Esposito (Syracuse, N.Y.: Syracuse University Press, 1980), 189–90.

33. Christelow, "Three Islamic Voices," 240.

34. J. A. Naude, "Islam in South Africa: A General Survey," *Journal, Institute of Muslim Minority Affairs* 6, no. 1 (January 1985): 21–23.

35. Farid Esack, "Three Islamic Strands in the South African Struggle for Justice," *Third World Quarterly* 10, no. 2 (April 1988): 486.

36. Ibid., 492.

37. Ibid., 498.

38. Naude, "Islam in South Africa," 32.

39. Ibrahim, "Egypt's Islamic Activism," 648.

PART VI

Asia

11.

Islam and the State: The Case of Pakistan

MUMTAZ AHMAD

This chapter focuses on the Islamization drive in Pakistan as it proceeded under three leaders who consecutively ruled that nation almost uninterrupted for thirty years: Field Marshal Mohammad Ayub Khan (1958–69), Zulfikar Ali Bhutto (1971–77), and General Zia-ul-Haq (1977–88). The first of these leaders, Ayub Khan, promoted a reformist version of Islam to enhance his goals of economic development, national unity, political stability, and regime loyalty. His efforts were resisted by the ulama (the body of mullahs), who resented Ayub Khan's attempt to "use" religion for political objectives. The struggle between Ayub Khan and the ulama, involving such issues as the Muslim Family Laws Ordinance (MFLO) and the nationalization of the *Auqaf* (religious endowments), set the stage for similar struggles in the Bhutto and Zia regimes.

Ayub Khan's Islamic Modernism and the Ulama's Response

The relationship between Islam, politics, and the state during the Ayub Khan era developed during three distinct periods into which his decade-long rule can be divided.[1] The first period, which began with the imposition of martial law in October 1958 and ended with the promulgation of a new constitution in June 1962, was marked by Ayub Khan's attempt to use Islam as a vehicle for socioeconomic development. During this period the martial law regime undertook a massive program of modernization and institutional reorganization of the state and economy, and presented Islam as a progressive and forward-looking religion.

The second period spanned from 1962 to 1965 and witnessed the revival of political activities under a new constitutional order with an indirectly elected presidential form of government. In the wake of the hectic and divisive politicking of this period, Ayub Khan underscored the value of Islam as a basis of national unity. The third period began with the September 1965 war with India, which marked the gradual political decline of the Ayub era. It ended in March 1969 after months of antigovernment agitation, mass rallies, violent processions, and nation-wide turmoil. It was during this period that Ayub Khan tried to use Islam as a basis of political stability and regime legitimacy.

Islam and National Development

The linkage between the programmatic emphases and political needs of the regime on the one hand, and the use of selective aspects of Islamic ideology on the other, was dictated more by political dynamics than by a conscious choice. While the first period was characterized by efforts to modernize Islam, however, the second and third periods witnessed an ideological reversal in which the emphasis shifted to more traditional Islamic values that were found more suitable to justifying a strong central government and the legitimacy of the regime.

Although Ayub Khan did occasionally pay rhetorical homage to Islam, saying, for example, that "a nation's advancement is incomplete without moral and spiritual progress" and that "without Islamic way of life, Pakistan is no more than a mere wasteland,"[2] his main priority was not Islam at all; he knew "only one miracle that can change the destiny of our nation, and that miracle is hard work, honest work, clean work."[3] Ayub Khan believed that the true Islamic spirit was "dynamism, prog-ress and development"; but over the centuries, Islam had become "more dogmatic and academic and less dynamic and practical."[4] In an Eid message in May 1961, Ayub said,

> One of the most dominating features of Islam is that its principles are timeless and eternal, and make it possible for every age to apply and implement them in the light of its requirements and environments. . . . They are a beacon-light for the faithful. . . . Beacon-lights are meant for guidance and not for stagnation. Stagnation is a manifestation of darkness and needs no light to grow and flourish. The secret of real progress is that we should

comprehend the basic principles of Islam, hold fast to them and under the search light of the past, discover fresh avenues for their application in the present and the future.[5]

Unlike President Zia, who emphasized that Pakistan was created to implement Islamic principles in the new state, Ayub emphasized the need to elevate the national character, as well as to build progress and prosperity for the people, as the goals of the regime.[6] He desired to build a "modern, progressive, united and strong Pakistan under the banner of Islam."[7] Thus, he identified economic development, national integration, and political stability as the three pillars on which the edifice of Islam was to be rebuilt in order to meet the requirements of modern times. In 1959, while giving details of the new Constitution, Ayub Khan reassured the people that it would reflect "the glorious principles of Islam" while, at the same time, methods and details would have to be in accordance with conditions prevailing in the world today: "We must go forward, keep pace with the modern scientific world; we cannot be backward by thousands of years."[8] Ayub Khan's approach throughout was to reduce all problems, be they political, social, cultural, educational, or religious, to their relevance to economic development and scientific progress. When controversy arose on the issue of national language in the early 1960s in the context of Pakistan's religious identity and national goals, Ayub's response was that "the problem has to be viewed essentially as an academic and scientific problem," that is, its relationship to the prospects for development of science and technology in the country.[9]

Ayub Khan clearly expressed his views on Islam and its role in Pakistan in a speech at Darul Uloom Islamiya in Sind within a few months after he assumed power. The president reminded the ulama that Islam had emerged more than thirteen hundred years ago as "a dynamic and progressive movement" that "gave a new meaning and purpose to man's endeavors." "Unfortunately," he observed, "with the passage of time, the Muslims at large sought to concentrate more on the dogmatic aspects of Islam and less on its inherent greatness as a movement." He lamented the fact that while every innovation came to be considered unIslamic and the innovators as nonbelievers, "those who clung to mere formality and dogma and remained static claimed to be true Muslims."[10] Later, in a letter to Mufti Mohammad Shafi of Darul Uloom, Karachi, Ayub Khan expressed his hope that the ulama would fulfill their new responsibilities of liberating "religion from the debris of wrong superstitions and prejudices" and making "it keep pace with the march of time."[11]

Reforming the Muslim Family Laws

The first real test of the ability of the state to effect changes in the traditional domain of the religious establishment came in 1961 when the government enacted the Muslim Family Laws Ordinance. It was the most controversial and important legislation in religious affairs passed up to that time and set the future direction for the relationship between Ayub Khan's government and the ulama. The ordinance provided for the restriction of polygamy, regulation of divorce procedures, and improvement of maintenance provisions for women. It also required that all marriages be registered with government authorities before they would be recognized as legally valid, and recognized the inheritance rights of orphaned grandchildren, who had been debarred from inheritance under the traditional law.[12]

The ordinance was hailed as progressive legislation by modern educated women and liberal circles but was severely opposed by the ulama of all schools of thought. In practice, it altered the daily lives of Pakistani women very little, but its challenge to the religious establishment was enormous. First, it established an important precedent whereby the state would appropriate the right to legislate in Islamic affairs. Second, in the view of the ulama and the fundamentalist Jamaat-i-Islami (JI), the ordinance had violated the sanctity of the traditional Islamic laws of marriage, divorce, and inheritance by introducing changes of a "fundamental nature."[13] Third, it directly challenged the monopoly of the ulama in Muslim family laws and transferred one of the most important remaining domains of their power to the state. The power to conduct marriages, pronounce judgments on the validity of divorce, and give authoritative views on inheritance and maintenance were now to be turned over to the secular authorities of the state. Fourth, and probably most important from the point of view of the JI, it underscored the ascendance of Islamic modernists, albeit under the sponsorship of the state, over both the traditionalists and fundamentalists.[14] The MFLO was thus seen as the first move in a series of measures that the new regime was planning to "modernize Islam" and to "liquidate" the traditional champions of Islamic orthodoxy.[15] Finally, the ordinance created administrative and judicial institutions within the structure of the state for adjudicating family disputes, which had been previously decided by the *fatwas* (religious decrees) of the private ulama. Thus the ulama, to remain in "business," were now being forced to accommodate themselves to, and collaborate with, the newly created institutions by seeking registration with the state authorities.

As expected, the ulama of all schools of thought and the JI joined hands to oppose the MFLO. Fourteen prominent ulama from Lahore issued a joint statement describing the ordinance as "against Islam" and asked the government to withdraw it forthwith. That the ulama were much more concerned about the loss of their influence rather than about the changes in the traditional formulation of Muslim family laws is evident from a statement by a group of prominent ulama of Karachi, in which they proposed that if the government appointed competent ulama as *Qazis* (religious judges) and registrars of marriages, "the problems and difficulties of jurisprudence and religion . . . [could] be overcome through mutual discussions."[16] For Ayub Khan and his modernist associates in the government, however, the MFLO was a test case of their ability and determination to "liberate Islam from the debris of wrong superstitions and prejudices," to "make it keep pace with the march of time," and to fight against the obscurantist forces in the religious establishment. The regime, therefore, used the full force of martial law to curb any criticism of the new legislation by the ulama and the fundamentalists. Mian Tufail Mohammad, the secretary-general of the JI, who had obtained and published the anti-Family Laws *fatwas* of the fourteen ulama from Lahore, was arrested and the booklet containing the *fatwas* was confiscated. The government also imposed a ban on any public criticism of the ordinance. In a letter to Mufti Mohammad Shafi of Darul Uloom Karachi regarding his objections to the MFLO, Ayub Khan was firm and blunt, especially on the question of polygamy: "I consider it [polygamy] a barbaric torture of the highest order. As the head of State, I just cannot close my eyes to it."[17]

Controlling the Religious Auqaf

Another aspect of the social organization of religion in Pakistan that Ayub Khan considered to be a major obstacle to his efforts to control the political and socioreligious life of society, build a strong state, and pursue the goals of modernization and development was the institution of sufi *pirs* (spiritual guides), shrines, and their *sajjada-nishins* (hereditary custodians of shrines).[18] The *sajjada-nishins,* who were either themselves big landlords or were associated with the traditional landowning interests as religious mentors, posed a challenge not only to Ayub Khan's socioeconomic reforms but also to his efforts to build both a nationally oriented bureaucratic administration and state structures that could reach the people unmediated by rural nobility and religious hierarchy. As a religious institution, the shrines represented what President Ayub often referred to as "the debris of wrong superstitions" and a decadent form of Islamic piety. The *pirs* and *sajjada-nishins* of major shrines in Punjab and Sind exercised enormous spiritual and political influence over their disciples and followers throughout the country, and controlled thousands of acres of landed property attached as *waqf* (religious endowment) to the shrines. Nationalization of the private *Auqaf* (plural of *waqf*) therefore constituted a prime case in which Ayub Khan's three major goals—a strong central government, economic development, and modernization of religious institutions—converged. In 1959, the government issued the West Pakistan Waqf Properties Ordinance, giving them the power to take over and manage shrines, mosques, and other properties associated with religious endowments. A separate Auqaf Department was created to manage the spiritual and financial affairs of the shrines and mosques taken over by the government. Another law issued in 1961 further extended the authority of the Auqaf Department by removing some of the legal obstacles to undercutting the political power of both the hereditary *pir* families and the ulama.[19] Although the main targets of *Auqaf* legislation were the hereditary *pirs* and *sajjada-nishins,* whom the orthodox ulama themselves considered as spiritually bankrupt and degenerate, the ulama saw the new legislation as a serious threat to the autonomy of the religious institutions. The establishment of a separate Auqaf Department, in particular, was seen as a move toward the gradual appropriation of religion and religious institutions by the state, as had occurred in many Middle Eastern Islamic societies. The ulama's apprehensions were not unfounded. Although the government initially confined its program of taking over religious endowments to major shrines only, in principle the legislation conferred wide powers on state authorities to bring any religious establishment under their control. As the ulama had feared, these powers were later extensively used to expand the reach of the Auqaf Department and to take control of hundreds of mosques in West Pakistan.[20]

Using Religious Leaders as Agents of Social Change

The strategy of the newly created Auqaf Department was "to develop a new ideology with respect to the saints and shrines."[21] This new ideology emphasized those aspects of sufism that conformed with the developmental goals of the regime: promoting national integration, economic development, social reform, a work ethic, and a universalist outlook. The annual *'urs* (anniversary) celebrations at major shrines, which are attended by hundreds of thousands of devotees, became forums for agricultural extension, industrial exhibitions, and dissemination of new techniques in animal husbandry. The new emphasis on scientific and technological activities at the shrines, as opposed to the previous practices of chanting, singing, dancing, or narrating miracles of the saints, reflected Ayub's vision of the role of Islam in Pakistani society. What better use of a shrine could there be than to teach villagers how to raise cattle, use improved seeds and fertilizer, and operate tractors and tube wells?

Ayub Khan's efforts were not confined to controlling the religious divines and the ulama; he also wanted to "reform" them for use in implementing his developmental goals. In 1961, he issued instructions to both provincial governments to "make constructive use of the Islamic religious leaders' abilities."[22] New and attractive pay scales were established for the *imams* and *khatibs* of the government-controlled mosques to attract young and aspiring graduates of the *madrasas*. A prominent Egyptian scholar was engaged to advise the government on setting up an academy for the training of the ulama. This academy was later established in Lahore under the auspices of the Auqaf Department of West Pakistan. The courses taught at the academy included the history, geography, and politics of Pakistan; international affairs; and problems of economic development, unity, and harmony among various Islamic sects. The ulama were also taken to visit various development projects and were apprised of their significance and contribution to national development. The Pakistan Academy for Rural Development in Peshawar, a US-AID funded training institution, launched a massive project of rural development with the help of the local *imams* and *khatibs* of mosques. The ulama associated with the project became agents of socioeconomic change in their respective localities: they operated adult literacy centers, acted as extension workers for the departments of agriculture, health, and animal husbandry, managed cooperative societies, and distributed fertilizer, improved seeds, and pesticides to the farmers.

Modernizing Islam

But while the government tried to utilize the services of the nonpolitical ulama for developmental purposes, the JI and the political ulama as represented by the Jamiyat Ulama-i-Islam (JUI) became increasingly critical of Ayub Khan's efforts to "modernize" Islam through government-controlled research institutions. Of particular concern to the ulama and the JI were the activities of the Central Institute of Islamic Research, which under the directorship of Professor Fazlur Rahman became one of the most productive and controversial religiointellectual centers in the 1960s. The purposes of the institute, as explained by the government, were "to define Islam in terms of its fundamentals in a rational and liberal manner . . . and to interpret the teachings of Islam in such a way as to bring out its dynamic character in the context of the intellectual and scientific progress of the modern world."[23] The ulama considered these terms of reference of the institute to be a blueprint for the beginning of secularism in Pakistan. As a major source of intellectual strength and justification for the modernization efforts of the regime, and because of its unorthodox views on a variety of issues ranging from social reform to doctrinal reformulations, the institute soon became a target of the ulama's hostility. The liberal-modernist orientation of the institute and its director manifested itself in such controversial issues as family laws, birth control, bank interest, and mechanical slaughter of animals. Some writings of Professor Fazlur Rahman on the nature of revelation and prophetic experience, the legal and historical status of *Hadith* (traditions of Prophet Muhammad), and the methodology and forum for formulating and interpreting Islamic laws, especially with reference to such methodologies as *ijma'* (consensus) and *ijtihad* (exercise of independent judgment), further convinced the ulama that the government wanted "to create dissensions and doubts even on those issues on which the *umma* has remained unanimous for centuries."[24] As one of the most intellectually competent and articulate spokesmen of Islamic modernism, Fazlur Rahman was engaged in what Mohammad Iqbal had earlier described as "the reconstruction of religious thought in Islam." His writings represented an attempt to show how Islam could accommodate Ayub Khan's modernism. The ulama and the JI saw "sinister motives" behind his intellectual formulations. They linked his views with government policies in the socioreligious sector and warned the people that this represented a broader "conspiracy" of the modernists and liberals to lead the country toward secularism.[25] In their *fatwa* issued against the proposed mechanical slaughter of animals, for example, the ulama observed that "the motive behind this official *fatwa* [Professor Fazlur Rahman's views on mechanical slaughter] is to lead the Muslims away from Islam and to make them an easy prey for atheism, Western culture, and communism."[26]

Islam and the 1962 Constitution

Yet another disappointment for the ulama was the new Constitution announced by President Ayub Khan in March 1962. First, the Constitution changed the name of the republic from the Islamic Republic of Pakistan to the Republic of Pakistan. Later, however, as a result of intense pressure from the ulama and the JI, the Constitution was amended to add the word "Islamic" to the name of the country. Second, the ulama and the JI were in favor of keeping the Islamic provisions of the 1956 Constitution, which they maintained provided the bare minimum legal structure necessary for an Islamic state. They had asked Ayub Khan to incorporate the "Basic Principles of an Islamic State"—popularly known as the ulama's twenty-two points drawn up in January 1951—as an operable part of the Constitution.[27] The new Constitution retained most of the Islamic provisions of the 1956 Constitution but did not make them mandatory. Third, the new Constitution replaced the phrase "Qur'an and Sunnah" with the word "Islam," a change that the ulama thought denied the authenticity of *Hadith* as a source of Islamic law and allowed a liberal and modernist interpretation of Islam.

The 1962 Constitution also contained a preamble similar to the one in the 1956 Constitution. The ulama and the JI welcomed this part of the Constitution, since it was based on the Objectives Resolution, both the harbinger and the symbol of their influence on constitution making in the 1950s.

In principles of lawmaking, the Constitution stated that "no law should be repugnant to Islam." The ulama and the JI had two major problems with this principle of lawmaking. First, in their view the word "Islam" should have been specified by mentioning the "Qur'an and Sunnah." Second, the ulama wanted the repugnancy clause to be made justiciable in the superior courts.[28] The Constitution, on the other hand, stated that the responsibility for deciding whether a proposed law did or did not disregard the repugnancy clause rested with the legislature concerned and that the validity of a law should not be called into question on the grounds that the law violated the principles of lawmaking.[29] Article 6 (2), however, provided that the lawmakers could refer to the Advisory Council of Islamic Ideology "for advice" any question that arose as to whether a proposed law disregarded these principles. The chapter on "Principles of Policy"—another nonjusticiable part of the Constitution—reproduced, with minor changes, all the Islamic provisions contained in the Directive Principles of State Policy of the 1956 Constitution. Article 9 provided that the president should be a Muslim.

Part 10 of the Constitution contained provisions for the two Islamic institutions. The first was the Advisory Council of Islamic Ideology, whose responsibility it was (1) to recommend means by which Muslims could live in accordance with the tenets of Islam, and (2) to advise the legislature or executive on any questions of the Islamicity of proposed laws. The other institution was the Islamic Research Institute, which was to undertake research and instruction to assist "in the reconstruction of Muslim society on a truly Islamic basis."[30]

Besides these constitutional issues, the major demands of the ulama and the JI, as always, had been the introduction of Islamic penal laws, elimination of *riba* (interest), and the prohibition of drinking, gambling, and the free mixing of sexes, the questions of least interest to President Ayub. Unlike the military regime of General Zia-ul-Haq, which appointed fifty-three different commissions and committees to make recommendations on various aspects of Islamic reforms from 1977 to 1985, the military government of Field Marshal Ayub Khan set up thirty-seven reform commissions and committees between 1958 and 1966 to review virtually all aspects of Pakistani society, economy, and government;[31] yet none of these commissions was directly concerned with Islamic issues. In 1958, Ayub Khan appointed the Law Reform Commission to suggest how justice might be better and speedily done and how to restructure the laws of procedures and evidence, as well as to recommend changes in the legal system. Indicative of the general thrust of the Ayub regime's ideological orientation, out of the 368 recommendations of the commission, not a single point dealt with the Islamization of laws or legal procedures.[32]

The Ulama and the Ayub Regime

Although the majority of the ulama disagreed with Ayub Khan's policies regarding the Muslim Family Laws Ordinance and birth control, and disapproved of the modernist Islamic scholarship coming out of the Islamic Research Institute, these disagreements did not necessarily result in a united front of *all* the ulama against Ayub's government. On the contrary, the majority of the Brelvi ulama remained solidly behind Ayub Khan and supported him during the presidential election of 1964.[33] These ulama, along with some belonging to other schools of thought, in fact, issued a *fatwa* delegitimizing the candidacy of his opponent, Miss Fatima Jinnah, saying that it was against Islam to appoint a woman as head of the state.[34] Even Maulana Ihtesham-ul-Haq Thanvi from the Deoband school, who in 1961 opposed the introduction of the MFLO and later launched a personal crusade against Professor Fazlur Rahman and the Islamic Research Institute, remained Ayub Khan's ardent supporter. The *pirs* and *mashaikhs* (spiritual guides), led by the *Pir* of Deval Sharif of West Pakistan and the *Pir* of Sarsina Sharif of East Pakistan, also helped Ayub Khan to counter the influence of the anti-Ayub ulama and the religious political parties associated with the candidacy of Miss Fatima Jinnah in the 1964 presidential elections. Ayub Khan also encouraged the activities of the nonpolitical reformist Islamic movement, the Tablighi Jamaat (TJ), in order to neutralize politically activist religious groups. Some ulama were also mobilized to support the idea of the strong central government envisaged in the new Constitution.[35]

Among the traditional ulama, consistent opposition came from the Deobandi ulama based in the Northwest Frontier Province (NWFP) and led by Maulana Mufti Mahmud of the JUI, the Ahli-Hadith ulama of Lahore and Karachi, and the ulama of the Nizam-i-Islam party of East Pakistan. However, this opposition never assumed the character of either a solidly united religious front or of an ulama-led mass movement, as it did against Prime Minister Bhutto in 1974 and in 1977. The ulama were still at a relatively rudimentary organizational stage, and their potential social constituency found Bhutto's rhetoric of Islamic socialism more attractive and responsive to their concerns than the ulama's call for *Shari'a* (Islamic law).

The Jamaat-i-Islami and the Ayub Regime

From among the religious groups, the most serious challenge to the Ayub regime came from the JI, which continued to criticize Ayub Khan's government throughout his reign. The JI also took the initiative in organizing the ulama in their opposition to the MFLO in 1961. The government reacted by arresting the secretary-general of the Jamaat,

Mian Tufail Muhammad. Although political parties were banned during the four years of martial law, the JI continued to operate as a religious organization. It used its publicity resources, workers' loyalty, nationwide organizational network consisting of hundreds of branches, and its "nonpolitical" subsidiary organizations of students, labor, and professionals, to launch a major offensive against the legitimacy of the regime even during the martial law period. The modernist ideas propounded by the government-controlled research centers constituted the primary target of their attack. As a counterideological measure against Ayub Khan's modernism, the JI published two special issues of its monthly magazine *Chiragh-i-Rah,* one entitled "Ideology of Pakistan" and the other entitled "Islamic Law." These two volumes became the most frequently quoted works on the Islamic basis of Pakistani statehood and the efficacy of *Shari'a.* However, the major weapons in Jamaat-i-Islami's ideological crusade against modernism were the works by its founder, Sayyid Abul Ala Maududi, especially *Islam and Birth Control, Parda* (Veil), *Sud* (Interest), *Family Relations in Islam, Islamic Law and Constitution,* and *Sunnat ki A'ini hassiyat* (The constitutional status of the *Sunnah*), which were reprinted in thousands and made widely available through the JI's nationwide marketing and distribution network. The Jamaat established its own research institute in 1963, the Islamic Research Academy in Karachi, to neutralize the effects of the modernist interpretations of Islam as presented by the Central Institute of Islamic Research, Institute of Islamic Culture, and the Auqaf Department.

The Jamaat-i-Islami was the first political party to resume its work when martial law was withdrawn in June 1962. It was also the first opposition group to issue a blistering critique of the 1962 Constitution.[36] The JI further intensified its politicoreligious opposition to Ayub Khan after the lifting of martial law and restoration of political activities. The Jamaat leaders undertook tours of all major cities and towns of the country to attack Ayub Khan's religious and political policies. As a consequence, when in October 1963 the JI held its national convention of workers in Lahore, it was marred by government-sponsored violence in which one JI worker was killed. Finding the JI's oppositional activities too menacing, the provincial governments of East and West Pakistan, through two separate orders in January 1964, declared the JI to be an illegal organization, locked its offices throughout the country, and confiscated its records and assets.[37] Simultaneously, all members of the Central Executive Council were arrested under the Maintenance of Public Order Ordinance. The Supreme Court, however, declared the official ban on the Jamaat illegal in September 1964, that is, just a few months before the proposed presidential election in January 1965, thus allowing it to participate in the election campaign in support of the candidacy of Miss Fatima Jinnah for the president of Pakistan.

The Jamaat accused the Ayub regime of promoting secularism; disregarding Islamic norms and way of life; violating traditional Muslim personal law; introducing family planning and birth control, which in Jamaat's view encouraged sexual permissiveness and licentiousness; and above all, vigorously trying to "modernize" Islam and to legitimize the Western way of life by "distorting" Islamic teachings.[38] The Jamaat's hostility toward Ayub was so strong that it was ready to reverse the position earlier taken by its founder, Maulana Maududi, that women were not allowed to hold public offices in an Islamic state. In October 1964, the Central Executive of the Jamaat adopted a resolution declaring that "in the present unusual situation the candidature of a woman as head of the state is not against the *Shari'at.*"[39]

The Challenge of the State and the Ulama's Response

The reforms of Ayub Khan in the religious sector may not, in retrospect, seem radical enough, but they represented an important attempt to break the hold of the ulama, the *pirs,* and the fundamentalists over the social and political life of the Muslim masses. What was not realized at the time, however, was the capability of the ulama and the fundamentalists to regroup themselves and join other disgruntled political forces to take their revenge. The fundamentalists responded to Ayub Khan's attempts to modernize Islam by mounting an effective challenge to Pakistan's state.

The ulama's response was most creative. First, they formed alliances with other political groups and thus demonstrated their ability to seek new allies, even among secular and left-wing parties, to protect their vital interests. Some Deobandi ulama of the JUI in Sind and Punjab became supporters of the Pakistan People's party (PPP), while in the NWFP the JUI entered into a formal political and electoral alliance with the secularly oriented National Awami party (NAP), as a result of which JUI was able to form a coalition government in this province in 1972 under the chief ministership of Maulana Mufti Mahmud.

The second response can be described as "organizational renewal." The JUI, the Jamiy at Ulama-i-Pakistan (JUP), and Jamiyat Ulama-i-Ahl-i-Hadith (JUAH) were primarily ulama organizations. They were never organized as political parties and did not contest elections before the 1960s. Only during the Ayub Khan period did the JUI and JUP organize themselves as modern political parties, establish regular headquarters, elect officeholders, collect funds, organize regional and city branches, set up executive committees and public relations departments, and start issuing policy statements on issues ranging from domestic inflation to foreign relations. They published their own daily newspapers and weeklies and put up their own candidates in local, provincial, and national elections. They also organized their students and youth wings under separate leadership and hierarchy. The impetus for this massive organizational renewal evidently came from the challenges of both the state and fundamentalist JI.

Third, the period also saw organizational renewal in the primary bases of power, that is, the mosques and the *madrasas*. The economic prosperity of the business community generated by Ayub Khan's "decade of development" had made considerable funds available for the building of new mosques, especially in the expanding urban centers of Punjab and the NWFP. Making use of the modern organizational and management techniques and taking advantage of the Societies Act, the ulama, in association with local business communities, established mosque management committees in the urban areas to preclude the possibility of the Auqaf takeover, to seek a closer alliance with the merchant class, and to ensure a regular flow of funds for the maintenance and staff of mosques. It was also during this period that mosques were clearly denominationalized and strict vigilance was maintained to make sure, for example, that a Brelvi mosque remained under the control of a Brelvi *'alim* (singular of ulama) and *imam,* a Deobandi mosque under a Deobandi *'alim* and *imam,* et cetera.

The Ayub period also witnessed immense growth in the number of new *madrasas*. This growth was reminiscent of past responses of the ulama in the face of threats to the centrality of their beliefs.[40] The number of higher *madrasas* doubled during this period, as is evident in Table 11.1.

Furthermore, to expand the recruitment base of students for higher *madrasas,* hundreds of "feeder" *madrasas* were established in small towns. Management practices and educational procedures of *madrasas* were rationalized, and all major schools of thought—Deobandis, Brelvis, Ahl-i-Hadith and Shi'a—organized separate federations of their respective *madrasas*. These federations provided additional organizational strength, increased the political power of the *madrasa* system, and

TABLE 11.1

Growth of Higher *Madrasas* in Pakistan, 1947–1971

Year	Madrasas	Teachers	Students
Before 1947	137	—	—
1950	210	—	—
1960	472	1,846	40,239
1971	908	3,185	55,238

Sources: Hafiz Nazar Ahmad, *Jaiza madaris-i-arabiya maghrabi Pakistan* (Lahore: Jamia Chishtia Trust, 1960), and *Jaiza madaris-i-arabiya maghrabi Pakistan 2* (Lahore: Muslim Academy, 1971); *Report, quami committee braa'y deeni madaris Pakistan* (Islamabad: Ministry of Religious Affairs, Government of Pakistan, 1979).

afforded the ulama an effective platform for coordinating their strategies aimed at countering the government's efforts to reduce their social and political influence and religious autonomy.[41] The bureaucratization of the *madrasa* system also included the rationalization and expansion of its financial resource base through the recruitment of the business community into its management structures. The expanding economy provided ample funds, and the new urban development schemes provided easy and cheap land for building new *madrasas* and expanding the existing ones. The spectacular expansion during the Ayub Khan era of Darul Uloom, Madrasa Arabiya Islamiya, and Darul Uloom Amjadiya of Karachi; Jami'a Ashrafiya, Jami'a Na'imiya, Jami'a Madina, and Darul Uloom Hizbul Ahnaf of Lahore; Madrasa Khairul Madaris and Madrasa Qasimul Uloom of Multlan; and Jami'a Ashrafiya and Darul Uloom Haqqaniya of Peshawar, gives clear evidence of the relationship between urban development, economic growth, and religious revival.[42] The rapid expansion of the economy during the decade of development provided the ulama with new and bigger sources of income. This not only mitigated the economic crisis experienced by the religious establishment from the time of the end of Muslim political power in India, but also lessened its dependence on the rural-based feudal class. Its new financiers were the bazaar merchants, small- and middle-level businessmen, commission agents, wholesalers, and in Karachi, people like Valika, Bhawani, and Adamji, members of the top twenty-two business families in Pakistan. This meant that the religious establishment now had the financial wherewithal not only to face the challenge of the state but also to adjust its structures in accordance with the new economic realities.

Parallel to the changes in the training patterns of the elite Civil Service of Pakistan (CSP) to cope with the new responsibilities of development administration were some important curriculum reforms in the *madrasas* as well. Among other things, the most important reform was the introduction of the English language and some other modern subjects, especially in the field of law, in major *madrasas*. Many *madrasas* linked their courses of study with the general education curriculum, thus enabling their students to acquire undergraduate and graduate degrees from government schools and colleges. Members of the younger generation of prominent ulama families were encouraged to acquire modern (English) education to prepare them to deal with the state authorities on one hand and their modernist and fundamentalist opponents on the other. This paid enormous dividends during the Bhutto and Zia periods, to which we now turn our attention.

Islam and the State in the Bhutto Era

Although most of the revivalist measures in Pakistan were introduced during the military regime of President General Zia-ul-Haq, they were rooted in the period of Zulfikar Ali Bhutto's rule. As paradoxical as it may seem, Mr. Bhutto—probably the most secular of all Pakistani leaders—opened the floodgates of Islamic revival in the process of his attempts to reinstate the ideological integrity and legitimacy of the Pakistani state in the aftermath of its dismemberment in the 1971 war with India. Bhutto also unleashed the forces of Islamic revival as a result of political bargaining with his opponents in the religious right. Although the Islamic measures introduced by Bhutto were piecemeal and peripheral to the core of his socioeconomic policies, their impact on subsequent Islamic developments was far-reaching. By incorporating extensive Islamic provisions in the 1973 Constitution, and later in 1974 declaring Ahmadis—a heretical sect founded by Mirza Ghulam Ahmad in the early part of this century in British India—as non-Muslims, Bhutto helped raise the expectations of the religious parties and prepared the ground for a full-grown movement for Islamization during Zia's regime.

Although Bhutto entered the political scenario of the last days of the Ayub era with a serious challenge to the centrality of Islam as the organizing principle of state formation in Pakistan, the traumatic events of the 1971 civil war and the loss of East Pakistan convinced him that a renewed quest for authenticity and national identity must be firmly anchored in Islamic ideology.

The powerful Islamic current evident at the level of civil society in the "New Pakistan" in early 1972 had a great impact on the Constitution adopted in 1973. This Constitution, which was unanimously approved by all the political parties in the National Assembly as a show of national solidarity, has been described as the most Islamic Constitution in the history of Pakistan. Professor Fazlur Rahman maintains that Bhutto's decision to adopt an Islamic constitution bears "the unmistakable impression of a man who had his eyes fixed on the gallery to which he played unceasingly" and represents nothing but "vain populism."[43] However, one can also argue that Bhutto was genuinely striving for a constitution that enjoyed unanimous approval of all political parties, including the religious political parties, and could provide the Pakistani state "religious moorings in a sea of uncertainty."[44]

Bhutto, unlike Ayub Khan before him, did not initiate any religious reforms (on the model of the Muslim Family Laws Ordinance); neither did he take any other action that would cause the ulama to launch an agitation against him. Given his bitter experience with the religious groups during the 1970 election campaign, Bhutto was fully aware of the potential power and influence of the ulama and the Jamaat-i-Islami. In view of this, he tried to avoid initiating any policy measures that would provoke the wrath of the religious groups. On the contrary, to appease the ulama and enhance the Islamic credentials of his government in the eyes of the masses, Bhutto initiated a series of Islamization measures on his own.

First of all, he almost completely dropped any reference to socialism—a core element of his 1970 election campaign—in his policy statements and instead started using Islamic idioms and symbols. But his Islamization went beyond employing powerful Islamic religious imagery and symbolism in his public speeches and statements. In 1973, his government provided institutional machinery for the printing of an "error-free" Qur'an. In 1974, Bhutto changed the name of the Pakistan Red Cross, which he described as a legacy of Christian colonialism, to the Pakistan Red Crescent. During the same year, Bhutto did the ultimate for the ulama and the Jamaat-i-Islami: he amended the Constitution to declare the Ahmadis a non-Muslim minority. For the first time in the modern history of Islam the institutional structures of the state were used to excommunicate a heretical sect or to pass authoritative judgment on doctrinal issues.

Bhutto also undertook the establishment of the Ministry of Religious Affairs at the federal level. This action was intended to provide the state authorities some measure of control over the country's religious establishment. The ministry was assigned the task of developing and supervising the teaching of Islamic studies at all levels; promoting research and teaching of Islam in the institutions of higher learning; giving advice to other government agencies on Islamic religious matters; seeking cooperation from the ulama for national development; formulating policy guidelines for the provincial *Auqaf* departments; and taking over management of the annual pilgrimage (*haj*) to Mecca.[45] Bhutto's most triumphant moment came in February 1974 when he hosted the Second Islamic Summit Conference in Lahore. This conference was attended by thirty-eight Muslim leaders, including six kings, twelve presidents, six prime ministers, eight foreign ministers, and many other heads of international Islamic organizations. The conference, which has been described as the biggest gathering of its kind in the post–World War II period, provided an unprecedented opportunity to Bhutto not only to enhance his Islamic legitimacy at home, but also to realize his long-cherished dream to establish his credentials as a prominent leader of the Islamic world.

Simultaneously with his attempts to impress the ulama with his Islamic accomplishments, Bhutto also tried to neutralize their influence in politics and society. First he launched a countermove to check the forces of orthodoxy and fundamentalism by reasserting the authenticity of popular and folk Islam with the help of official channels, especially the state-controlled *Auqaf* agencies. Second, an attempt was made to mobilize the nonpolitical ulama and the ulama employed by the *Auqaf* departments in support of the government and its policies. In 1977, the government seriously contemplated taking over a few major *madrasas* as a test case, but the reaction of the ulama to this proposal was so swift and strong that the government abandoned the idea. The Ministry of Religious Affairs also contemplated the organization of the *Zakat* (obligatory alms tax) under the auspices of the state. The ulama, fearing that this would deprive their *madrasas* of one of the major sources of income, strongly opposed the move. As a result, the government decided to postpone the implementation of the *Zakat* scheme until after the March 1977 elections.[46] Bhutto's last, and perhaps most desperate, attempt to appease the ulama and the Jamaat-i-Islami came in the midst of the religiously charged mass movement of March–July 1977, when violent processions, demonstrations, and barricade fighting between the opposition political parties and the security forces had already created a serious and increasingly uncontrollable law-and-order situation. Responding to the ulama's campaign for the establishment of a truly Islamic system, Bhutto issued his own package of Islamization measures by banning alcoholic drinks, gambling, horse-racing, and dance and nightclubs; promising to reconstitute the Council of Islamic Ideology to include ulama acceptable to JI, JUI, and JUP; and committing himself to revise all existing laws in accordance with the teachings of Islam within a period of six months. The religious parties rejected his Islamization measures by describing them as "too little and too late."

That all these measures failed to enhance Bhutto's Islamic legitimacy among the religious groups and a majority of the people raises the important questions of who could use Islam more effectively and under what conditions. As paradoxical as it may appear, General Zia, who took the reigns of government from Bhutto in a military coup in July 1977, was much more successful in using Islam as a major source for the legitimacy of his government and its domestic and foreign policies. The relative success of General Zia in establishing this Islamic legitimacy can be explained not only by his strategic moves to seek support from the religious groups, but also by the structural imperatives of the state.

Islam and the Military in the Zia Era

The introduction of Islamic socioeconomic measures sponsored by the state, which was firmly in the hands of the military-bureaucratic oligarchy during the Zia period, raises important questions about what Hamza Alvi describes as the alternative modes of articulation of power by the state. It also opens new perspectives on the role of the military in the sociopolitical developments of "new" nations, as well as on Islam and the legitimation of power in a given social context.

The recent Pakistani experience runs counter to the popular notion of modernization theory—propounded most vigorously by Lucian Pye, among others, in the 1960s—that the military elite in the excolonial countries possess organizational and technical skills and beliefs that enhance their capabilities to play an important role in the process of modernization and development.[47] Besides belonging to a highly professional, rationally organized institution, the military elite also have been described as a modernizing force because of their social origins. It has been argued that the military in the post–World War II era in developing countries reflects the reformist outlook of a new breed of middle-class, urban-born officers who are socially and intellectually separated from the landed and business interests of their societies. Manfred Halpern, for example, has cited the modernization experiments of Mustafa Kemal of Turkey and Gamal Nasser of Egypt to argue that the new middle-class-based military officials in new states could initiate progressive changes in the socioeconomic conditions of their societies.[48]

Contrary to the expectations of the modernization theorists, the military in Pakistan, which has been the dominant partner in the ruling oligarchy since the late 1950s, has been less known for its concern for social reform than for the maintenance of its own power and privileged position. Drawn largely from the traditional landed families of Punjab and the lower districts of the NWFP and trained at Sandhurst Military Academy, senior military officers shared the ideology of Muslim nationalism with the civilian bureaucracy and the Muslim League leadership but had no sympathy either for the demands for fundamental structural transformation of society or for the revivalist ideology of the Jamaat-i-Islami and the ulama. The political influence and strength of the military as an institution increased significantly in the second half of the first decade of independence, when the interregional power struggle and the intraelite rivalries within the ruling sectors created a political stalemate, blocking the path toward a viable constitutional order and resolution of regional conflicts. Its power was further consolidated during the second decade when it directly assumed the control of the state apparatus under the leadership of Field Marshall Ayub Khan. The military then formed a coalition with the higher cadres of the civilian bureaucracy and became the basic referent in the new programs of socioeconomic and political development. The decade of Ayub Khan witnessed the formalization of a highly centralized rule largely dependent on the military–Civil Service coalition. Pakistan's membership in the Western defense system (SEATO and CENTO), and the U.S. military aid that accompanied this membership, further enhanced the organizational and technical skills and the coercive power of the military. With its prominent members assuming the highest political and administrative positions in the country, the primary concern of the military, henceforth, became the maintenance of the political status quo and the socioeconomic conditions under which it had emerged as the strongest political force in the country.

During the 1960s, the military-bureaucratic oligarchy used the ideology of developmentalism to enhance its political control and strengthen its fiscal resource base, and also to perpetuate the socioeconomic conditions and political arrangements that had given rise to its unmitigated control of the state apparatus.

The 1970s witnessed a series of crises for the state and its guardians—the military and the higher Civil Service. Economic development, political authoritarianism, and administrative centralization were the three pillars on which the ruling oligarchy had built its edifice of power and control during the 1960s. The 1968–69 anti-Ayub mass movement, led by Zulfikar Ali Bhutto in West Pakistan and Sheikh Mujibur Rahman in East Pakistan, challenged both the legitimacy and the efficacy of these pillars. The dismemberment of the country in 1971 as a result of the successful assault by the regionalist forces in East Pakistan against the central state further deepened this crisis. First, the guardians of the state were badly bruised and humiliated for their failure to protect the territorial integrity of the state. Second, the loss of East Pakistan brought new, popular political forces into power in the "New Pakistan," forces that represented the aspirations and interests of the nonelites. This new political leadership came with a popular mandate to enact major structural changes in the economy, polity, and society. Third, the legitimacy and the *raison d'être* of the state itself were challenged in the wake of the East Pakistan tragedy. This legitimacy crisis was primarily linked to the question of Pakistan's national identity and the ideological basis of the state. Fourth, the regional and ethnic separatist interests in the remaining parts of Pakistan, emboldened by the experience of East Pakistan and cognizant of the vulnerability of the state, became more assertive in challenging the authority of the state. All these developments compounded the general crisis of the state, which in accordance with the calculations and perceptions of the military-bureaucratic oligarchy, the populist and erratic political leadership of Zulfikar Ali Bhutto was unable to resolve. On the contrary, Bhutto was held responsible for unleashing the sociopolitical forces and initiating economic and administrative policies that, in the oligarchy's view, had further aggravated the crisis of the state.

One can argue, therefore, that the state- (or military-) sponsored Islamization during the Zia regime (1977–88), like the 1958 coup d'état of Ayub Khan, was an attempt on the part of the traditional guardians of the Pakistani state to regain control over the direction of change and to bring some order and management to the processes of change that had been essentially haphazard, erratic, and unpredictable during the Bhutto era. Islamization can thus be viewed as an efficient and necessary mode of articulation of power by the state at its critical juncture in the late 1970s. The civil and military bureaucratic elites did not oppose economic and social development; they only wanted to ensure that these developments took place in accordance with *their* preferences and interests and did not bring into the political arena those elements who could challenge the status quo or who enjoyed an independent, popular support base. Hence, the most important element in the Islamization strategy of the military regime was restoration of the authority of the state, which had eroded as a result of the populist rhetorics and policies of Bhutto, and also by the continuous agitational politics perpetrated by the opposition political parties. This restoration of authority was achieved through a combination of ideological and punitive measures: Islamic normative ideals (harmony of interests between the civil society and the state, obedience to state authorities as an Islamic virtue, and legitimation of the authority of the state itself in Islamic terms); Islamic penal laws; and martial law regulations (delegitimation of political dissent, detentions, imprisonments, corporal punishments, and executions for violations).

Another important objective of Islamization policies was to bring order into the productive sectors of society, to guarantee the sanctity of private property in order to restore confidence among private investors, and to find ways and means to meet the rising expectations associated with the welfare demands of the underprivileged classes that were encouraged during the Bhutto era. It was also necessary to ensure a steady and predictable flow of funds from the productive sectors of society for the fiscal stability of the state, which was facing a serious financial crisis as a result of declining investments, low savings rates, decreasing flow of foreign aid, and enormous budget deficits and trade imbalances. These objectives were achieved by providing constitutional guarantees for the protection of private property "in accordance with the principles of Islam"; by introducing the system of compulsory collection of *Zakat* and *Ushr* (bringing enough funds not only to distribute among needy individuals, but also to take care of the budget deficits of all social welfare, education, and health departments of the provincial governments);[49] by deregulating and denationalizing industrial and commercial enterprises to encourage private investment and, as a consequence, expand the tax base of the economy ("Islam encourages private initiatives," Zia told the Pakistan Chamber of Commerce and Industry);[50]

and by introducing the Islamic system of interest-free financing and banking, thus ensuring a greater control over the credit supply through the nationalized banks.

In view of the above conditions, the explanation for the rise of Islamic revivalist/fundamentalist ideology and its adoption by rulers as a means to respond to the structural crisis of the state becomes plausible. But this phenomenon is not peculiar to Islam. It appears that both Marxism-Leninism (in the cases of Ethiopia and Mozambique) and Islamic fundamentalism (in the cases of Iran[51] and Pakistan) have performed similar functions as far as the needs for legitimacy and imperatives of the reassertion of authority of the state are concerned.

In the case of Pakistan, one can argue that Islamic revival as a state-sponsored ideology emerged at a very critical time in the history of the Pakistani state. It helped facilitate the reconsolidation of political power in the monolithic structure of the state, through both ideological rationalization and institutional changes. Notwithstanding Bhutto's actual policies, his rhetoric had certainly created a psychopolitical climate conducive to more radical demands for popular participation, regional autonomy, and socioeconomic reforms, thus threatening the power and privileged position of the military-bureaucratic complex. The degree of radicalism and militancy that Bhutto had helped introduce into the political process was equally threatening. Islamic revivalism as an ideological instrument in the hands of the military rulers helped them in countering the militancy of the groups mobilized during the Bhutto regime. It also provided the rulers with a powerful ideological justification to delegitimize the political aspirations of the nonelite militant groups on the basis of their alleged anti-Islamic orientations. Simultaneously, Islamic revivalist/fundamentalist ideology and the Islamization measures adopted under its rubric, helped the guardians of the state to mobilize, as a countermeasure, important segments of society (religious political groups, nonpolitical ulama, lower sections of the new middle classes, and traditional petty bourgeoisie) as a solid support base for their power and policies.

When the military and the Civil Service intervened in the political process in the wake of the civil disturbances and decided to appropriate the Islamic revivalist ideology of the *Nizam-e-Mustafa* (the system of Prophet Muhammad) movement, they apparently were responding primarily to the crisis created by Bhutto's efforts to restructure the locus of power in the postcolonial state.

Throughout Pakistan's independent existence—from bourgeois

parliamentary regime to Ayub Khan's development-oriented dictatorship, from Bhutto's populist regime to Zia's conservative and authoritarian military rule—the social forces that supported and benefited from
the military–Civil Service oligarchic domination of the state, and the
dominant ideological overtones that gave legitimacy to this oligarchy,
have more or less remained the same. In broad structural terms, there
was no difference between General Zia's Islamic-oriented military regime and Field Marshal Ayub's development-oriented military
regime—only the mode of articulation of power changed from economic development to Islamic revivalism.

It is difficult to distinguish clearly between a situation in which a
particular religious movement—consciously or as a result of the unin-
tended consequences of its sociopolitical ideology—tends to reinforce
the existing socioeconomic formations of a society and one in which
traditional religious ideas are used by the rulers to perpetuate, legitimize, and strengthen their power position. There may be situations in
which the ideal interests of the religious groups and the structural
imperatives of the state, as represented by the power interests of the
existing political authorities, become clearly identical. One example of
this is the issue of political and cultural autonomy of the smaller regions
in Pakistan. The doctrinal orientation of the Islamic groups, which
predisposes them to view society in undifferentiated terms as Islamic
umma, is in direct conflict with the present political reality in which
certain regional communities do not consider that their "Muslimness"
obliterates their distinct ethnic and linguistic identities or invalidates
their demands for autonomy. The guardians of the state, on the other
hand, who view such demands as a prelude to a more equitable distribution of political power and economic resources across the various regions
of the country and, therefore, as detrimental to their own hegemonic
domination, resort to the use of Islam as a means to suppress regional demands. Ayub Khan used the notion of the unity of *umma* to strengthen
his highly centralized authoritarian control in the wake of demands for
regional autonomy by East Pakistan and other smaller provinces in West
Pakistan. Even a man with such secular views as General Yahya Khan
resorted to the invocation of Islamic ideology to justify his military
action against the autonomy movement in East Pakistan and, as a result,
was able to elicit active support in this regard from the Jamaat-i-Islami
and other religious parties. The notions of Islamic unity, solidarity, and
brotherhood also figured prominently in the speeches of General Zia-ul-
Haq.

The above analysis, however, does not preclude the possibility that among the ruling oligarchy there may be certain individuals—General Zia being the most prominent—whose Islamic commitment is genuine. In speaking of General Zia as an individual, for instance, it is difficult to isolate the elements of personal piety from the considerations of political expediency in his attitude and behavior with regard to his programs of Islamization. His personal religiosity undoubtedly affected the policies of his regime. The increasing sympathy for Islamic fundamentalist ideology among the middle stratum of the military establishment, especially in noncombat services, because of their changing social backgrounds and career patterns also had an effect. However, whatever degree of genuine religious enthusiasm and missionary zeal one may be able to identify in General Zia and some other military officers, it was certainly inextricably linked to their use of popular Islamic symbols to legitimize their continued grip on political power and safeguard the interests of social forces that constituted their bases of support. It is no wonder, then, that among the Islamic measures introduced by General Zia—the Islamic penal code; the system of *Zakat* and *Ushr* and interest-free banking holidays on Fridays; the Islamic university in Islamabad; *Shari'a* benches; prayer breaks during working hours; the wearing of *chadors* (veils that cover face and body) by female newscasters on TV; penal laws; revision of textbooks; holding of Islamic conferences; and patronization of religious festivals—virtually nothing threatened the status quo; the existing structure of social and economic power and political domination remained completely unaffected. On the contrary, most of these measures were, ideologically as well as functionally, necessary for the perpetuation and strengthening of the power position of the rulers and their support groups. *Zakat* and *Ushr* were used to ward off the welfare and distributive demands on the state and to legitimize the inequitable economic relations in society. Interest-free deposits were used to encourage savings in a faltering economy and to provide investments for the highly mismanaged public sector. *Zakat* and *Ushr* also helped alleviate the fiscal crisis of the state. Laws on theft and robbery were meant to assert the sanctity of private property. Penal laws (involving punishment with whipping) were intended to help the state authorities deal more effectively with the system-challenging elements in society. Rhetoric about an Islamic political system was a convenient cover to postpone free democratic elections, impose press censorship, detain political opponents, and ban political parties. Thus, seen from the perspective of the state, Islamization policies of the military regime could not have been devised otherwise. From political control and stability to ideological hegemony, from revenue extraction to regime legitimation, Islamization proved the most efficient ideological and institutional means to resolve the crises the Pakistani state faced in the late 1970s.

Conclusion

Among Muslim societies, the Pakistani case of the interaction of religion and state is most instructive. Being the very *raison d'être* of the new state carved out of the Muslim India, Islam has played a major role in the political development of Pakistan. The Pakistani case is also unique in that while Islam was used by the religious groups to challenge the hegemony of the state apparatus during the Ayub Khan and Bhutto periods, it also became a major source for the legitimacy of the state apparatus during the Zia period, when the military rulers used its symbols and institutional structures to rebuild their power base and meet the challenge of their opponents. The Zia government sought the moral commitment of the people by propagating an ideology that linked the destiny of both Islam and Pakistan to a strong, centralized state. Coming into power in the wake of the worldwide resurgence of Islam as a sociopolitical ideology, the Zia regime met the challenge of Islam, not by opposing it, but by selectively accommodating it within the authoritative structures of the state. The appropriation of Islam by the state during the Zia period helped facilitate more effective government control over the religious establishment than was possible during the Ayub and Bhutto eras, when relations between the state and religious groups were primarily conflictual.

Notes

1. This periodization of the Ayub era has been suggested by both Philip Jones and Lawrence Ziring; see Jones's "The Pakistan People's Party: Social Group Response and Party Development in an Era of Mass Participation" (Ph.D. diss., Fletcher School of Law and Diplomacy, 1979), 180–81, and Ziring's *The Ayub Khan Era: Politics in Pakistan, 1958–1969* (Syracuse, N.Y.: Syracuse University Press, 1971), 10–22.

2. *Dawn* (Karachi), February 26, 1959, 3.

3. Ibid.

4. Quoted in Edgar A. and Kathryn R. Schuler, *Public Opinion and*

Constitution Making in Pakistan 1958–1962 (East Lansing: Michigan State University Press, 1967), 13.

5. Mohammad Ayub Khan, *Speeches and Statements,* vol. 3 (Karachi: Pakistan Publications) (July 1960–June 1961): 135.

6. Mohammad Ayub Khan, *Pakistan Perspective* (Washington, D.C.: Embassy of Pakistan, n.d.), ix.

7. Quoted in Schuler, *Public Opinion,* 119.

8. Ibid., 43.

9. Mohammad Ayub Khan, *Friends Not Masters* (Karachi: Oxford University Press, 1967), 102.

10. *Dawn* (Karachi), May 4, 1959, quoted in Schuler, *Public Opinion,* 29–30.

11. Mohammad Ayub Khan, *Speeches and Statements* 3: 137, 140.

12. Freeland K. Abbot, "Pakistan's New Marriage Law: A Reflection of Quranic Interpretation," *Asian Survey* 3 (January 1962): 26–32.

13. Mian Tufail Mohammad, ed., *Muslim Family Laws Ordinance: The Opinion of the Ulama* (Lahore: n.p., 1961), 3.

14. Traditionalists, as represented by the *madrasa* (educated ulama), are primarily concerned with the preservation of the historical legacy of Islam, both as doctrine and social organization. The fundamentalists, as represented by the Jamaat-i-Islami, on the other hand, tend to emphasize the political role of Islam and strive for the establishment of our Islamic state, a state based on the principles of Islamic law (*Shari'a*). For a detailed discussion of the differences among the Islamic modernists, traditionalists, and fundamentalists, see this author's chapter on "Islamic Fundamentalism in South Asia: The Jamaat-i-Islami and the Tablighi Jamaat of South Asia" in Martin Marty and R. Scott Appleby, eds., *Fundamentalisms Observed* (Chicago: University of Chicago Press, 1991).

15. Ibid., 3–7.

16. *Dawn* (Karachi), March 8, 1961, 6, quoted in Schuler, *Public Opinion,* 97.

17. Mohammad Ayub Khan, *Speeches and Statements* 3:137.

18. Katherine Ewing, "The Politics of Sufism: Redefining the Saints of Pakistan," *Journal of Asian Studies* 42, no. 2 (February 1983): 251–53.

19. Ibid., 258.

20. By the late 1970s, the *Auqaf* departments of the four provinces of Pakistan and the federal government controlled more than eight hundred religious establishments, which included shrines, mosques and *madrasas.*

21. Ewing, "The Politics of Sufism," 259ff.

22. Schuler, *Public Opinion,* 111.

23. *The Forward March* (Karachi: Government of Pakistan, Department of Films and Publications, n.d.), 19. Article 207 of the 1962 Constitution also provided for the establishment of an Islamic Research Institute to "undertake Islamic research and instruction."

24. Jamaat-i-Islami, *Kiya jhatka halal hey?* (Is mechanical slaughter permissible?) (Karachi: Department of Publicity, Jamaat-i-Islami, n.d.), 4.

25. Ibid., 6, 32. It should be noted here that the majority of the ulama, either unknowingly or deliberately, tend to equate Islamic modernists with secularists.

26. Ibid., 4. This *fatwa,* which was signed by the ulama of all schools of thought, caused the government to withdraw its plan to introduce mechanical slaughter of animals in the country.

27. For details of the Islamic provisions of the 1956 Constitution, see Leonard Binder, *Religion and Politics in Pakistan* (Berkeley: University of California Press, 1968), 216–17, 227–32 and 271–72.

28. The power to determine whether a particular law is "repugnant to the teachings of Islam" has now been given to the Federal Shariat Court under a constitutional amendment enacted during the Zia period.

29. *The Constitution of the Republic of Pakistan* (Karachi: Superintendent of Government Printing, Government of Pakistan, 1962), Article 6 (1–2).

30. Ibid., Chapter 10, Article 207.

31. Ziring, *Ayub Khan Era,* 217.

32. See *Law Commission Report* (Karachi: Superintendent of Government Printing, 1959). During the entire ten-year rule of President Ayub Khan, there was only one attempt by a religious scholar, who was a member of the West Pakistan Assembly, to introduce a bill for the enforcement of Islamic penal laws. Its object was to punish married adulterers by stoning and unmarried adulterers by flogging [see *Gazette of West Pakistan* (Lahore, July 1, 1964)]. The bill made no progress due to lack of support and eventually was forgotten. Herbert Feldman, commenting on the demise of this bill, wrote in 1967: "It is, to say the least, unlikely that legislation of this character will ever find a place on the statute books of Pakistan." [Herbert Feldman, *Revolution in Pakistan: A Study of the Martial Law Administration* (London: Oxford University Press, 1967), 123.] What seemed "unlikely" in 1967 became a reality in 1979.

33. The Brelvis, a South Asian subdivision of Sunni Muslims, put more emphasis on saint veneration and other ceremonial aspects of religion than on *Shari'a* and orthodox rituals.

34. *Dawn* (Karachi), September 25, 1964, 1, quoted in Karl von Vorys, *Political Development in Pakistan* (Princeton, N.J.: Princeton University Press, 1971), 275; and Feldman, *Revolution in Pakistan,* 124.

35. Schuler, *Public Opinion,* 178.

36. Von Vorys, *Political Development in Pakistan,* 259–60.

37. Among other things, the government also accused in its press note that the JI had tried to damage Pakistan's friendship with Iran by criticizing the shah's assault on Qom and his decision to send Ayatollah Rohullah Khomeini into exile.

38. See the speech of Maulana Maududi in November 1964 in Karachi

published in a pamphlet, *Ayub Khan ka dauri-i-hakumat* (Ayub Khan's rule) (Karachi: Jamaat-i-Islami, 1964), 2–14.

39. *Pakistan Observer* (Dacca) October 3, 1964, 1, quoted in Von Vorys, *Political Development in Pakistan,* 275.

40. For similar cases of revival of orthodoxy through the *madrasas,* see H.A.R. Gibb, *Studies on the Civilization of Islam* (Boston: Beacon Press, 1962), 23–27; G. E. von Grunebaum, *Classical Islam* (Chicago: Aldine, 1970), 166–67; and Bernard Lewis, *Islam in History* (New York: Library Press, 1973), p. 223. For a different view on this, see Fazlur Rahman, *Islam* (New York: Doubleday, 1968), 221–25 and George Makdisi, "Remarks on Traditionalism in Islamic Religious History," in *The Conflict of Traditionalism and Modernism in the Muslim Middle East* (Austin, Tex.: University of Texas Press, 1966), 82–84.

41. These federations later fought successfully against the Bhutto regime in its attempt to control the *madrasas.*

42. The history of the growth and expansion of these *madrasas* can be seen in Hafiz Nazar Ahmad, *Jaiza madaris-i-arabiya,* 2d ed. (Lahore: Muslim Academy, 1972). The present author also collected various publications of these *madrasas* in 1975, which provide details of the expansion of their physical facilities and affiliated feeder *madrasas* during the 1960s.

43. Fazlur Rahman, "Islam in Pakistan," *Journal of South Asian and Middle Eastern Studies* 8 (Summer 1985): 50–51.

44. Mir Zuhair Husain, "Politics of Islamic Revivalism" (Ph.D. diss., University of Pennsylvania, 1985), 330.

45. Interview with Maulana Kausar Niazi, minister for religious affairs in the Bhutto government, Islamabad, August 30, 1979.

46. Later, when the collection and distribution of *Zakat* was taken over by the government during the Zia period, the ulama were assured that their *madrasas* would continue to receive funds from the provincial *Zakat* administrations in the form of student grants.

47. Lucian Pye, "Armies in the Process of Political Modernization," in J. J. Johnson, ed., *The Role of the Military in Under-Developed Countries* (Princeton, N.J.: Princeton University Press, 1962), 80–89.

48. Manfred Halpern, "Middle Eastern Armies and the New Middle Class," in Johnson, *Role of the Military,* 277–315.

49. *Zakat* and *Ushr* collections are now approximately equivalent to all federal government subsidies. It is also important to note that since 1988, *Zakat* and *Ushr* funds have been formally integrated into the federal revenue accounts.

50. *Dawn* (Karachi), December 18, 1979.

51. Leonard Binder, *Revolution in Iran,* Middle East Review Special Studies, no. 1 (1980), 18–40.

12.

Religion and Modernization in Gorbachev's Soviet Union: An Indirect Challenge to Secular Authority

JAMES W. WARHOLA

With the collapse of the Marxist-Leninist model, the Soviet Union is not left with Western modernism or postmodernism as its only alternatives. As Allen Kassof wrote, "The leading drama of our age is the exhaustion of socialism as a political and economic doctrine. For the first time in more than a century, there is no great alternative to the Western model of modernization—unless one counts religious fundamentalism."[1]

The persistence of religious vitality in the Soviet Union is undisputed, even by the regime itself. This represents a rather different type of challenge to secular authority than that posed by modernization or some other forms of contemporary politicized religiosity, such as Latin American Liberation Theology, Islamic political assertiveness, or the activities of the American New Christian Right. On one hand, the religious challenge in the Soviet Union is more oblique: there is as yet no "moral majority" there, no religiously inspired guerrilla underground, and as of this writing, little in the way of politicized Moslem assertiveness that might directly challenge the institutions of Soviet power.

However, the challenge to secular authority posed by invigorated religiosity in the USSR represents one of the gravest threats to the essence of Soviet power ever faced by the regime. One noted scholar long attentive to this theme summed up the situation in the late 1980s:

One of the most intractable dilemmas facing the Gorbachev leadership is the problem of religion. . . . The Gorbachev leadership remains confronted with a problem for which the Soviet government has not yet found a solution. Not only is religion alive and well in Soviet society, but it is handily surviving, and at times flourishing under, the best efforts of the state to suppress or even contain it. . . .

One thing is certain. If there is a religious revival under way in the USSR, and the evidence is increasingly persuasive that there is, then the nation and the society are on the brink of profound changes.[2]

This chapter maintains that a variety of factors have sustained the force of religiosity in the USSR; that the way in which the USSR came into the modern world gave secularizing tendencies a peculiar political twist; and that Soviet historical experience has spawned indirectly a resurgence of religiosity intrinsically threatening to the political legitimacy of the Soviet regime even without staging an overt political offensive against it. The aphorism frequently expressed by party functionaries not long after the Revolution—"either communism will win in the end, or Christianity will"—may turn out to be the most accurate point in the revolutionary catechism. Specifically, "forced secularization" was imposed as a critical dimension of modernization and was one of the sociopolitical pillars of "communist construction." Forced secularization (or "coerced atheization," as some Soviet commentators now label it) not only failed, but was counterproductive as an inhibitor of religiosity. An examination of how it failed illumines our understanding of the interplay of politics, social change, and religion in the USSR and elsewhere. The theme has only assumed greater significance with the Communist party's surrender of its monopoly on political power in February 1990. That concrete political surrender was preceded by an ideological capitulation not unrelated to the enduring strength of religion as a social and political force.

Soviet Policy and Practice toward Religion

The perdurability of religious vitality in the Soviet Union despite periodic episodes of concerted opposition has been noted by outside observers since the early years of Soviet power. Yet as one surveys the relatively sparse corpus of literature dealing with the topic since the 1940s, an element of surprise at the tenacity of religious commitment is often not far from the surface, even in major scholarly works.[3] And so it has remained until very recently. Even the most cursory examination of religion in the Soviet Union and formerly Communist Eastern European polities pointed to evidence of an undercurrent of religious vitality that appeared only to grow despite various forms of governmental repression. However, the Soviet regime's current acquiescence to religious vigor is not only unprecedented, but also a sharp reversal of official posture for virtually the entire Soviet era. This reversal is reflected in several revealing statements by Gorbachev made well after the package of radical reforms was launched in 1986. By June of 1988, the season of the Millennium of Christianity in Russia, Gorbachev asserted the following:

> We do not conceal our attitude toward the religious world view as being nonmaterialistic and unscientific. But this is no reason for a disrespectful attitude toward the spiritual worldview of believers, and still less for applying any sorts of administrative pressure for the affirmation of materialistic views.[4]

In retrospect, this statement clearly reflected a significant shift in the regime's orientation. If there were any question about the direction of the high leadership's posture toward religion after that assertion, it was removed by Gorbachev's subsequent policies of easing restrictions on religious practice. If there were any question about the mentality behind those policies, clarification was provided in a remark by Gorbachev in December 1989 in Rome:

> We have changed our attitude toward problems that, I admit, we used to approach simplistically—religion, for example. Its initial rejection characterizes not only our revolution but also, to one degree or another, all major social upheavals in other countries.
>
> In our country today, the church and the state are separate. But today *we proceed* not only from the assumption that faith is a matter of conscience for each person and something in which no one should interfere, but also *from the assumption that the moral values that religion has developed and embodied over the centuries can serve and are already serving the cause of renewal in our country.*[5]

This change, and what it may reveal about the *political* role of religiosity under conditions of a rapidly modernizing society, is explored in greater detail below.

A detailed chronicle of Soviet official attitudes and policies toward religion for most of the Soviet era is not necessary, as the academic literature is rather comprehensive.[6] It is sufficient to note the following points, some of which are common knowledge: (1) the general posture of the Soviet regime since the October Revolution has been to discourage religion both as a public phenomenon *and* as a matter of private belief; (2) periodically, severe and concerted efforts have been exerted by the regime to extirpate religious practice from Soviet life, using violence as well as verbal persuasion; and (3) from all evidence available, we may conclude that religiosity has retained a remarkable and growing degree of vitality for a significant portion of the Soviet population. In light of these general considerations, the phenomenon of deepening religiosity in the face of what might be termed *forced, rapid modernization* begs closer inspection.

The question involves first of all the role of the state in the religious dimension of social life. What are we to make of previous Soviet denials of religious persecution? It may be useful to bear in mind that European society has generally experienced a less distinct separation of church and state in the modern era (i.e., since the American and French revolutions) than has the United States. Therefore when examining what appear to be highly repressive state influences upon religious practice, American commentators may be operating from a somewhat skewed frame of reference. Note, for example, the following comment from a European scholar:

> Does the concept of separation of church and state still have any function in Europe today? The answer is that in terms of the liberal conception of this separation there is none. The decline of the liberal concept of separation of church and state in Europe, however, . . . does not necessarily mean there has been a decline in the separatist tradition *tout court*. The concept of church-state separation is a very deeply felt issue that goes well beyond the historical and juridical forms that it has assumed from time to time in specific social and political systems.[7]

Thus while it is undeniable that the Soviet regime has intruded into religious affairs to a far greater degree than the American state, the traditional Soviet denial of religious persecution should be understood from this comparative perspective. If the basis of comparison is Europe (even Western Europe) in the entire modern era, then Soviet statist intrusion into religious affairs appears not as severe, at least from an administrative perspective, as when the basis of comparison is the United States. Thus, while not diminishing the severity of the Soviet regime's antireligious posture, this point should be borne in mind when considering the domestic policy ramifications of Gorbachev's concept of incorporating the USSR into a "common European home." This concept is the most important element of Gorbachev's "new thinking" that impinges most directly on the new character of Soviet state-church relations.

The intention behind the Bolshevik seizure of power in October 1917 was to create a modern socialist democracy that would serve as the foundation for "communist construction," or the creation of full communism. Two points are especially critical: first, throughout Soviet history the leadership has heavily emphasized acceleration of economic and social development as an essential component of Communist construction. Under Brezhnev this was usually referred to as "laying the material-technical base of communism." To date this imperative has not abated under Gorbachev, although restructuring has changed the tactics dramatically.

Second, in the conventional Soviet view social development includes the adoption of a "mature worldview" by individual citizens. Public policy has been accordingly designed to encourage such a worldview. Thus in the USSR we observe a sort of forced modernization, with a particularly heavy emphasis on personal and societal secularization. While most modern or modernizing regimes have tended to experience some form of societal secularization willy-nilly, traditional Soviet conceptions of development have included a formal commitment to the secularization of both society and individual citizens' worldview. The statutes of the Communist party of the Soviet Union clearly reflect this commitment:

Section I. PARTY MEMBERS, THEIR DUTIES AND RIGHTS:
    2. It is the duty of a Party member . . .

        (d) to master Marxist-Leninist theory, to expand his political and cultural horizons, and to promote in every way an increase in Soviet people's consciousness and their ideological and moral growth. To wage a resolute struggle against all manifestations of bourgeois ideology, private-property mentality, religious prejudices and other views and customs that are alien to the socialist way of life.[8]

Strictly speaking, *any* adherence to religion or espousal of a religious worldview could have been—and usually was—tantamount to harboring a "religious prejudice," since that adherence contradicted dialectical materialism.

Thus, historically at the core of the overall Soviet political program was a formal commitment to rapid economic modernization and to secularization of society. The core questions thus become (1) just what is meant by secularization in the Soviet context? (2) what demonstrable effect, if any, has this "forced modernization" had upon religiosity in the USSR? and (3) what theoretical conclusions might be drawn from the Soviet case to deepen our understanding of religion and modernization in other national contexts?

Roots and Consequences of Soviet Forced Secularization

Despite official Soviet disclaimers predating glasnost, persecution of religion in varying degrees has characterized church-state relations in the Soviet Union since the earliest days of the regime. Governmental actions following the decree on "Separation of the Church from the State" in January 1918 demonstrate that the very concept has meant something quite different in the Soviet Union than in the Western world in general, and certainly in the American constitutional experience.[9] In the Soviet case, separation of church and state has meant in practice a rather clear subordination of nearly every aspect of religion to official purview by the regime—arguably the opposite of the original intention of the founders of the American republic, where disestablishment was seen as salutary for religion and thereby for the public good.[10]

At this point it is useful to consider religion as a social phenomenon in two distinct but related dimensions, each of which must be properly considered to understand the nature of the religious challenge to secular authority in the USSR.[11] The Latin etymological roots of the term *religion* suggest these two dimensions: (1) a set of private beliefs; and (2) a "public bond," from the two component roots, *res* (the public thing, as in republic) and *ligio* (as in ligament, ligation, ligatory, etc.). The eighteenth-century Enlightenment (of which both liberal democracy and Marxism are intellectual progenies) stood in reaction against *both* religious dogma and the institutionalization of religious power as de facto or de jure civil authority. However, in the subsequent course of the Western world, religion as a "public bond" came increasingly under legal proscription—what is commonly referred to as the "separation of church and state," though that separation has varied widely in the actual practice of pluralist democracy from one national context to the next. The more direct role of the Enlightenment in setting the course for church-state relations in East and West is taken up again below.

Religion as a set of private beliefs has been conventionally relegated to individual conscience both in law and in practice in the conduct of pluralist democracy. Not so in the USSR, despite the official, formal "separation of church and state" legally in force since January 1918. Given the programmatic orientation of the Communist party, and given the party's traditional claim for the scientific status of dialectical materialism, both types of religion have been fair game for the forced secularization process since the earliest days of Soviet power, although the concerted, forcible efforts to eradicate religion did not begin until the Stalin era.

Thus the secularization that has willy-nilly attended deepening modernization since the eighteenth century has had a peculiar and much more comprehensive character about itself in the USSR than in the pluralist Western democracies that had pioneered social and economic modernization in the first place. The Soviet regime insisted upon forcing in that country what appeared to be occurring spontaneously in the advanced capitalist countries, where proletarian revolution was forecast by Marx to occur first.

Yet the experience of secularization in both the West and the Soviet Union raises serious theoretical questions about the so-called secularization hypothesis which generally asserted that as a society modernizes, secularization broadens and deepens.[12] How satisfactory has this hypothesis proven as a long-range description of social change, and of the character of religion and politics under modern conditions? By the late twentieth century the hypothesis appears ready for critical reexamination.

While this hypothesis has come under close critical scrutiny for some time, few would dispute that since the eighteenth-century Enlightenment (and to some degree because of it), a form of secularization *had* deepened and broadened in the West, up to a point. At the very least, religion had come to play a rather different social and political function. Also, following Weber, certain aspects of secularization appear more or less directly related to socioeconomic modernization.[13]

Yet this pattern was generally *not* characteristic of the prerevolutionary Russian empire. It was certainly not true in any significant political, constitutional sense, beyond superficial concessions in the direction of religious toleration granted after the Revolution of 1905–6.[14] Nevertheless, a form of de facto "secularization" apparently occurred among the Russian Orthodox population some time prior to the October 1917 Revolution, with some of the population having become positively hostile or indifferent to formal religion.[15] In this respect early twentieth-century Russia differed sharply from much of Western Europe and North America concerning secularization of political authority, if not in popular attitudes.

During this social climate the Bolshevik regime assumed the task of inculcating a materialistic, nonreligious worldview into Soviet citizens. This task eventually took on a broad scope and grim measures, especially after passage of Stalin's comprehensive Law on Cults of 1928. The Stalin regime clearly felt that religiosity in nearly any form was at variance with official goals, was incompatible with the type of society being created, and that active measures against it were necessary.

Two important questions emerge. First, why did the Soviet regime feel the necessity of actively combating religion, given the ideological presumption that it would ultimately wither away along with other negative superstructural phenomena? Second, how is the remarkable durability of religious vitality in the USSR to be explained? Understanding these two questions will shed light on the contemporary religious challenge to secular authority in the USSR.

In answer to the first question, modernization in the USSR clearly took the form of *direct* confrontation with religion as an integral part of Stalin's revolution from above.[16] Significantly, the scope, duration, and determination of the regime's confrontation with religion was without historical precedent, even in the premodern era. Again the question is why. At least part of the answer is surely to be found in the personal animus of Lenin (and Marx) against religion. Another part is to be found in the intellectual roots of Leninism traceable to Peter Lavrov, Peter Tkachev, and other nineteenth-century Russian revolutionaries who insisted upon a "transitional dictatorship" on the way to socialism. Clearly no such "transitional dictatorship" could allow competing bases of genuine social power of any sort, and certainly not least that of the Russian Orthodox church's privileged position before the October Revolution.

However, Soviet leaders must have realized by the late 1920s that religious forces represented no explicit, direct political challenge to Soviet power. The civil war and foreign intervention were over; the

Russian Orthodox church had publicly, officially capitulated from its early privileged position; even the ideologically suspect National Bolsheviks and troublesome Moslem Basmachis had been militarily and politically throttled by the end of the 1920s. Why then the continued animus, and determination to force the process of secularization beyond that which—they believed—would occur spontaneously with the overall maturation of society into socialism?

Soviet hostility toward religion can also be traced, in part, to a widespread indifference or even hostility toward Russian Orthodoxy prevalent during the World War I era, as noted above. Representing something of a de facto secularization, this attitude may partially explain the popular support given to the avowedly atheistic party. Russia's general social conditions probably contributed to popular acquiescence in a plan of forced modernization, too. But it is impossible to judge accurately how deep and widespread this antireligious hostility was. It is not an empirical question and can hardly explain in full the vengeful persecution initiated in the late 1920s; in any case, public opinion determined Stalin's policies in no area. By that time Soviet power was clearly free of direct threat from religionists or practically anyone else, Stalin's paranoia notwithstanding. Nor can the fierce campaign against religion be explained solely in terms of that paranoia: Khrushchev's antireligion campaign was similar if less savage, and was not driven by any clearly demonstrable paranoia. That is, unless Khrushchev is imagined to have foreseen the current threat posed by religion in the USSR; significantly, he did not couch his campaign in those terms.

The important point is that some other underlying sociopolitical force appears to have been at work to give the regime's continuous antireligious orientation such a pronounced character. To be sure, the party's doctrinal basis—dialectical materialism—was most directly responsible for the insistence on a secular society. But again the question is, why the insistence on forcing what was believed to be historical inevitability, that is, the ultimate secularization of society and of individuals' worldview? We move closer to understanding that underlying force by considering the Russian empire's mode of entering the modern, post-Enlightenment political world.

Here the influence of the eighteenth-century Enlightenment upon religiosity in the modern world merits a closer look. In a broad sense the intellectual roots of both Western liberal democracy and Marxism are found in some of the core ideas of the Enlightenment: the emphasis upon reason, observation, and experimentation as avenues to knowledge instead of divine revelation; equality as opposed to established privileges for classes or individuals; a broad scope of civil and political liberties, including freedom of conscience and religious practice; and, by implication at least, the disestablishment of officially sanctioned religious authority in the civil realm. Yet few, with the major exception of Hegel in his "Lectures on the Philosophy of Religion" near the end of his life, have foreseen the possibility of Enlightenment ideals having gone so far in the direction of supporting antireligious tyranny. Kolakowski for one sees a direct link between these ideals and the particular form of secularization under Soviet communism:

> Communism was indeed the degenerate progeny [of the Enlightenment]. Progeny, even when degenerate, nevertheless retains a variety of discernible genetic traits, and these were also discernible in communism. The Enlightenment gave birth to rationalism, contempt for tradition, and hatred of the entire mythological layer in culture. The brutal persecution of religion was not the only form in which these trends blossomed in communism; they also found expression in the principle, put into practice rather than voiced outright, whereby human individuals are entirely exchangeable, the life of those individuals counting only insofar as they are tools of the higher cause, namely the state, since there is no rational basis for attributing any kind of special, noninstrumental status to the human personality.[17]

Beyond these intellectual roots of Soviet antireligious policy there was also a distinct social-class dimension to the change in religion's sociopolitical role as the Russian empire moved into the modern world. In the West, religious toleration expanded with the development of the bourgeoisie capitalist class and with world trade. This did not happen in the Russian empire. Yet curiously, the rising political force of religion in the USSR today has a social-class dimension. In the Western case the reasons were perhaps more directly connected with commercial interests of the emerging middle and upper social strata; in the USSR the reasons appear more to do with the same strata's intellectual and emotional disillusionment with the failed ideology.

One study dealing with the emergence of political and religious toleration in the modern world summed up the transition in the West at the genesis of the modern era as follows:

At its highest level, secularism expressed itself in the conscious indifference of governments to religious confessions. The absolute rulers of the seventeenth century were devoted primarily to the interests of the secular state, and tended to adopt a permissive attitude to all sects that did not disturb society. At the same time trading communities in both Catholic and Protestant countries came to accept the dogma that religious affiliations were irrelevant to the maintenance and promotion of commerce. Despite retrogressive developments in several countries, the general mood by the end of the seventeenth century was one of hope and in a few instances, irenicism. [18]

In other words, one major effect of socioeconomic modernization was the contraction of state interference in religion and a concomitant expansion of religious tolerance. In this regard the contrast between the direction of the Western world and the Russian empire could hardly be more stark, despite the sporadic and irregular expansion of religious toleration in the West. The role of commerce and social-class formation in the West and Russia varied enormously, with broad social and political ramifications that closely affected the political role of religion. [19]

As a partial result of Russia's late entry into the world of social modernization, and especially after decades of deliberate political reaction by the late-nineteenth-century autocracy, when these modernizing influences did come they assumed a profoundly radical character, including the determination to forcibly secularize that society. The familiar Russian historical theme since Peter the Great of catching up with the West was made the official Soviet industrial goal by the early 1930s. As the late and dependent character of industrialization in the Russian empire contributed to the radicalization of that process, so also the explicit political-legal reaction of latter-day autocracy contributed to the political circumstances in which Enlightenment ideals assumed a profoundly more radical *political* character than they had in the Western world. This in turn engendered in the new Soviet state the determination to forcibly secularize that admittedly backward society. Thus long-term sociological reasons, as well as ideological ones, contributed both to the antireligious posture of the regime from the start, and to its deepening severity after the regime was reasonably secure from foreign and domestic threat. The entire complex of political motives for deliberately suppressing religiosity since the October Revolution was perhaps best summarized by Michael Bourdeaux in 1984, on the eve of the

Gorbachev era: "The full evidence is still lacking in why the Soviet state is still so actively hostile to religion—still, indeed, committed to diminishing it completely—while the circumstances of 1917 have entirely changed. One deep seated reason is that religion provided the *only legal alternative ideology to communism in the Soviet Union.*"[20] Thus a variety of factors operating at different levels and at different times contributed to the regime's pronounced antireligious orientation—until Gorbachev's radical reforms came to fruition, and particularly after summer 1988. Each of these factors involved some degree of perceived threat to the regime's program. Ironically, with the sense of security that made glasnost and democratization possible, religion appears to represent more of a challenge than ever before. A brief examination of the survival of religious belief and practice in such inhospitable political circumstances explains this anomaly.

How is the perdurability of religious vitality in the USSR to be accounted for in the face of decades of official discouragement ranging from administrative harassment to periodic bloody persecution? This question moves us closer to the heart of the larger issue, namely the manner in which religion poses a threat to secular authority in the contemporary USSR. In other words, *why* religiosity has survived so tenaciously provides clues about the nature of the political challenge it represents. Transcendental explanations, whatever intrinsic value they may or may not possess, are not treated here because the question is essentially political.[21]

Why did the regime's efforts to eliminate religion fail? First, and perhaps paradoxically, persecution has historically served to strengthen religious communities. Not surprisingly, the same result has ensued in the USSR, despite the exceptionally brutal character the persecution assumed at various periods. Significantly, Soviet leaders have been much more willing to recognize this after the obvious (long-term) failure of Khrushchev's antireligious campaign beginning in 1959.[22] The moral dynamics of this phenomenon are interesting, but beyond the scope of this essay; one should note, however, that the Gorbachev leadership came to recognize and publicly acknowledge the counterproductive nature of religious persecution. Even in the early period of Gorbachev's radical reforms the regime adopted a much more conciliatory attitude, even if only for tactical reasons of more effectively reducing the influence of religion.[23] Only later, after the Millennium celebrations of summer 1988, did a more pragmatic, even utilitarian orientation begin to evolve: after that time, talk of the "socially useful role of religion" became more frequent, more earnest, and eventually the official posture.

Yet there are clearly other reasons for the dogged persistence of religious vitality in the USSR beyond the energizing force of persecution; even in the most relaxed periods of governmental intrusion into religious belief and practice an uncommon religious dynamism persisted. Many observers have attributed the tenacity of religion in the USSR to the humdrum, cloistered, and banal character of Soviet society before Gorbachev. These conditions may well have invited a search for meaning that led many to religion. Regardless of whether the cloistered character of Soviet society was justified on grounds of "capitalist encirclement," "bourgeoisie influences," or "capitalist-imperialist intrigues," it apparently contributed to the turn (or return) to religion for many. Soviet socialism, after all, had explicitly promised decade after decade eventual material abundance as well as existential fulfillment. [24] One would be hard-pressed to find much evidence of either in the USSR by the time of Gorbachev's radical reforms.

Finally, and most important for this essay, the failed "cultic function" of the Communist party and its doctrines is often viewed as largely responsible for the increasing interest and practice of religion in Soviet society. The return to Russian Orthodoxy by many educated, professional, and well-placed individuals was perhaps most emblematic of the utter failure of the official ideology to command allegiance. Disillusionment with the official ideology is often considered a major reason for the growing interest and practice of religion among all social classes. Among the upper social stratum this turn toward religion by many apparently had more or less direct political ramifications, including a more conciliatory posture on religion by the regime. [25]

Of these three most plausible sociological reasons for the tenacity of religion in the USSR—active persecution; lack of personal, existential fulfillment in a stagnant society; and reaction against a moribund but official ideology—the third clearly represents the greatest political challenge to the form that secular authority had historically assumed in the USSR. Soviet efforts to eradicate both major dimensions of religion—the set of an individual's personal beliefs, and the ideational-normative bonds tying a group together—patently failed. Politically, the failure was bad enough in itself, given the heavy emphasis that this dimension of "communist construction" had received from 1929 until 1988. What is much worse, and in fact an oblique but increasingly powerful challenge to secular authority, is *how* the regime has failed in this regard: at best, the officially enforced worldview proved unpopular, unworkable, and increasingly irrelevant for a significant portion of the population. The nature of this oblique challenge is now explored more closely.

The Challenge of Religious Vitality and Regime Accommodation

The core issue of this chapter is the manner in which the enduring, growing base of religiosity in the USSR represents a challenge to the authority and power of the Soviet regime. Much evidence points to a general resurgence of religiosity in the USSR virtually across the board: no social class is exempt; no territory is exempt; and one would be hard-pressed to find a traditional confession that has not experienced some measure of increased vitality. The occurrence itself represents a phenomenon; our concern, however, is the political fallout from it.

The challenge is multifaceted, but reducible to two broad dimensions. First, growing religious vitality—of whatever confessional stripe—represented a direct repudiation of the formerly authoritative worldview of the Communist party. Denied this authoritative worldview, the party no longer enjoyed its legitimate claim to authority. Once this ideological mandate was gone or even practically unenforceable, as it clearly was by early 1990, so eventually was its actual political power. If dialectical materialism is unacceptable philosophically, the demise of political power deriving from it was inevitable.

It is particularly important to recall that religion was the only tolerated opposition in Soviet history, though until Gorbachev that toleration was concessionary. To the extent that the force of history is determined by the clash of ideas, Soviet Marxism-Leninism appears to have lost the ideological war to religion. The paradox is that, unlike most other challenges to secular authority examined in this volume, religion (even Islam) had never really cast itself in the role of explicit political opponent of the regime. That is, at least not since the official but coerced recantations of the Russian Orthodox church leadership after the Bolshevik victory in the Russian civil war (1918–21). But if there were no explicit threat beyond the realm of competing ideas, where the direct threat?

The other major dimension of political challenge, beyond the ideological challenge to dialectical materialism, comes from the complex of public policy issues of extraordinary difficulty for whatever regime emerges from the outworking of Gorbachev's set of radical reforms. Failure to manage these would spell the end of the USSR.

This complex of issues is itself multifaceted but is coming from two major directions, each representing a somewhat different type of challenge. The first is from among the various Christian denominations, mostly in the Slavic lands; and second, among the traditionally Moslem peoples, mostly located in the southern USSR (see Table 12.1 for a demographic representation of religion in the USSR). Each of these two basic religious orientations has experienced not only a clear resurgence of significant popular adherence in recent times, but also a substantially greater degree of political autonomy as well.

Christianity does not now pose a threat to Soviet power in the form of direct armed popular uprising, and likely will not in the future. The core of its challenge has come rather from its basic philosophical incompatibility with Marxism-Leninism as an authoritative foundation for political authority, and thereby from its recasting of political issues ostensibly "resolved" while the Communist Party of the Soviet Union (CPSU) ruled the land.[26] The philosophical incompatibility would not have been a political issue if religious belief and practice were "withering away" and popular faith in dialectical materialism strong. But we have no evidence whatever of that, and much evidence that the opposite is occurring. In some respects the worst scenario imaginable for the old regime appears to be developing: greater religious vitality among the various Christian denominations on nearly every front combined with deepening disenchantment with the old regime and its ideology. They are increasing in numbers and in numbers of officially registered places of worship; the intellectual vitality of faith as a way of life is reflected with increased sophistication in the public realms of literature and the arts; religious communities are being permitted to conduct charitable work legally for the first time since official prohibitions in Stalin's Law on Cults of 1928; clerics have been elected to posts in lower-level soviets, the Supreme Soviet, and the Congress of Peoples' Deputies, including three Orthodox priests in high ecclesiastical positions elected to the Congress of Peoples' Deputies in March 1989.

This all signals more than an increasing political irrelevance of the Communist party, the former self-styled "leading and guiding force in Soviet society." It signals also the emergence of a vibrant rethinking and reenactment of the fundamental political-theoretic notions upon which public order is founded. Religion had been the only officially tolerated opposition in the USSR, as noted earlier; the religious dimension of the

TABLE 12.1

Demographics of Religion in the USSR

	General Religious Background of USSR	Estimates of Those Practicing (millions)	Registered Places of Worship as of mid-1988
Christian	105,510,000	—	—
Russian Orthodox	90,710,000	30–50	8,000
Protestant	9,360,000	3–5	—
Roman Catholic	5,340,000	3.5	—
Moslem (Islam)	34,330,000	50	—
Jewish	3,120,000	—	—
Buddhist	—	±0.5	—
Nonreligious	85,430,000	—	—
Atheist	58,900,000	—	—
Other	510,000	—	—
Total	—	—	20,000

Sources: 1990 Britannica Annual: *Current Digest of the Soviet Press* 40, no. 2 (May 11, 1988): 2; *The Soviet Union*, 2d ed., *Congressional Quarterly*, 1986:172–74.
Note: Numbers are based on the preliminary 1989 census results for a total population of 286,717,000.

surge of public activity since 1987 may be seen as a type of no-confidence vote. Seen in this light, the regime's accommodationist posture since summer 1988 represents a dramatically changed political reality, informed among other things by the secular power of religious belief and practice.

The growing politicized force of Christianity will compel the regime to deal with areas previously unproblematic due to the rule by fiat of the party, particularly at lower administrative levels. The replacement of Karchev as minister of religious affairs (1984–89) for failing to adequately perform may signal the gravity of this challenge, although the circumstances of his dismissal remain obscure and under dispute within the USSR itself.[27] Difficult questions of church-state relations common to pluralist democracies—such as church rights, taxation of property and clergy, the proper scope of religious liberty, the precise meaning of "establishment of religion"—must now necessarily be handled by Moscow with the interested parties wielding a substantial share of the political power involved. Precisely how they will be resolved is impossible to predict. The important point is that the challenge of religious vitality is certain to shape their resolution differently in the future.

The second major direction of religious challenge to secular authority is from the persistent, increasing vitality of Islam, mostly in the southern USSR. (Most Soviet Moslems are Sunnites, but in Soviet Azerbaidzhan most Moslems are Shi'ites.) Much has been written on this threat; the wave of religiosity does not bode well for Moscow's long-term assertion of authority in these regions, as partly evidenced by the turmoil beginning with the Alma-Ata riots in December 1986.[28] Yet here the challenge is somewhat different from that posed by Christianity. It is impossible to predict an outbreak of militant, politicized Islam as a direct challenge to Soviet authority, although this appears more likely than one from any of the Christian denominations (including Russian Orthodoxy), or from the other religious groups in Soviet society, such as Jews, Molokans, or Buddhists.

Yet even without an outbreak of armed insurgency, every challenge presented to the regime's authority by various forms of Christianity applies to Islam as well. However, with respect to Islam the matter is complicated by several other concerns: the role and interpretation of the *Shari'a* (Islamic legal code) in Soviet life; the larger relationship of civil law and religious law in Soviet society; the federal problem of spatial/geographic spheres of authority (e.g., specifically where will Moscow's authority over religious issues end with respect to Islam, in contrast with other religious groups?); relations with other Moslem countries in secular concerns such as terms of trade, diplomatic recognition, or patterns of foreign aid. This is but to name a few of the more obvious. The point is that increased politicization of Moslem identity will create conditions under which these issues will no longer be settled by central diktat.

Finally, the frightening prospect of a politically "reconstructed" Christian Slavic area in collision with "reconstructed" Islam in the southern areas is unlikely but not beyond possibility.[29]

The overall political challenge in both dimensions—the force of Christianity and Islam—is seriously compounded by the close relationship of nationalism with religiosity. Particularly for ethnic minorities, religion has often been a preservative agent for nationalist identity. It is therefore not surprising that with the increased general religiosity in the USSR minority nationalist assertiveness has increased as well. This is proving true in the Baltic areas, the Caucasus, Ukraine, in central Asia, and with particular force even in Russia itself. Again, the political challenge comes not only from popular rejection of the previously official ideology, but from the complex of concrete public policy issues resulting from the "deideologization" of Soviet society under conditions of heightened political salience for religion.

Thus Soviet "forced secularization" did not succeed but rather gave rise in part to the gravest threat to the ideological hegemony of the party since the civil war of 1918–21. In the Soviet case modernization did not give rise to a secularized society; the manner in which it occurred appears to have contributed to the "new religious wave," to use the expression more and more frequent in Soviet commentary. The Western *Encyclopaedia of the Social Sciences* published in 1937, the year Stalin's Constitution went into effect (such as it did), deals with "modernism" as a phenomenon involving in essence deepening secularization of society.[30] Yet now the connection between modernization and secularization seems as indirect, or even as chimeral, as the pathetically inoperative ideals of the Stalin Constitution.

The "secularization hypothesis" seems to have been repudiated by the aggregate global experiences of the late twentieth century, or at the very least in need of essential revision. Political modernization has come to include, as a rule, the disestablishment of the religious base of civil authority. But socioeconomic modernization of society has not necessarily led to deepened secularization of the popular consciousness, nor necessarily to the attenuation of the religious dimension of communal identity. Particularly in the Soviet case forced secularization as a component of forced modernization appears to have helped create the opposite effect.

Paradoxically, it is clearly not the Soviet popular consciousness that is undergoing secularization, but after more than seventy years of quasi-religious claims to political legitimacy by the regime, the governing regime itself. The paradox is that this form of political secularization is being spawned, among other things, by an increasingly religious population pressing for the expansion of civil liberties, if not for direct political power. (See Table 12.2 for a chronology of major events.) This suggests a markedly different role for religion than that in the previous regimes—czarist and Bolshevik. Even if the "reconstructionists" gain

TABLE 12.2

Religion in the USSR: Chronology of Major Events

Kievan Rus' adopts Eastern Rite Christianity as official religion	June 988
Official split between Eastern and Western Christianity (Eastern Orthodoxy and Roman Catholicism)	1054
Tatar Mongol invasions and occupation of Russia	1220s–late 1400s
Constantinople, center of Orthodoxy, falls to Turks	1453
Moscow emerges as political, military, and religious center of Russia	mid–late 1400s
Russian Orthodox Patriarchate established	1589
Peter the Great abolishes the Patriarchate and establishes the Synod, under czarist administration	1721
October Revolution, Bolsheviks take power	October 1917
Decree on Separation of Church from State	January 23, 1918
Period of "New Economic Policy" (continuous confrontation with Orthodox church; relative tolerance of various sects)	1921–1928
"Law on Religious Associations" (modified slightly in 1975) put into effect	1929
Intense persecution of all religions	1929–1941
State–Church rapprochement	September 1943
Establishment of Christian Peace Conference in Czechoslovakia	1958
Khrushchev's vigorous antireligious campaign	1959–1964
Official pressure on registered Baptist church gives rise to internal church split, formation of "unregistered Baptists" group, headed by Georgi Vins	1961
Deposing of Khrushchev, general return in religious affairs to 1943–59 status quo	October 1964
Christian Seminar on Problems of the Religious Renaissance founded by Aleksandr Ogorodnikov	1974
Christian Committee for the Defense of Believer's Rights in the USSR founded by Fr. Gleb Yakunin	1976

TABLE 12.2 (*Continued*)

General de facto governmental policy shift in favor of direct intervention in religious affairs, rather than earlier pressure on religious leaders to throttle religious dissent	1978–1979
Slight but general increase of known incarcerations of Christian believers	1979–early 1980s
Gorbachev calls for increase in antireligious propagandization (first direct call since Khrushchev)	late 1985
Glasnost results in general loosening in many areas of religious life	early 1986
Celebration of Millennium of Christianity in Russia	June 1988
Election of three Russian Orthodox clergy (patriarch and two metropolitans) to the Congress of Peoples' Deputies	March 1989
Progressive loosening of administrative and ideological strictures against religion, culminating in speech by Gorbachev in Italy on the salutary moral effects of religion on Soviet society	December 1989
Passage of legislation guaranteeing a broad range of religious liberties	October 1990

significant political influence, the role of religion will not be the same as in either previous regime.

The Soviet case underscores the ongoing problematic of religion and politics in the modern era, which more or less requires constitutional disestablishment of religion but has proved less than capable of eliminating the political effluent of popular religious impulses. One would be hard-pressed indeed to produce a case in which the effort to eliminate religion was more comprehensive, more determined, and more longstanding than in the USSR from 1918 to 1988.

The possible connection between the Enlightenment and the secular impulse was noted earlier. That movement placed a premium on reason, liberty, rationality, and the expansion of toleration, among other civic virtues. Yet not all at the time saw the general denigration of religious influences on society and the state as leading exclusively to the public good. Perhaps not accidentally, the closing words of Hegel's *The*

Philosophy of Right, issued as a "science of the state," reflect his general criticism of certain antireligious strains in the Enlightenment. They appear increasingly appropriate to the troubled Soviet leviathan:

> The realm of fact has discarded its barbarity and unrighteous caprice, while the realm of truth has abandoned the world of beyond and its arbitrary force, so that the true reconciliation which discloses the state as the image and actuality of reason has become objective. In the state, self-consciousness finds in an organic development the actuality of its substantive knowing and willing; in religion, it finds the feeling and the representation of this its own truth as an ideal essentiality; while in philosophic science, it finds the free comprehension and knowledge of this truth as one and the same in its mutually complementary manifestations, i.e., in the state, in nature, and in the ideal world.[31]

Seen in this light, properly constituted modern state authority should feel little long-term threat from religion—and vice versa.

Notes

1. Allen Kassof, "For American and Soviet Scholars, 'Glasnost' Is Creating Unprecedented Opportunities—and Some Dangers," *Chronicle of Higher Education* 35 (April 15, 1989): 30, A44.

2. William C. Fletcher, "Religion and the Soviet Future," in *The Soviet Union and the Challenge of the Future,* ed. Alexander Shtromas and Morton A. Kaplan (New York: Paragon House, 1988), vol. 3, *Ideology, Culture, and Nationality,* 176, 197.

3. For example, see Robert Conquest, *Religion in the Soviet Union* (New York: Praeger, 1968); Walter Kolarz, *Religion in the Soviet Union* (London: Macmillan, 1961); Max Hayward and William C. Fletcher, eds., *Religion and the Soviet State: A Dilemma of Power* (New York: Praeger, 1969); Nicholas Zernov, *The Russian Religious Renaissance in the Twentieth-Century* (New York: Harper & Row, 1963); R. F. Miller and T. H. Rigby, *Religion and Politics in Communist States,* Occasional Paper no. 19 (Canberra: Australian National University, 1986).

4. This was spoken by Gorbachev at the nineteenth Conference of the CPSU, June 1988, and quoted from *Current Digest of the Soviet Press* 40, no. 26 (1989): 13.

5. *Current Digest of the Soviet Press* 41, no. 48, (1989): 7. Emphasis added.

6. The major works include Trevor Beeson, *Discretion and Valor: Religious*

Conditions in Russia and Eastern Europe (Glasgow: Fontana Books, 1974); David Powell, *Anti-Religious Propaganda in the USSR* (Cambridge: MIT Press, 1975); Christel Lane, *Christian Religion in the Soviet Union: A Sociological Study* (Albany: State University of New York Press, 1978); Pedro Ramet, *Cross and Commissar: The Politics of Religion in Eastern Europe and the USSR* (Bloomington: Indiana University Press, 1987); of particular significance in this regard is T. H. Rigby, "Regime and Religion in the USSR," in Miller and Rigby, *Religion and Politics.*

7. Silvio Ferrari, "Separation of Church and State in Contemporary European Society," *Journal of Church and State* 30, no. 3 (Autumn 1988): 542.

8. These are from Section I, Article 2, of the Party Statutes, adopted at the 27th Congress of the Communist Party of the Soviet Union in 1986, although this aspect of the statutes represented nothing novel. "Religious prejudices" in the traditional Soviet usage (antedating Gorbachev's glasnost) cover a much broader set of beliefs and practices than implied in English usage: nearly any religious conception at variance with dialectical materialism was fair game for this politically opprobrious label.

9. Specific examples of early Soviet practices of "separation of church and state" include confiscation of church property, circumscriptions of religious expression (written and oral), and with Stalin's Law on Cults of 1928, strict prohibition of religious instruction, severe restrictions on activities of religious organizations, and others. See Powell, *Anti-Religious Propaganda in the Soviet Union,* chap. 2; Conquest, *Religion in the Soviet Union,* chap. 1; and Rigby and Miller, *Religion and Politics,* 17–20.

10. For example, see Mark DeWolfe Howe, *The Garden and the Wilderness: Religion and Government in American Constitutional History* (Chicago: University of Chicago Press, 1965). For a more recent statement of a similar position, see Michael W. McConnell, "Taking Religious Freedom Seriously," *First Things,* no. 3 (May 1990): 30–37.

11. See J. H. Miller, "Ethnicity and Religion under Communism: USSR," in Rigby and Miller, *Religion and Politics,* 28–48.

12. For example, see Ronald J. McAllister, "Religion in the Public Arena: A Paradox of Secularization," *Journal of Church and State* 30, no. 1 (Winter 1988): 15–32.

13. The classic work positing a causal relation between Protestantism and the emergence of capitalism is Max Weber, *The Protestant Ethic and the Spirit of Capitalism,* trans. Talcott Parsons (New York: Scribners, 1958). With respect to the relevance of this view to the USSR and Eastern Europe, Pedro Ramet notes that

> Weber suggested in his study of Protestantism, that one great advantage it enjoyed was that it was better suited to the emergent free enterprise society than was Catholicism. Economic modernization, in short, was making ecclesiastical and theological notions of stability and unchanging verity a handicap. That suggests that under the pressures of moderniza-

tion, religious organizations may tend to assimilate ideas of progress, displacing ideas of stability. Confessional fragmentation, theological heterogeneity, and pressures for grass-roots participation can be dated to the very origins of Christianity. Modernization, however, has provided an additional stimulus to these trends, and thus has further complicated the religious picture. [*Cross and Commissar,* 186.]

14. See, for example, Alfred Levin, "Toward the End of the Old Regime: State, Church, and Duma," in *Religion and Modernization in the Soviet Union,* ed. Dennis J. Dunn (Boulder, Colo.: Westview Press, 1977): 23–59.

15. Ibid.; see also William C. Fletcher, "Backwards from Reactionism: The De-modernization of the Russian Orthodox Church," in Dunn, ed., *Religion and Modernization in the USSR,* 205–10.

16. Zvi Gitelman, "Judaism and Modernization," in Dunn, ed., *Religion and Modernization in the USSR,* 285.

17. Leszek Kolakowski, "Communism as a Cultural Phenomenon," in Shtromas and Kaplan, eds., *The Soviet Union and the Challenge of the Future,* vol. 1, *Status and Change,* 80.

18. Henry Kamen, *The Rise of Toleration* (London: Wiedenfeld and Nicholson, World University Library, 1967), 228.

19. See W. W. Rostow, *Politics and the Stages of Growth* (Cambridge: Cambridge University Press, 1971); Barrington Moore, *The Social Origins of Dictatorship and Democracy: Lord and Serf in the Making of the Modern World* (Boston: Beacon Press, 1965); Alexander Gerschenkron, *Economic Backwardness in Historical Perspective* (Cambridge: Cambridge University Press, 1961); and James R. Kurth, "Industrial Change and Political Change: A European Perspective," in *The New Authoritarianism in Latin America,* ed. David Collier (Princeton, N.J.: Princeton University Press, 1979), 319–63.

20. Michael Bourdeaux, *Religious Minorities in the USSR: A Report,* rev., 4th ed. (London: Minority Rights Group, 1984), 4. Emphasis added.

21. We seek here to explain the *political* question of how religion as a social phenomenon impinges on civil authority. The fact that it does is given. The philosophical and specifically metaphysical question of possible transcendent causes for a given religion's perdurability are of a somewhat different, though perhaps no less significant, character.

22. Bourdeaux, *Religious Minorities,* 3.

23. For more on the tactical abandonment of persecution, see Alexander Ilyich Klibanov, "Historian Sees No Need to Overemphasize Fight against Religion," *Current Digest of the Soviet Press* 40, no. 15 (May 11, 1988), 4, 5; and Oxana Antic, *Radio Liberty Research Bulletin,* no. 179/88 (May 4, 1988).

24. For comments on the character of Soviet society itself as a catalyst for religiosity, see D. Hammer, "Alternative Visions of the Russian Future: Religious and Nationalist," *Studies in Comparative Communism* 20, nos. 3–4 (Au-

tumn/Winter 1987): 265–75; Christel Lane, "Russian Piety among Contemporary Russian Orthodox," *Journal for the Scientific Study of Religion* 14 (1975): 139–58; William Fletcher, *Soviet Believers: The Religious Sector of the Population* (Lawrence: Regents' Press of Kansas, 1981).

25. See John Dunlop, "Gorbachev and Russian Orthodoxy," *Problems of Communism* 38, no. 4 (July–August 1989): 96–117.

25. Much has been written on this philosophical incompatibility; for trenchant commentary and notes concerning some of the classic works see Mary-Barbara Zeldin, "The Religious Nature of Russian Marxism," *Journal for the Scientific Study of Religion* 8:111, which concludes, "Regardless of 'spiritual heresies' on the part of Marxism or secularization on the part of Christianity, the two sides in the controversy can reach a higher synthesis not by both being transcended, *aufgehoben,* but only if one of them is willing entirely to give up its essential nature and thus its very existence."

27. *Current Digest of the Soviet Press* 42, no. 11 (April 18, 1990): 22–23, 31.

28. See Michael Rywkin, *Moscow's Muslim Challenge: Soviet Central Asia* (Armonk, N.Y.: M. E. Sharpe, 1982); William Fierman, "Religion and Nationalism in Soviet Central Asia" (review of four books on the general topic); *Problems of Communism* 34, no. 4 (July–August 1989): 123–27; "Greater Tolerance for Islam?" *Radio Liberty Research Bulletin,* no. 197/88 (May 9, 1988).

29. For a less than sympathetic overview of the various strains of reconstructionism in the United States, see John Richard Neuhaus, "Why Wait for the Kingdom? The Theonomist Temptation," *First Things* 3 (May 1990): 13–21.

30. "Modernism indeed might be described as the endeavor to harmonize the relations between the older institutions of civilization and science. . . . In religion this is notoriously the case. Modernism entered that institution with the French Revolution." *Encyclopaedia of the Social Sciences,* S.V. "modernism."

31. *Hegel's Philosophy of Right,* trans. with notes by T. M. Knox (Oxford: Oxford University Press, 1980), 222–23.

Contributors

MUMTAZ AHMAD is associate professor of political science at Hampton University in Virginia. He studied at American University in Beirut before receiving his Ph.D. from the University of Chicago. His research interests and publications focus on Islam in South Asia, principally Pakistan and Bangladesh.

DONALD E. BAIN is professor of history and the director of strategic, military, and diplomatic studies at St. John Fisher College in Rochester, New York. His research interests and publications are primarily in the areas of national defense and international security. In 1989, he was a visiting scholar at the Defense Intelligence Agency of the Defense Intelligence College.

MARK BARTHOLOMEW is associate professor of political science at the University of Maine, Farmington. His publications have focused on German social democracy, the Socialist International, nuclear arms control in Europe, and problems of the welfare state.

DAMIÁN J. FERNÁNDEZ is assistant professor of international relations at Florida International University. He is the author of *Cuba's Foreign Policy in the Middle East* (Westview, 1988), and the editor of *Central America and the Middle East: The Internationalization of the Crises* (University of Florida Press, 1990).

LOWELL S. GUSTAFSON is assistant professor of political science at Villanova University. He has received research grants from the Fulbright Commission and the National Endowment for the Humanities, and is author of *The Sovereignty Dispute over the Falkland (Malvinas) Islands* (Oxford University Press, 1988). In addition, he has contributed to such professional journals as *Inter-American Economic Affairs, Political Science Quarterly, Social Science Quarterly,* and *Publius: The Journal of Federalism.*

ANN M. LESCH is associate professor of political science at Villanova University. She lived in Egypt from 1980–87, where she was a program officer for the Ford Foundation, and then a research associate for Universities Field Staff International. In addition to service on the board of directors of the Middle East Studies Association, Middle East Watch, and *Middle East Report,* she has recently authored (with Mark Tessler) *Israel, Egypt and the Palestinians: From Camp David to Intifada* (Indiana University Press, 1989).

ALLAN METZ is assistant professor/assistant subject specialist for Latin America at the library of the University of Illinois at Urbana-Champaign. He has published articles on Argentine intellectual history, Jewish refugee settlement in Central America, and the treatment of Jews in South America.

MATTHEW C. MOEN is assistant professor of political science at the University of Maine. A former Congressional Fellow, he is author of *The Christian Right and Congress* (University of Alabama Press, 1989) and has contributed to such professional journals as *Social Science Quarterly, Sociological Quarterly, Comparative Strategy, Social Science Journal,* and *Presidential Studies Quarterly.*

JOHN O. VOLL is professor of history at the University of New Hampshire, where he teaches Middle Eastern and world history. He has written numerous articles and chapters on the contemporary Islamic resurgence and modern Sudanese history, and is the author of *Islam: Continuity and Change in the Modern World* (Westview, 1982).

JAMES W. WARHOLA is associate professor of political science at the University of Maine. He received his Ph.D. from Ohio State University and has published articles on the Soviet Union dealing with ethnic relations, church-state issues, and foreign policy.